"At the centre of debates on populist politics in Latin America, this book's combination of impressive knowledge and careful argument will make it a touchstone reference for understanding Venezuela's contemporary transformation. It offers fresh and vital new insight on the past, present, and future of the Bolivarian project."

—Adam David Morton, *The University of Nottingham*

"Ryan Brading brings an original and imaginative perspective to an issue of fundamental concern to discourse analysis: the role of the state and ideology in legitimizing current Venezuela's military populism. The result is a highly suggestive work which will have to be confronted on one level or another by any future study of populism in Latin American societies. It is a book that well worth the reading.

—Luis Ricardo Davila, *Harvard University*

"This book provides a rigorous and well-researched study of one of the most important national-popular regimes that have emerged in Latin America over the last fifteen years: Chavez's Venezuela. Brading's work constitutes a remarkable contribution to the understanding of one of the most original political movements of our time, and it is bound to become a necessary reference for the scholars working in the field of Latin American politics."

—Ernesto Laclau, *Northwestern University*

Populism in Venezuela

Populism in Venezuela analyzes the emergence, formation, reproduction and resistance to a left-wing populist project in a major world oil producer.

For readers who seek to understand the historical, economical and sociological contexts that gave rise to a 38 year-old mestizo-mulato Lieutenant Colonel who stormed the presidential palace in a bloody coup d'état in 1992, subsequently returned to the same palace in 1998, but this time, as a democratically elected President, and has been in power since, this book is the right place to start. In spite of opposition attempts to oust President Hugo Chávez and his political machinery from power, this 'socialism of the twenty-first century' hegemonic project has succeeded in creating an institutional structure designed to improve the lives of the previously excluded population. An in-depth fieldwork study of a Cuban healthcare program named Barrio Adentro (deep in the slums) in Venezuela's poor and rural areas, and the nonviolence Manos Blancas (white hands) opposition student movement - provides a descriptive and analytical account of people's problems from both sides in a deeply polarized society. The concluding chapter of this book examines Chávez's intention to stay in power until 2031.

An original resource for scholars, students and general readers; this book not only furthers our understanding of populism in Venezuela but also provides a sound method to analyze populist practices in other contexts.

Ryan Brading is a Post-Doctoral Fellow at University of Essex, UK.

Routledge Studies in Latin American Politics

1 Research and International Trade Policy Negotiations
Knowledge and Power in Latin America
Edited by Mercedes Botto

2 The United Nations in Latin America
Aiding Development
Francis Adams

3 Fear and Crime in Latin America
Redefining State-Society Relations
Lucía Dammert

4 Populism in Venezuela
Ryan Brading

Populism in Venezuela

Ryan Brading

LONDON AND NEW YORK

First published 2013
by Routledge
711 Third Avenue, New York, NY 10017

Simultaneously published in the UK
by Routledge
2 Park Square, Milton Park, Abingdon, Oxfordshire OX14 4RN

First issued in paperback 2014

*Routledge is an imprint of the Taylor & Francis Group,
an informa business*

© 2013 Taylor & Francis

The right of Ryan Brading to be identified as author of this work has been
asserted by him in accordance with sections 77 and 78 of the Copyright,
Designs and Patents Act 1988.

All rights reserved. No part of this book may be reprinted or reproduced or
utilised in any form or by any electronic, mechanical, or other means, now
known or hereafter invented, including photocopying and recording, or in
any information storage or retrieval system, without permission in writing
from the publishers.

Trademark Notice: Product or corporate names may be trademarks or
registered trademarks, and are used only for identification and explanation
without intent to infringe.

Library of Congress Cataloging-in-Publication Data
Brading, Ryan.
  Populism in Venezuela / Ryan Brading.
    p. cm. — (Routledge studies in Latin American politics ; 4)
  Includes bibliographical references.
  1. Venezuela—Politics and government—1999– 2. Populism—
Venezuela. 3. Chávez Frías, Hugo. I. Title.
  JL3831.B72 2012
  320.56'620987—dc23
  2012016419

ISBN 978-0-415-52297-7 (hbk)
ISBN 978-1-138-88651-3 (pbk)
ISBN 978-0-203-09859-2 (ebk)

Typeset in Sabon
by IBT Global.

Contents

Diagrams	ix
Acknowledgments	xi
Introduction	1
1 Populism, Theories, and Logics: A Theoretical and Methodological Approach	8
2 The Venezuelan State: Its Formation, Consolidation, and Decline	43
3 The Process of Deinstitutionalizing the Power Structure and Institutionalizing Venezuela's Bolivarian Project	61
4 A Healthcare Program in Excluded Areas: A Community Participative Model Constructs Healthcare with Cuban Medics in Venezuela	89
5 The Anti-Bolivarian Student Movement: New Social Actors Challenge the Advancement of Venezuela's Bolivarian Radicalism	114
6 Indefinite Re-Election, Gerrymandering, Chávez's Cancer, Grand Missions, and a United Opposition Force	135
Conclusion	158
Notes	165
Bibliography	197
Index	203

Diagrams

1.1	A request is satisfied.	28
1.2	Multiple requests are rejected.	28
1.3	A nodal point arrests the flow of differences in an equivalential chain.	29
1.4	A fighting demand against a common enemy.	30
1.5	Methodological framework.	38

Acknowledgments

It would not have been possible to do this investigation without the critique and guidance of Dr. Aletta Norval and Dr. David Howarth. I would like to express my sincere gratitude for their full support. The Ideology Discourse Analysis (IDA) program provided me an enjoyable working academic environment. The 'Essex School' post-structuralist discourse theory and methodological schema have been pivotal in unfolding this in-depth empirical analysis of populist practices in Venezuela. I would also like to thank all of those in the Department of Government at the University of Essex for running such an inspiring academic department. I thank Professor Ernesto Laclau for his theoretical guidance during our discussions and during IDA workshops and conferences. Furthermore, many thanks go to Dr. Steven Griggs (De Mortfort University) for his helpful suggestions.

I want to express my gratitude to Freddy Chacon (*la mugre*), Ramon Vallve, the Mújica family, and those who contributed to the enrichment of this investigation. I thank Enrique Suarez Cabrera for his help in many aspects, Domingo Fontiveros for his economic and socio-political opinions about Venezuelan affairs in recent years, and other family members who have been with me, tooth and nail, as I tried to unravel and demonstrate the nature of the political phenomenon Venezuela has faced in the last 25 years. I would also like to express my appreciation to Jane Tang for her help throughout the years. Last, but certainly not least, I want to thank my wife Wen-Hao for her personal understanding, support, and patience in dealing with me while I conducted this research and wrote the book. I dedicate this book to Ricardo Fontiveros, who taught me at an early age the importance of clean and honest politics in a sharply divided society.

Introduction

The rapid change of social and political practices in Venezuela in the past two decades is hard to grasp. This country, previously known abroad either for its oil wealth or its success at international beauty contests like Miss Universe and World, started to change. By the late 1980s, the image of a wealthy and prosperous nation enhanced by the beauty of its women was no longer the best way to describe this tropical South American country with more than 1,700 miles of Caribbean coastline.

My relationship with Venezuela goes back to the late 1970s. As a kid, I remember people's feel-good attitude towards social, political, and economic affairs in Venezuela. Regularly, adults talked about corruption in the government, but that appeared to be nothing else but a topic people liked to talk about. I always laughed when I heard the nickname '*Toronto*' (a hazelnut coated in milk chocolate) given to the president elected for office from December 1978 until 1983. The chubby President Luis Herrera (*Toronto*) Campins was known for his '*Toronto*' appetite. With a sense of sarcasm, people compared Campin's '*Torontos*' with corrupt practices. During that period, Venezuela was very proud of its success in beauty contests and the inauguration of projects like the Metro (underground system) in Caracas. This euphoric period ended when the Bolívar (local currency) was devalued on February 18, 1983—known as the '*Viernes Negro*' (Black Friday). Oil revenues decreased, foreign debt increased, and political clientelism, business cronies combined with government projects, and national expenditure grew. Devaluation was a wake-up call to the nation.

Jaime Lusinchi, from the party *Acción Democrática* (AD), promised during his December 1983 presidential campaign to pay off every penny of Venezuela's foreign debt. In other words, he would fix the mess politicians created. Initial attempts to correct the system were in vain. Lusinchi's administration opted to borrow more money and let his successor deal with it. The ex-president (1973–78), Carlos Andrés Pérez of AD, was re-elected in December 1988. People voted in hopes of a return to the opulent period enjoyed during Pérez's 1970s oil bonanza administration. However, circumstances had changed. I clearly remember listening to the radio after Pérez took office, hearing that the new government would borrow U.S. $4.5

2 Populism in Venezuela

billion, and that the financial crisis would be dealt with using neoliberal 'Washington Consensus' reforms. I was confused. Why don't they pay off the debt rather than borrowing more, which would be in keeping with the emergent discourse? Days later, Venezuela changed forever.

On February 27, 1989, the popular mass protested in Caracas. The steep increase of petrol prices (neoliberal reform) caused uproar as people from underprivileged sectors, spontaneously, started protesting, rioting, and looting. Anger, hunger, and despair took the streets of Caracas. I recall watching the news, seeing people looting supermarkets, shops (e.g. a man carrying a beef carcass on his shoulder, washing machines being taken out of shops), etc. Later on, the armed forces restored order by firing on the people. At night, I clearly heard gunshots from the slums in the hills of Petare in Caracas. It sounded like a war zone in the slums. News reports changed to corpses being moved by fellow slum dwellers, friends and relatives describing how their loved ones were killed for no reason, and a mass grave in a cemetery in the west of Caracas where many bodies were buried. It became obvious to me that people would never forgive nor forget this incident.

I returned to England in August 1989. Not being in Venezuela, I couldn't get a good insight into people's reaction to the neoliberal reforms the government implemented. On February 4, 1992, I was informed of a coup d'état in Miraflores (the Presidential Palace). In the evening, watching the BBC news, I saw some brief footage of the coup leader, Lieutenant Colonel Hugo Chávez, in the Presidential Palace asking other officers in other positions of the country to surrender. This was the second blow to Venezuela's institutional structure. Chávez's brief speech shocked me. Rather comfortably, the symbolic name of Simón Bolívar, Venezuela's and part of Latin America's liberator from Spanish rule in the 1800s, was used to trademark this subversive undemocratic movement. Chávez, a young mulato-mestizo (African, European, and Indian), appeared to be a strong-minded and determined character who took everyone by surprise. He meant business. The coup resonated with the social uprising known as the '*Caracazo*' on February 27, 1989. In spite of its undemocratic nature, the unsuccessful coup led by Chávez signified radical change to a discredited and repressive institutional system. To the common Venezuelan in the slums, Chávez was one of them.

The happy-go-lucky oil-based society of the 1970s turned into one of social revolts in the late 1980s and coup d'états in the early 1990s (the second coup was on November 27, 1992). For a number of years, Venezuela was a model of democracy for other Latin American countries.[1] By the 1990s, this institution was unsustainable. All the efforts politicians from the establishment made to resuscitate it were just facelifts. These political attempts are described and analyzed in Chapter 2. In March 1994, Chávez was pardoned and set free with no restrictions whatsoever on his participation in any political activities. In December 1998, he comfortably won the presidential elections with 56.2 percent of the vote. He returned to Miraflores, but this time as a democratically elected representative of the people.

Why was an insurgent coup leader that tried to oust Venezuela's president in 1992 elected president six years later? To understand what lies behind this phenomenon, a series of social, political, and cultural problems in Venezuela need to be contextualized. Since 1958, Venezuela seemed to be a country constructing a robust party democratic system. However, by the 1990s this institutional system was in tatters. These conditions of institutional fragmentation opened a platform for a new political project with a discourse of radical change to emerge and win the presidential elections in 1998. This investigation aims to analyze, and thus carefully unpack, the 'core of the problem' rather than do an interpretive description. This aftermath seemed to be, on the one hand, punishment to some, but on the other, emancipation to those that wanted radical change.

Richard Gott, who claims to have a close friendship with Chávez, thinks that Fidel Castro and Chávez have a number of similarities. Chávez has stirred up nationalist sentiments with the people in the slums of Venezuela. He has challenged 'the acceptance of neo-liberalism and globalization' by reviving 'radical nationalism', exalting 'the figure of Simón Bolivar in much the same way as Castro used the example of the Cuban patriot José Martí'. As Bolívar and Martí fought against Spanish rule, Castro and Chávez 'campaign against the US attempt to rule the world'. This 'has not been approved by Venezuela's rich and tiny elite'.[2] According to Tariq Ali, Chávez, a charismatic commander, 'was elected in a landslide election . . . riding in on the desires of the population intent on banishing the corruption-tainted parties of the past'.[3] In other words, 'electing Chávez was the revenge of the dispossessed'. Ali notes:

> The majority of Venezuelans opposed the economic policies then in force, which consisted of a frontal assault on the poor and the less privileged in order to shore up a swollen, parasitical oligarchy and a corrupt, reactionary civilian and oil-industry bureaucracy. . . . They hated the arrogance of the Venezuelan elite, which used wealth and a lighter-skin color to sustain itself at the expense of the poor, dark-skinned majority. They condemned this same elite's blind mimicry of all the values—social, political, imperial, cultural, economic—held dear by its US counterparts. None of this is secret.[4]

According to Sujatha Fernandes, 'Chávez gives voice to the marginalized'. Discursively, it is a 'newfound sense of hope, retribution for social injustices, and dignity for the urban poor. Chavismo has found strength by tapping into the deep reservoir of daily humiliation and anger felt by people of the lower classes'. Fernandes claims that Chávez has the 'ability to speak to the poor, to show that he understands their feelings of exclusion, that endears him to them'.[5] Cristina Marcano and Alberto Barrera Tyszka mention that Chávez likes to act like a warrior and always thrives on confrontation. Easily, he finds 'people who would take his bait and get caught in conflict with him:

4 Populism in Venezuela

the communications media, the Church, trade unions, the United States . . . [p]uffed up by his tremendous popularity, he has always revelled in provoking his adversaries with irreverent, over-the-top remarks. "Christ is with the Revolution!" he would cry, and the church would lunge at him'.[6] Chávez's discourse is 'deeply reviled by a certain sector of the middle class who consider him vulgar and common'. However, on the other side of the spectrum, Chávez 'incites the fervour of Venezuela's more impoverished citizens, who gave him carte blanche to do what he wanted'.[7] Populism is often used to describe the Bolivarian project. Nonetheless, I haven't found a convincing explanation of why populism refers to the Venezuelan phenomenon.

As Kirk Hawkins points out, 'many scholars, journalists, and policy-makers use the word populist to describe Chávez and his movement'. In Hawkin's review of 'about 40 academic journal articles published between 2000 and 2006 that study Chávez . . . about half also use the word populist or populism'. However, 'none of these observers really clarify the meaning of this term or why it applies to Chávez, and they ultimately fail to say what it reveals about the unique causes and consequences of Chavismo'.[8] Hawkins claims that 'populism is a set of fundamental beliefs about the nature of the political world—a worldview or, to use a more rarified term, a "discourse"—that perceives history as a Manichaean struggle between Good and Evil, one in which the side of Good is the "will of the people," or the natural, common interest of the citizens once they are allowed to form their own opinions, while the side of Evil is a conspiring elite that has subverted this will'.[9]

Gerry Stoker sees Chávez as a former officer elected on a left-leaning populist platform. He 'promotes a coalition of support around populist ideas derived from the leader Simón Bolívar . . . [h]e relies heavily on his ability to communicate his ideas directly to many parts of society from the poor, through the middle classes to significant sections of the army'.[10] Stoker claims that 'politics and politicians are challenged now more than in the past'. Populism has a tendency 'to demonise its opponents'. Many populists do not like to listen. They 'portray opponents as evil rather than simply people with different interests or values, often taking an emotive tone that can undermine the role of reason'.[11]

Populism is generally seen as a negative term. Critics seek to politically discredit the project by describing it as a discursive tactic that uses inflammatory and loaded language to get the support of disgruntled sectors of the population. People are hypnotized: 'people become mass, and mass becomes the mob (la chusma)'.[12] Without a shadow of a doubt, social and economic polarization in Venezuela has led to alarming and ever-growing levels of tension in this society. An in-depth academic analysis that seeks to unpack the nature, practices, and theoretical approaches to populism, searches for methodological tools to categorize populist practices, and applies them to the Venezuelan case in a wider context can provide new insights into the emergence of this phenomenon and the practices that make it so effective.

Introduction 5

This investigation seeks to answer two research questions. First, I shall employ Ernesto Laclau's theoretical approach to populism and determine to what degree the case of Venezuela constitutes instances of populist politics. I intend to use this case study in order to provide a fuller and more general understanding of the phenomenon of populism. Here I will be concerned to investigate the key factors that account for the emergence and reproduction of populism, and to differentiate between populism as a mode of opposition and populism as a mode of governance. Second, I am concerned to explore whether or not a more general account of populism can be applied to this case and used to evaluate existing theories of populism, e.g. those proposed by Margaret Canovan and Paul Taggart. The above theoretical approaches are discussed and analyzed in Chapter 1. Furthermore, in the sub-section 'Research strategy' in Chapter 1 (see pages 69–74), these research questions are further contextualized.

In Chapter 1, Laclau's theory of populism is readdressed in order to tie these theoretical elements with Jason Glynos and David Howarth's methodological 'logics approach' schema. The arguments and claims raised in this investigation use an Essex School post-structuralist discourse theory and methodological framework to select and analyze historical accounts and categorical techniques to formulate and contextualize this populist phenomenon. This in-depth analysis does not seek to test nor defend theoretical or methodological positions. It is problem-driven research that contributes, with an in-depth analysis, an explanation of how a new populist political project managed to displace an institutional system, install a new constitution designed to serve the well-being of the people, construct an institutional structure, and reproduce itself, as well as how opposition forces resist the sedimentation of this new hegemonic order. In-depth fieldwork research is conducted analyzing the nature of agents that support two opposite camps in a deeply polarized society. This post-structuralist qualitative investigation is divided into six chapters.

THE STRUCTURE OF THIS BOOK

The first section of Chapter 1 addresses the literature of populism, drawing on theorists like Margaret Canovan and others. A sub-section follows evaluating three theoretical approaches. The second section discusses Ernesto Laclau's theoretical approach combined with Jason Glynos and David Howarth's methodological schema. This chapter puts forward a category called 'logic' which is sub-divided into three logics: social, political, and fantasmatic. These sub-categories provide the methodological model required to classify and analyze populist elements. Nonetheless, a vital component of these logics category-model is Laclau's theoretical framework. Theoretical elements with these sub-categories are discussed throughout this chapter.

6 *Populism in Venezuela*

Chapter 2 presents the genealogical basis of this in-depth analysis. The first section presents a historical review of Venezuela from its independence in 1821, to the restoration of democracy in 1958, through to the February 1989 popular revolt. The second section contextualizes the degree of social inequality and how neoliberal reforms in the 1990s further 'excluded' the poor. I describe what provoked Chávez's movement organize a coup and overthrow the government in 1992, and analyze the extent of social support to the failed attempt after Chávez's brief surrender speech. A focal point in this section is to narrate and thus analyze the context upon which small/medium political parties and social/business groups constructed a new political platform that promised to challenge and displace the institutional structure.

The first section of Chapter 3 discusses how the Bolivarian Government managed to displace and instate an institution. Interviews with key political figures that constructed and invested in this new political project, but later left because they rejected the degree of radicalism Chávez and his faction wanted to implement once in government, give us an interesting discursive insight into the internal problems between moderates and radicals in this populist project. The second section discusses the events that occurred after the Bolivarian moderates left in January 2002, and the attacks the opposition organized to oust Chávez from power (e.g. the coup in April 2002 and national oil strike in December 2002–January 2003) as they realized there was no room for dialogue. The third section evaluates the second phase of institutional radicalism that started in April 2003. This phase consists of a variety of social programs in poor and remote excluded sectors designed to help Venezuela's underprivileged classes. The fourth section describes the emergence and success of three new opposition forces: a political party that ends its alliance with the Bolivarian project; General Raúl Baduel, Chávez's long-trusted friend, political ally, and military colleague, who publicly denounces in November 2007 his rejection of Chávez's socialist idea and run for re-election indefinitely (in a constitutional reform referendum held on December 2, 2007); and a student movement that challenges both Chávez's decision not to renew a broadcasting license of a TV channel in May 2007 and the constitutional reforms in the December 2007 referendum.

Chapter 4 is a fieldwork-based analysis of one of the social programs addressed in the third section of Chapter 3. This chapter provides an in-depth account explaining how the Bolivarian project constructed (with Cuban medical involvement) a comprehensive healthcare program to improve the living conditions of people in poor and marginalized sectors. This analysis illustrates the extent of community participation in the creation of new popular social programs. It also contextualizes how healthcare public services deteriorated in the last two decades and how the displaced institutional structure tries to contest the sedimentation of the Bolivarian institutional structure. This chapter helps us contextualize and thus understand the discursive articulation that formed a new phase of the populist

Introduction 7

Bolivarian project with direct grassroots popular participation. Divergent interpretations of this healthcare program are addressed and analyzed. My claim is that this popular program has radically transformed healthcare in Venezuela. With information gathered in three different regions of the country, I unfold people's opinions and the symbolic meaning of this 'free of charge' healthcare service. Furthermore, I show that, after years of the program's existence, the discourse of workers who are distressed about the future of the program due to poor management practices demonstrates important concerns about the fate of this healthcare program.

Chapter 5 is also a fieldwork-based analysis that investigates the student movement addressed in the 'New Opposition Forces' section in Chapter 3. Its formation and demands, and its methods of challenging the consolidation of the new institutional regime, are analyzed. This chapter investigates the discourse used to symbolize youth, an apolitical stance, innocence, and so on, in an effort to contest the expansion of the Bolivarian project. What I claim in this chapter is that this student movement, while it begins with many possibilities and seems to constitute a challenge to the new hegemonic project, ultimately loses focus and is absorbed into other opposition political parties. I explain why this movement, which displayed a great deal of initial optimism, failed to crystallize and effectively contest the Bolivarian project beyond its initial phase.

The last chapter of this investigation analyzes the referendum that took place on February 15, 2009. This referendum bypassed the incumbent's defeat in the constitutional referendum in December 2007, giving Chávez the right to stand for re-election indefinitely. The 'gerrymandering' district adjustments before the September 26, 2010, parliamentarian election are discussed. Chávez's health conditions and popularity after being diagnosed with cancer, the formation of four more 'mission' social programs—all occurring before the October 2012 presidential election—as well as Chávez's close relation with the symbol of Simon Bolívar are analyzed in the second section of this chapter. The concluding section starts with an interview with Leopoldo López, an influential opposition political leader who has Bolívar blood, and an analysis of the *Mesa Unidad Democratica* (MUD) unified opposition force, the five candidates who ran for the February 2012 opposition presidential primary election, and the celebratory speech of Henrique Capriles Randonski, who won with almost two-thirds of the vote.

News and information used in this book were gathered before March 2012.

1 Populism, Theories, and Logics
A Theoretical and Methodological Approach

This chapter starts with a section addressing general characteristics of the literature on populism. Margaret Canovan's theoretical approach to populism and other authors are addressed here. The following sub-section evaluates three theoretical populist approaches that could potentially provide an analytical structure for this in-depth investigation. First, Paul Taggart's 'heartland & chameleon' theoretical approach to populism is evaluated, followed by Francisco Panizza's theoretical propositions and Ernesto Laclau's theoretical characteristics of populism. The second section discusses Laclau's theoretical approach combined with Jason Glynos and David Howarth's 'logics approach' methodological schema. This chapter seeks to achieve two important objectives. First, it addresses different theoretical approaches to populism in the literature and determines which theories to use in order to identify instances of populist politics and categorize the key elements of such politics. Second, it selects a methodological model in which key elements from a case study can be categorized and offers a new approach to understanding the dynamics of populist political practices in a deeply polarized society.

1.1 THE CONCEPT OF POPULISM

For many years, the study of populism has been held back by the complex problem of framing a clear methodological schema. Some analysts have offered definitions or listed essential characteristics of populism, and others have found only dubious connections and weak similarities between different populist practices. Attempts to offer a general characterization of populism have been contentious.[1] According to Margaret Canovan, the definitions formed 'suggest affinities with ideological movements like socialism, liberalism or nationalism. But although all these other "isms" range over widely varied phenomena, each gains a degree of coherence to identify themselves by the name, distinctive principles and policies'. However, 'populism does not fit this pattern'.[2]

The abstract nature of populism is clearly fleshed out in Canovan's seven analytical sub-categories, published in 1981, which are: (1) farmers' radicalism,

(2) peasant movements, (3) intellectual agrarian socialism, (4) populist dictatorship, (5) populist democracy, (6) reactionary populism, and (7) politician's populism. The first three fall into the 'agrarian populisms' category, and the remaining four fall into the 'political populisms' category.[3] Canovan refers in brackets to a case in each sub-category. She emphasizes that this classification is a typology of populisms; thus the 'types suggested are analytical constructs—real-life examples may well overlap several categories'.[4] This classification was an attempt to simplify the nature of populist practice; nonetheless, choosing one sub-category while recognizing the possibility that cases might overlap does not provide much clarity to an investigation on a case study that appears to be populist. Furthermore, there is only a descriptive narrative, but no methodological structure to analyze what is behind these operations, explaining how and in what context these different types of populism are constructed and crystallized.

Canovan has worked extensively trying to unpack what makes this concept work. She notes that while the interpretations of others overlap and resemble one another across the broad phenomenon, they seem 'to have little in common apart from its rhetoric element of appeals to "the people"'.[5] Canovan points out that 'recent studies have underlined the importance of that populist discourse and shown that paying more attention to it can help both in understanding particular cases and in analyzing populist phenomena more generally'.[6] Once 'discourses of "the people"' have been analyzed, 'the next step is to investigate the range of meanings made available to populists by "the people's" ambiguities'.[7]

Canovan uses the phrase 'new populism' to describe what is in the news today. These new populist movements 'claim to speak for the forgotten mass of ordinary people'. New populists 'campaign for and the values they express depend on local concerns and the kind of political establishment they are challenging'. These new populists 'claim to say aloud what people think especially if it has been deemed by the elite to be unmentionable'. Confrontational in style, populists emphasize their 'closeness to the grassroots and their distance from the political establishment by using colorful and undiplomatic language'. Populists believe that they 'represent the rightful source of legitimate power to the people'.[8] Describing a phenomenon that appears to be populist is interesting; however, the prerogative is to find a methodology that classifies the social, political, and emotional elements that construct and articulate populist practices.

Canovan argues that to understand populism in modern democracy we need to be aware that 'democratic politics does not and cannot make sense to most of the people it aims to empower'.[9] Politics is mostly inclusive and democracy needs 'ideological' transparency. The politics communicated to the people is systematically misleading. 'This contradiction between ideology and practice is a standing invitation to populists to raise the cry of democracy betrayed, and to mobilize the discontented behind the banner of restoring politics to the people'.[10] Canovan's interpretation of populism and

10   *Populism in Venezuela*

modern democracy appears logical; nonetheless, how a populist political force demanding the restoration of a 'true democracy' (articulating popular participation) is constructed needs explaining.

According to Torcuato Di Tella, 'populist' also applies to conservative politicians who appeal to popular feelings and prejudices. 'Unimpeachable establishment leaders' like Ronald Reagan and Margaret Thatcher have been labeled populist. 'Though one should not quarrel about names, this exceedingly wide usage is not fruitful, because it can end by applying to almost any politician capable of winning an election'.[11] Di Tella states that the 'bad shape of the economy in Latin America can breed discontent and possibly populism. Admittedly, discontent can help to build a solid Left'. In Europe, new political projects that are 'often branded populist, should be put in a different category, because they are not aimed against the dominant groups but rather against the underprivileged ones they see as threatening'.[12]

In America, Michael Kazin claims that with populism 'Americans have been able to protest social and economic inequalities without calling the entire system into question'. Americans believe 'that mass democracy can topple any haughty foe means avoiding gloomy thoughts about entrenched structures of capital and the state that often frustrate the most determined movement. Populism is thus a grand form of rhetorical optimism; once mobilized, there is nothing ordinary Americans cannot accomplish'.[13] According to Kazin's definition, populism is 'more an impulse than ideology . . . too elastic and promiscuous . . . people [populists during American politics in the twentieth century] employed populism as a flexible mode of persuasion. They used traditional kinds of expressions, tropes, themes, and images to convince large numbers of Americans to join their side or to endorse their views on particular issues'.[14] In my view, dichotomy in America's society is not polarized enough for social and political unrest to emerge and challenge the institutional structure as a whole. Populist demands succeed in changing conditions via democratic processes without de-instituting the establishment. In other words, these kinds of political practices are better classified as moderate populism.

I have discussed some interpretations of populism, highlighting the ambiguity of this political phenomenon. Nonetheless, I cannot find a methodological approach with a theoretical structure that explains the explanandum posed in the introduction of this investigation. Canovan uses the phrase new populism to describe what is in the news today. In my view, this is only a naming exercise without sufficient methodological grounds to explain the shift from 'Traditional to New Populism' (e.g. democratic appeal to the people only scratches the surface), and Canovan claims that we should acknowledge that 'recent stress on populist rhetoric raises an issue that goes beyond matters of definition'.[15]

The theories I discuss below could provide the framework to analyze this in-depth case study. First, Taggart's theoretical proposition is addressed, followed by a discussion of Francisco Panizza's theoretical interpretation of

Populism, Theories, and Logics 11

populism. This section concludes with Ernesto Laclau's theoretical understanding of populist practices. I aim to select methods that could help me unpack what populism entails and comprehend the necessary conditions for populist practices to emerge, who invests in a populist project, why and how they do so, and how this project crystallizes itself. I'll explain at the end of each sub-section the value of each theoretical approach.

1.1.1 Taggart's Theoretical Approach: 'Heartland & Chameleon'

Paul Taggart describes 'populism as an unusual concept' with an 'essential impalpability and awkward conceptual slipperiness'. Taggart claims that populism appears to be 'revolutionary . . . offering the potential to radically transform politics'.[16] Taggart stresses that 'populism is a difficult, slippery concept'. It 'lacks features that would make it more tangible'. Thus, 'it is profoundly difficult to construct a generalised description, let alone a universal and comprehensive definition of populism as an idea or as a political movement'.[17] Taggart tries to define this phenomenon 'by exploring six key themes that run through populism':

- Populists as hostile to representative politics
- Populists identifying themselves with an idealized heartland within the community they favor
- Populism as an ideology lacking core values
- Populism as a powerful reaction to a sense of extreme crisis
- Populism as containing fundamental dilemmas that make it self-limiting
- Populism as a chameleon, adopting the colors of its environment

These six themes can interlink with each other in different ways. Based upon the context of the researched case, these themes can cast light on the particularities of a populist involvement.[18]

Taggart points out that a populist practice 'excludes elements it sees as alien, corrupt or debased, and works on a distinction between the things which are wholesome and those which are not'.[19] In this context, Taggart describes 'heartland' (mentioned in the second theme above) and the margins. 'It is a notion that is constructed by looking inward and backward'. 'Heartland' creates 'a world that embodies the collective ways and wisdom of the people who construct it, usually with reference to what has gone before (even if that is idealized)'. The heartland 'is populated by "the people" and gives meaning to constructions and invocations of the people by populists'.[20] Taggart claims that populism has an essentially 'chameleonic' quality—taking 'on the hue of the environment in which it occurs'.[21] This is not a disguise or camouflage, but an ability to adapt to the circumstances it encounters. 'Populism has primary and secondary features, and one of its primary features is that it takes on, as a matter of course, secondary

12 *Populism in Venezuela*

features from its context'. Ideologies tend to do this, whereas 'populism constructs narratives, myths and symbols', with the need to 'resonate with the heartland draw[ing] on the surroundings to a fundamental degree'.[22]

Taggart notes that populism 'lacks universal key values, it is chameleonic, taking on attributes of its environment, and, in practice, is episodic. Populism is an episodic, anti-political, empty-hearted, chameleonic celebration of the heartland in the face of crisis'.[23] Furthermore, Taggart states that 'populism serves many masters and mistresses . . . it has been a force for change, against change, a creature of progressive politics of the left . . . a companion of the extreme right'.[24] The reason for its adaptability lies in the 'empty-heart' of populism, lacking a commitment to key values. 'While other ideologies contain, either implicitly or explicitly, a focus on one or more values such as equality, liberty and justice, populism has no such core to it'. This explains why a wide range of political practices can be defined as populist.[25] Taggart argues that in the politics of the 'heartland', 'populist rhetoric uses the language of the people not because this expresses democratic convictions about the sovereignty of the masses, but because "the people" are the occupants of the heartland and this is what populists are trying to evoke'.[26] In other words, populist rhetoric, in the name of the occupants of the heartland, discursively emphasizes in a political dimension what they (people) perceive of their heartland.

Heartland can be categorized as a territory of the imagination. In spite of the abstracted nature of heartland, it is a powerful mechanism that reminds 'native' people the damage immigrants have caused to their traditional way of life, and politically defends those national qualities that are threatened by foreign subjects that have invaded and intoxicated the cultural fabric of their land. Populists projecting the heartland 'use their imaginative glances backward in an attempt to construct what has been lost by the present'.[27] This is a sentimental evocation that is not 'necessarily either rationalized or rationalizable'. To Taggart, 'the heartland is constructed not only with reference to the past, but also through the establishment of its frontiers', justifying 'the exclusion of the demonized'. The lines of inclusion are fuzzy but those of exclusion are usually much clearer.[28] Exclusion refers to groups that practice foreign customs, therefore intruding into and invading the harmony in the heartland.

The relation between Taggart's populist heartland concept and nationalistic sentiments is to 'exclude those outside the nation and it does not include all those in the nation'. This is clearly a category to dichotomize the population. It 'explicitly excludes a series of social groups and is based around the idea of an organic community that has some natural solidarity and therefore is more circumscribed than the sort of community contained within the national boundaries'.[29] I interpret 'natural' as referring to those communities that fully practice and enjoy a national hegemonic order. 'Populism will identify with nationalism when nationalism is an expression of the values of the heartland'.[30] Taggart's theoretical approach highlights interesting characteristics about

Populism, Theories, and Logics   13

this ('slippery') phenomenon. The term 'idealized heartland' tries to describe nationalistic populism, but more theoretical components defining two dichotomous views of national hegemony in a nation could make this term useful. Taggart's explanation what 'universal key values' entails is not convincing. The term 'chameleonic' (referring to attributes of its environment) has too many loose ends because it does not theoretically address social subjects and political elements in populist practices. Perhaps Francisco Panizza's theoretical views of populism could shed light on interesting and crucial characteristics of this phenomenon.

1.1.2 Panizza's Theoretical Propositions

According to Panizza, the core of populism is the constitution of the people as a political actor. Populism works 'as an anti-status quo discourse that simplifies the political space by symbolically dividing society between "people" (as the "underdogs") and its "*other*"'.[31] These two camps are constituted on the basis of antagonism rather than sociological categories. Antagonism is what constructs this political project. 'This is the mode of identification in which the relation between its form (the people as signifier) and its content (the people as signified) . . . establish who the enemies of the people (and therefore the people itself) are'. Populism constructs popular identities seeking to 'politically defeat "*the other*" that is deemed to oppress or exploit the people and therefore to impede its full presence'.[32] This oppressive '*other*' against the 'underdog' can be politically or economically constructed ('or a combination of both') as representing the '"oligarchy", "the politicians" . . . "the Washington insiders", "the plutocracy" or any other group that prevents the people achieving plenitude'.[33]

Panizza notes that 'populists are well aware that politics always consists of the creation of an '"Us" versus a "Them"'.[34] In other words, a populist empathizes with the antagonized population because 'we' (us: the people) struggle in a dichotomized society. 'Populist practices emerge out of the failure of existing and political institutions to confine and regulate political subjects into a relatively stable social order'. The terrain of 'politics as usual' is no longer sustainable. Based upon the 'mode of identification' earlier mentioned, a populist project articulates 'a political appeal that seeks to change the terms of political discourse, articulate new social relations, redefine political frontiers and constitute new identities'.[35]

To contextualize what he implies with the terms 'identification' and 'political appeal', Panizza states that 'populist practices operate within a social space in which people have grievances, desires, needs and wants that have not yet been constituted as political demands or, to put it in another way, people do not know how to name what they are lacking'.[36] A populist project successfully incorporates all these 'private wants and needs' and is 'transformed into public demands by the leader's action of bringing them into public discourse'. This process opens new forms of identification. It is like

14   *Populism in Venezuela*

a 'metaphor of awakening a dormant identity that was "already there", but the "awakening" can be best understood as the constitution of new political identities and the politicization of issues that had previously not been part of the political agenda'.[37]

Panizza argues that 'populism is not just about a crisis of representation in which people are weaned off their old identities and embrace a new "popular" one'. This political project provides an opportunity for those 'who have never been represented because of their class, religion, ethnicity or geographical location'.[38] People identify with a populist project because it provides a political framework that identifies their problems and can collectively represent them. Under these conditions, populism opens new forms of identification and 'becomes a dominant mode of identification'. For example, high inflation produces deep social dislocation. 'Breakdowns of social order can also be produced by civil wars, ethnic conflict or natural catastrophes. But crises are often a combination of the economic and the political'.[39]

The meaning of 'people' in this context is primarily 'identified as *the plebs, el vulgo, the populace*; that is, as the lowest sectors of society defined in terms of their intellectual, cultural and socio-economic inferiority in relation to the civilized society'.[40] Panizza stresses that 'at the heart of populist identification is an image of the fullness of the people, which is always incomplete, achieved by the exclusion of an outside that can never be fully vanquished'.[41] The exclusion represents the *'other'*, those responsible for what people are lacking: the regime, oligarchs, corrupt politicians, and so on. The 'Us versus Them' configuration in populist politics constitutes populist identities and sets up new political frontiers.

Another crucial element is the role of leadership in a populist project. Panizza explains that a 'leader functions as a signifier to which a multiplicity of meanings can be attributed, as Jason Glynos put it, as an enigma that promises meaning: the promise of a fully reconciled people'.[42] Panizza notes that 'if populism can be redefined as a process of naming that retroactively determines what is the name of the "people", the name that best fills the symbolic void through which identification takes place is that of the leader himself'.[43] In other words, the leader is not only a political representative, but also a receiving symbolic figure that incorporates and provides a name for all the needs, wants, problems, etc., of the 'people' antagonized by the *'other'*. For example, 'people identify with a leader chiefly through the stories he or she relates not only with words but more broadly, by the use of symbols, including the leader's own body and personal life'.[44]

Panizza adds another important element: 'imaginary identification' with the leader- follower relationship. According to Slavoj Žižek, 'that imaginary identification is identification with the image in which we appear likeable to ourselves. Žižek points out that the trait by which we identify with someone is by no means necessarily a glamorous feature. This trait can also be a certain failure, weakness or even the guilt of the other, so that by pointing out the failure we can unwittingly reinforce the identification'.[45] This sense of identification and the failure of the *'other'* with respect to *'we'* (the people) 'explains

Populism, Theories, and Logics 15

why it is that the more their adversaries demonize the populist leaders, the more it usually reinforces the people's identification with them'.[46]

A final point to examine in Panizza's theoretical approach is the relation between populism and democracy. He stresses that 'populism has traditionally been regarded as a threat to democracy'. That relation of 'raw passion' between a populist leader and supporters, and its 'disregard for political institutions and the rule of law—all make populism an easy target for those who use it as a term of derision'.[47] Panizza quotes Canovan's 'disturbing question when she asks why, if notions of popular power and popular decision are central to democracy, are populists not acknowledged as the true democrats they say they are'.[48] Populist practices do indeed flesh out the 'blind spots' of liberal democracy. Nonetheless, 'the relation between populism and democracy is also problematic'. Because there are different versions of who the people are and who their legitimate speaker is, the notion of popular sovereignty is provisional; 'therefore the argument for the toleration of differences is not a liberal argument but a democratic argument as well'.[49]

As Claude Lefort puts it, 'democracy power is an "empty place" that can only be provisionally occupied'.[50] Problems occur when a political discourse doesn't want to respect that 'empty' element in democracy: 'claiming to speak for the people as its unmediated representative', thus appropriating the place of power, 'it is democracy itself, and not just liberalism, that is being denied. Taken to the extreme populism descends into totalitarianism'.[51] Panizza's theoretical basis sheds light on crucial features of populist practices. His analysis of the 'Us' versus 'Them' mode of identification, the meaning of the people, leadership as a signifier, and the composition of populism with democratic practices—all can be applied to this in-depth case study. Rather than stating that populism is an 'appeal to the people' discourse, Panizza has provided methods to apply a discursive analysis to a case that appears to be populist. The next and final sub-section addresses Ernesto Laclau's theoretical approach to populism.

1.1.3 Laclau's Theoretical Characteristics of Populism

Laclau's first theoretical work on populism was published in 1977. Since then, Laclau has refined his theoretical approach by incorporating new concepts into his framework and providing better devices to define and thus understand populist positions and practices. In his book *On Populist Reason*, published in 2005, Laclau pulls together concepts explored in other works in order to frame a new theoretical concept of populism.[52] In this sub-section, I address Laclau's general outlook on populism and concepts such as empty signifiers, hegemony, and logics of difference and equivalence. I examine the role of these concepts in his updated theoretical structure.

According to Laclau, populism is often categorized with some pejorative labels. 'Those pejorative connotations can be maintained only if one accepts, as a starting point of the analysis, a set of questionable assumptions':

16 *Populism in Venezuela*

(1) That populism is vague and indeterminate in the audience to which it addresses itself, in its discourse, and in its political postulates; (2) that populism is mere rhetoric. To this I (Laclau) opposed two different possibilities: (1) that vagueness and indeterminacy are not shortcomings of a discourse about social reality, but, in some circumstances, inscribed in social reality as such; (2) that rhetoric is not epiphenomenal vis-à-vis a self-contained conceptual structure, for no conceptual structure finds its internal cohesion without appealing to rhetorical devices. If this is so, the conclusion would be that populism is the royal road to understanding something about the ontological constitution of the political as such.[53]

Laclau seeks to articulate a theoretical framework and offer a way to understand the core of political populist practices. To start with, some general ontological assumptions, which have been explored in Laclau's preliminary works, will be discussed. The three sets of categories that are central to this theoretical approach are:

1. *Discourse*: Laclau has attempted to clarify the meaning of discourse several times. He states that it 'is not something that is essentially restricted to the areas of speech and writing; but any complex of elements in which *relations* play the represented role'. This means that the elements are constituted through the 'relational complex' construction process. 'Thus "relation" and "objectivity" are synonymous'. Laclau argues that 'there is no beyond the play of differences, no ground which would a priori privilege some elements of the whole over the others. Whatever centrality an element acquires, it has to be explained by the play of differences as such'.[54] He calls '*articulation* any practice establishing a relation among elements such that their identity is modified as a result of the articulatory practice. The structured totality resulting from the articulatory practice, we (Laclau and Mouffe) call *discourse*'.[55] Discourse is articulated and its socio-political significance is emphasized in Laclau's attention to differences, how new practices are crystallized, thus modifying identities and articulating a terrain of totality. This creates a sense of dichotomy, an 'us-them' axis. Discourse plays a key role in this process.
2. *Empty signifiers and hegemony*: these categories are mentioned briefly in this theoretical framework. A detailed explanation can be found in 'Why Do Empty Signifiers Matter to Politics?'[56] As Laclau puts it:

   (i) Given that we are dealing with purely differential identities, we have, in some way, to determine the whole within which those identities, as different, are constituted (the problem would not, obviously, arise if we were dealing with positive, only externally related, identities).
   (ii) Since we are not postulating any necessary structural center, endowed with a priori 'determination in the last instance' capacity, 'centering' effects that manage to constitute a precarious totalizing horizon have to proceed from the interaction of the differences themselves.[57]

Populism, Theories, and Logics   17

We have to discursively understand what Laclau tries to explain by stating: 'to determine the whole within which those identities are different'. He argues that what is external to those identities (categorized by *Them* [not one of *Us*] as *other* identities) performs a vital role in this process. In this context, the totalizing horizon is constructed. Empty signifiers are structured in the following five steps:

I. Even though we have a gathering of different identities, 'totality has to be present in each individual act of signification. Conceptually grasping that totality', and hence collectively constituting what they stand for as one force and what they seek to signify, is necessary.[58]

II. 'To grasp that totality', it is important to be aware that there are limitations because it has to differentiate in relation to something else '*other* than itself'. Nevertheless, this is only a difference, but as the aim is to construct 'a totality that embraces *all* the differences, this *other* difference represents the outside'—providing the necessary condition to construct that totality: the internal versus the external. Without demarcating what the *other* (us-them difference) is, it would be difficult to construct that sense of totality as such.[59]

III. 'The only possibility of having a true outside would be that the outside is not simply one more, neutral element but an *excluded* one,' something that is strongly rejected by *them* (the people) in order to construct itself.[60] For example, by politically claiming that the *other* section of the population is evil (demonization) 'the society reaches a sense of its own cohesion'. Those that do not support 'totality' are the *excluded* identity. Those that share that sense of identity constructed when totality was formed, is what Laclau calls equivalence. 'Equivalence is precisely what subverts differences, so all identity is constructed within this tension between the differential and the equivalential logics'.[61]

IV. As there is tension in the locus of the totality, 'what we have, ultimately, is a failed totality, the place for an irretrievable fullness. The totality is an object which is both impossible and necessary'. It is impossible because that tension between equivalence and difference is 'ultimately insurmountable'. It is necessary because without some closure, regardless of how ambiguous it might be, there is neither meaning nor identity.[62]

V. As there is no need to strictly and fully determine that object, the representation involved needs to be represented in one way or another, because simply creating that totality is not enough. 'The need remains for this impossible object somehow to have access to the field of representation. Representation has, however, as it only means, particular differences'. This point moves to the 'possibility that one difference, without ceasing to be a *particular* difference, assumes the representation of an incommensurable totality'.[63]

18 *Populism in Venezuela*

A totality that assembles *all* differences with a common outside makes totality possible. The outside is not just another neutral element but one that is clearly expelled (an *excluded* one). If a political project demonizes a section of the population, this helps society (totality) constitute its own cohesion. As Laclau points out, 'identity is constructed within this tension between the differential and the equivalential logics'.[64] However, in the locus of totality there is tension, which creates a failed totality. This represents an inconsolable fullness where an impossible object becomes the entry to the field of representation. Regardless of its ambiguity, there would be neither meaning nor identity without totality. The impossible object that has access to the field of representation is accepted by particular differences without eliminating their differences. In this context, we have an incommensurable totality; Laclau calls it 'universal signification'.[65]

According to Laclau, *'hegemony'* is 'this operation of taking up by particularity of an incommensurable universal signification'.[66] This 'embodied totality or universality is an impossible object, the hegemonic identity becomes something of the order of an *empty* signifier, its own particularity embodying an unachievable fullness'.[67] Laclau remarks that this category of totality cannot end because this failed totality is only 'a horizon not a ground'. Under these settings, 'a hegemonic totalization requires a radical investment' which may not be clear at the start, but signifies something different; 'affective dimension plays a central role here'.[68] These theoretical lenses can shed light on the operations that make populist practices effective. For example, they can illuminate how equivalence subverts particular differences in order to construct a new *hegemony*. Also, upon this new horizon, this hegemonic totalization requires radical investment, which involves a sense of affection. The third category is *rhetoric*.

> 3. *Rhetoric*: Laclau argues that 'there is a rhetorical displacement whenever a literal term is substituted by a figural one'. To explain this point he uses Cicero's reflection on the origin of rhetorical devices.[69] Let us imagine an undeveloped (primitive stage) society with more things to be named than the words available in that particular language, so words are used in more than one sense, 'deviating them from their literal, primordial meaning'. To Cicero, 'this shortage of words represented a purely empirical lack'.[70] However, 'this lack is not empirical, it is linked to *constitutive* blockage in that language which requires naming something which is *essentially* unnameable as a condition of language functioning'. In this context, 'the original language would not be literal but figural, for without giving names to the unnameable there would no language at all'.[71]

In classical rhetoric, when a figural cannot be replaced by a literal term we have *'catachresis'*. According to Laclau, 'if the empty signifier arises from the need to name an object which is both impossible and necessary ... the hegemonic

Populism, Theories, and Logics   19

operation will be catachrestical through and through'. Therefore, 'the political construction of the "the people" is, for that reason, essentially catachrestical'.[72] This is the generalization of its root by the need to express something that the literal term cannot communicate. So, catachresis is not only a particular figure, but also 'the common denominator of rhetoricity'.[73] The limitations in a language constitute a sense of catachresis, and the same phenomenon occurs in the hegemonic operation and the construction of a 'popular' political platform. To Laclau, these are the preconditions to a discussion of populism.[74]

The way to analyze populism is by observing if there is a unified formation of a group. '"The people" is not something of a nature of an ideological expression, but a real relation between social agents. It is, in other terms, one way of constituting the unity of the group'. Some social agents could have necessities and identities and thus support projects 'different to the populist one'. To understand a populist articulatory practice, we have to isolate units smaller than the group and investigate what kind of units identify with a populist project. For example, 'the smallest unit from which we will start corresponds to the category of "social demand"'.[75] The idea of demand can be unclear as it can also mean a 'claim as demanding an explanation to something'. Misunderstanding its content is useful 'because it is in the transition from request to claim that we are going to find one of the first defining features of populism'.[76] These points are carefully addressed and analyzed in the next section (see Diagram 1.4 on page 30).

Demands have particularities and have a different nature (*logic of difference*). However, when particularities are partially subverted and declare what all particularities have equivalentially in common, we have the construction of an antagonistic frontier, which is the *logic of equivalence*. For this totalization to come into effect, particularities are subverted and link its equivalential bond with all other particularities. 'The partial totalization that the hegemonic link manages to create does not eliminate that split but, on the contrary, has to operate out of the structural possibilities deriving from it. So both difference and equivalence have to reflect themselves with each other'.[77] Populist totalization creates an excluded frontier to divide society into two camps. '"The people" ... is something less than the totality of the members of the community: it is a partial component which nevertheless aspires to be conceived as the only legitimate totality'.[78] The members of a partial totality camp with subverted differences link together because they have something in common. 'The people can be conceived as *populus*, the body of all citizens; or as *plebs*, the underprivileged'. For populism to emerge, *plebs* must claim to be the only legitimate *populus*, seeking to 'function as the totality of the community'.[79]

Let's analyze how *populus*, *plebs* or underprivileged agents articulate demands. First, we have a clear dichotomic terrain between unfulfilled social demands and an unresponsive power. This is the reason 'why plebs sees itself as the *populus*, the part as the whole'. This kind of 'fullness of the community is merely the imaginary reverse of a situation lived as *deficient beings*'. The underprivileged claim that 'those who are responsible for this

20   *Populism in Venezuela*

cannot be a legitimate part of the community, the chasm between them is irretrievable'.[80] In other words, the underprivileged create a dichotomic frontier to contest an unresponsive power responsible for their *deficient being* status. As Laclau states:

> Populism involves the division of the social scene into two camps. This division presupposes the presence of some privileged signifiers which condense in themselves the signification of a whole antagonistic camp (the 'regime' the 'oligarchy', the 'dominant groups', and so on, for the enemy; the 'people', the 'nation', the 'silent majority', and so on, for the oppressed underdog—these signifiers acquire this articulating role according, obviously, to a contextual history).[81]

'The tension between differences and equivalence inside a complex of demands becomes "popular" through their articulation'.[82] This inscription gives the demand the substance it would not otherwise have. These practices are crucial to these particular demands because they are linked to others through the 'equivalential chain', which was discursively materialized. The progress of populism is very much related to the future of the political frontier that is constructed with the equivalential links of dissolution demands. 'If the frontier collapses, the "people" as a historical actor disintegrates'.[83] For populism to crystallize and challenge the regime, 'people's' radical investment is crucial. Without dissolution demands, there is no populism.

Two aspects are required for popular identities to be constituted:

> First, the demand which the popular identity crystallizes is internally split: on the one hand, it remains a particular demand; on the other, its own particularity comes to signify something quite different from itself: the total chain of equivalential demands.
>
> Secondly, our argument had to dovetail, at this point . . . about the production of 'empty signifiers'. Any popular identity needs to be condensed around some signifiers (words, images) which refer to the equivalential chain as a totality. The more extended the chain, the less these signifiers will be attached to their original particularistic demands. That is to say, the function of representing the relative 'universality' of the chain will prevail over that of expressing the particular claim . . . popular identity becomes increasingly full . . . representing an even larger chain of demands; but it becomes *intensionally* poorer, for it has to dispossess itself of particularistic contents in order to embrace social demands which are quite heterogeneous.[84]

Laclau points out that popular identity alters when more particularities adopt the equivalential chain as a totality. The extension of the equivalential chain weakens the chosen signifier that aims to embody all particularistic demands. Popular identities are affected when the chain is extended,

Regarding the role of leadership in a populist project, Laclau claims that we must analyze 'whether there is not something in the equivalential bond which already pre-announces key aspects of the leader's function'. We must recognize that 'the popular subject position does not simply *express* a unity of demands constituted outside and before itself, but is the decisive moment in establishing unity'.[85] The moment of naming the totality is important. Coherent articulation in the chain from the radical heterogeneity of the links entering into the equivalential chain 'exists only in so far as one of its links plays the role of considering all the others, in that case the unity of the discursive formation is transferred from the conceptual order (logic of difference) to the nominal one'. In this case, the name becomes the ground of the thing. Identification of unity (chain) uses the name of the leader. For example, 'Nelson Mandela's role as the symbol of the nation was compatible with a great deal of pluralism within his movement . . . the symbolic unification of the group around an individuality is inherent to the formation of a "people"'.[86]

According to Laclau, 'a rhetorical displacement or aggregation has precisely the function of emancipating a name from its univocal conceptual attachments. . . . This relation of contiguity will start to shade into one of analogy, the metonymy into metaphor'.[87] Thus, leader rhetoric (symbolizing the name) can re-constitute the equivalential chain. In this context, 'this becomes the name of a *concrete* social agent, whose only essence is the specific articulation of heterogeneous elements which, through the name, crystallize in a unified collective will'.[88] That is, an empty signifier (e.g. words, images, symbols) crystallizes the populist collective will of particularities.

With respect to the materialization of populist practices, Laclau reaffirms that 'the emergence of the "people" requires the passage—via equivalences—from isolated, heterogeneous demands to a "global" demand which involves the formation of political frontiers and the discursive construction of power as an antagonistic force'.[89] However, 'this passage does not follow from a mere analysis of the heterogeneous demands themselves'. There is 'no logical, dialectical or semiotic transition from one level to the other—something qualitatively has to intervene'. As Laclau notes, '"naming" can have the retroactive effect. This qualitatively differentiated and irreducible moment' is what Laclau calls 'radical investment'.[90]

This idea of investment in different signifying operations casts light on the forms the investment takes, but what makes that investment go forward is unknown. That needs to be explored in a case study. Obviously, 'an entity becomes the object of investment as in being in love, or in hatred, therefore the investment belongs essentially to the order of *affect*'.[91] Affect is the formation of different condensed emotions that go into a signifying chain. This is the meaning of 'investment'. This network of differential and equivalential logics constituted by 'discursive or hegemonic formations' would be unintelligible without the feelings and emotions 'the affective component' provides.[92]

22   *Populism in Venezuela*

We have to be clear that no social fullness is achievable except through hegemony, and that hegemony is created by investing in a partial object, of a fullness which will always confuse us because it is simply a fantasy, like thinking of the absolute opposite of being labeled 'deficient being'. Laclau's theoretical analysis states that there would be no populism without affective investment in a partial object. Nonetheless, there is a need to constitute what the 'people' signify as *plebs* for it to claim to be *populus*. This can be done when there is no fullness so the partial object within that society becomes coherent when aims, figures, and symbols are emotionally gripped together, thus becoming the 'name' of its absence. This is why affect is so important in populism.[93]

Thus, a popular identity requires the presence of an empty signifier expressing and constituting an equivalential chain. That equivalential articulation links a plurality of demands in a hegemonic totalization, constructed by different particularities that affectively participate in the *'radical investment'* (affect) process. These practices crystallize the 'popular' political collective 'will' that demands fullness to the antagonistic camp. The name of the leader can be the symbol in the equivalential chain that unifies particularities as a collective will. It is vital to discursively construct a dichotomized society between the excluded, underprivileged, underdog (antagonistic) camp and the unresponsive/repressive regime, the oligarchs, elite, and so on. The latter camp is labeled the 'enemy', responsible for people's misfortunes. This populist dimension is constructed upon a process of *discourse, empty signifiers,* and *hegemonic formation.* Laclau's *difference* and *equivalence logics* schema offers a set of useful analytical components, which serve as themes to contextualize a case study, investigate the grounds upon which this phenomenon can be categorized as 'populist', and analyze the social and political terrain that constructs and articulates these practices.

This section examined three theoretical approaches to populism and selected the one that provides a comprehensive approach to evaluate social and political practices articulated in the Venezuelan context. Taggart provides two interesting terms (heartland and chameleon), but this theoretical proposition fails to unpack and theoretically analyze elements related with these terms. Panizza argues that the analogy between the leader and the people works as a symbolic figure that effectively captures and names the meaning of the 'people' in that particular context. The concept 'imaginary identification' describes what Panizza wants to imply with the leader-people relation. Also, Panizza's analysis of how democracy and populism are entangled raises important issues that need to be considered to understand populist practices. Panizza's theoretical contribution will be revisited with descriptive material throughout the following chapters.

Laclau's theory of populism is a detailed analytical examination that casts light on a variety of social and political elements. Laclau offers an interesting and convincing insight into this 'vague and unclear' political concept. For example, Laclau describes how excluded, underprivileged social groups can crystallize a universal demand against a 'common enemy'. The concept of an empty signifier is a theoretical tool that provides a way to unpack those

Populism, Theories, and Logics 23

elusive mechanisms that construct and crystallize a populist project. All these internal processes are the operations behind what Laclau names 'hegemonic totalization'. All particular demands are condensed and reconstituted as an equivalential chain, which is the 'totality' of different links, as one collective will. This is 'popular identity'. The concept of *'hegemony'*, as a 'populist' and 'neoliberal-opposition' position, will be used throughout this investigation. The aim is to socially, politically, and ideologically explain how forces from both camps articulate in Venezuela's polarized society. This analytical method will be discussed in the next section of this chapter.

Furthermore, contextualizing 'radical investment' as a new political platform in Venezuela, one that constructed an equivalential chain of particularistic demands against a non-responsive/oppressive regime (demonization), helps unfold the conditions where populist practices emerged, and the discursive articulation that reproduces it. The next section presents the methodological schema I'll use in this investigation. I'll draw on Laclau's theory of populism in order to complement it with Jason Glynos and David Howarth's methodology: 'a logics approach'.

1.2 STRUCTURAL-METHODOLOGICAL AND THEORETICAL SCHEMA: A LOGICS APPROACH

Following the previous section's discussion of populism and various theoretical frameworks, this section focuses on what methods and theoretical tools can help us observe events and/or subjects from a different context and select the right empirical information from a particular case that seems to be experiencing populist practices. For instance, historical events can unearth key episodes of a deeply polarized society today and thus better explain why a country is experiencing a significant degree of populism. It is vital to highlight why sectors of a society feel antagonized and identify with the emerging discourse of radical institutional change a new political movement articulates.

In order to understand populist practices, it is important to go beyond the common practice of obliviously stating that populist success is rooted in manipulative charismatic leaders promising the masses a new form of a magical power if elected. There might be a degree of truth in this perception, but it is crucial to figure out if there are other hidden elements involved before implying that populism is simply a rather degraded tactic of electoral manipulation. For instance, unhealed social unrest can easily remind a society of past grievances and be used as an element to move the masses and crystallize a new political project. Thus, these types of factors require empirical-historical hindsight, which can unfold the elements that have contributed towards the emergence of a phenomenon that appears to be populist.

For these reasons, it is significant that the following chapters discuss these elements and thus flesh out the conditions for antagonistic sentiments (the term used by Laclau, discussed earlier in the theoretical section) to emerge, develop, and progressively form a political articulation against an oppressive/elitist

24   *Populism in Venezuela*

institutional structure. Thus, within this context, some well-defined questions need to be addressed:

1. Are there any categories available in the literature that can effectively help us construct a methodological model and integrate all the significant populist elements?
2. If there is a methodological model in the literature, what is the theoretical framework that helps us identify vital populist elements?
3. On which category (if there are any) of that model should each element be classified?

These three questions highlight key aspects that need to be answered in this section. It is considered that any contribution this research can offer lies in a methodological model where key elements from this case study can be carefully analyzed and which can offer a new approach towards populism. Let us be aware that the type of data/resources required to analyze the nature of this type of political practice is highly abstract and compatible with an analysis of populism from a discursive theoretical perspective.[94] The structure of this chapter is centered on presenting how the existing literature can help us answer the above questions and thus develop a theoretical schema for this investigation. The first question above is related to the search for a set of mechanisms/categories in the current literature that will hopefully offer a methodological structure for this analysis.

Before addressing the three questions mentioned earlier, I must discuss fundamental components in the existing literature. This section begins by discussing a methodological model which is considered suitable for this analytical research on populist practices. I consider this model useful because the authors make use of discursive terms also used in one of the theoretical approaches discussed in the previous section. In other words, a contextual criterion for populist elements can be constructed upon the category of 'logics'. I'll discuss various ways this category can be articulated, placing central emphasis upon the meaning of social, political, and fantasmatic logics. The articulation of these logics represents fundamental categories that help me answer the above questions, as well as provide a full-bodied structure for my argument on populist practices in various chapters of the investigation. Still, how can these category 'logics' be useful for an investigation of a phenomenon that appears to be populist?

This methodological model was developed by Jason Glynos and David Howarth, Ernesto Laclau's successors in the Essex Discourse Analysis School he founded in 1982; much of it rests on Laclau's theoretical concepts. Laclau's theory of populism was discussed in the previous section of this chapter. However, it is vital to revisit his 'logic of equivalence' category (see pages 17–21) to supplement it in this chapter with Glynos and Howarth's 'logics of critical explanation'. The co-authors add elements that develop and enhance Laclau's novel theoretical approach to the study of populism. For instance, Glynos and Howarth employ one of Laclau's key theoretical terms, which is the notion of

Populism, Theories, and Logics 25

'logic'. This approach provides resourceful instruments, or as they name it, a 'conception' that offers a suitable methodological model for this empirical and theoretical in-depth case study. Nonetheless, before presenting Glynos and Howarth's model, I'll address an article written by Howarth[95] that draws on method-articulation. By analyzing Howarth's earlier work (which addresses the South African context), his connection with Laclau's populist theoretical framework can be fleshed out.

1.2.1 Logics

First of all, the category of logics means, in general terms, the rules put forward as a central focus of a practice, institution, or system regarding the association or interaction between objects. This category also includes the 'kinds entities (and their relations) presupposed by the operation of such rules'.[96] For instance, Howarth uses the 'logic of the market' to explain the set of rules bringing together buyers and sellers of commodities and how aspects like price mechanisms make this practice of exchange work. These conditions explain how social and political logics within post-Marxist discourse theory function. The presupposed relation of the market as such automatically implements fundamental rules in this practice thus transforming the social and political logics.[97] The importance of the 'logics' approach in this populist research is its ability to capture different aspects of a practice. This classification method works by dividing key elements into several sub-categories: social, political, and fantasmatic logics. I'll elaborate on these conceptions later.

Howarth further explains his understanding of 'logics' by focusing on the South African case. For example, 'social logics are conditional and historically specific systems of sedimented practice, such as the "logic of the market"; the "logic of bureaucracy" or; the "logic of apartheid" [South African term], political logics refer to special kinds of practice that constitute and contest these social logics'.[98] Howarth argues further that 'political logics thus fulfill a role analogous to "fundamental ontology"' (a term from Heidegger's philosophy), as the landscape to construct and shape 'the rules governing any particular social logic'.[99] 'The (social) logic of apartheid', which was 'later challenged by precise political logics',[100] aimed to prevent social disruption in South Africa. Apartheid created a '"system of differences" through which particular ethnic and national groups were allocated separate and formally equal institutions and territorial spaces wherein they could exercise their legitimate "demands" for political and cultural self-determination'.[101] Their motive was to suppress any grounds for 'logics of equivalence and differences [to] emerge'.[102] These 'logics' were earlier discussed in Laclau's theoretical framework in the previous section (logics of equivalence: see pages 17–21; logics of difference: pages 17–20). The differences that divided and structured social space in South Africa sought to maintain the isolation of these groups from each other and minimize an attempt to create some form of hegemony. In other words, the differences sought to prevent any forms of linkage between these groups.[103]

26 *Populism in Venezuela*

As we have seen, the category of logic is used in different forms that inter-connect with each other. For instance, Howarth uses the 'logic of the market' and describes, based on practices of exchange, how social and political logics emerge. Moreover, Laclau's term 'logics of difference and equivalence' covers key theoretical factors, hence providing a potential methodological tool to this investigation. Thus, if there is a methodological model centering on the notion of 'logic', which provides a framework where socio-political elements within a society can be precisely identified and categorized, that is the model this investigation needs.

Before going any further, we need to address the question as to why certain past events or periods remain 'emotionally' significant to a society. My intention is to argue that regardless of the particularity of discontent in this in-depth case study, the articulation and reactivation of those emotions could strongly contribute to the emergence of populist practices. In other words, the process of 'identity re-articulation' centered on cultural, ethnical, and socio-economic elements links together various forms of un-fulfilled subjects. When these elements are politically put forward, the notion of radical change signifies them as one (unity). These types of political practices divide the society into two opposing camps: those who support radical change and those who don't. I argue that this is not a simple party-support procedure in a democratic framework. There are many elements that must be considered in order to comprehend why populist practices are democratically so effective.

1.2.2 Social Logics

Howarth discusses social logics in the South African context, but what does 'logic' mean? Let us review this concept again. As Howarth points out, 'social logics are conditional and historically specific systems of sedimented practice such as the logic of the market . . . or the logic of apartheid', as discussed earlier.[104] In a more in-depth explanation, Glynos and Howarth view 'logic' as a method that manages to precisely conceptualize what is at stake 'as it allows us to simultaneously hold on to the idea of a pattern and an open-endedness'.[105] To them, the emphasis on the specificity of the rules elaborates a sense of a thorough analysis of the social logics being practiced. However, it is fundamental to be aware that 'rules are not reified entities that subsume practices and discourses'.[106] But, they provide us with a point of emphasis in which there can be an analysis describing and characterizing the type and pattern of discourse used. It is important to be aware that social logics are not classified as an empirically driven conception only. Social logics have the scope of linking with other logics. For example, 'social logics of competition might describe the way that actors interact with, and understand, each other as competitors'.[107] Thus, Glynos and Howarth state that 'social logics of individualization might capture those patterns of discursive articulations which, in the self-understanding of actors, individuate persons, isolating them from each other'.[108]

Populism, Theories, and Logics   27

In general terms, the objective is to search for and analyze the type of communication within a specific social context. Thus, the conception of social logics helps us recognize the character of the relations practiced in a social situation demanding change. In other words, it is a way to analyze how the social domain is articulated—and how a regime-institution tries to either reject or eradicate social mechanisms demanding radical change.

An essential question that needs to be discussed at this stage is: how can this social logic be attached to a populist theoretical framework? This is when a structural schema is needed and, as mentioned earlier, Laclau's theory of populism is of potential value to this investigation. It is valuable not only as a theory, but also because it interlinks with Glynos and Howarth's methodological model. This link opens another point in relation to developing the needed structure, which is precisely the second question in the introduction of this section.

1.2.3   Laclau's Theory of Populism

Let's review the theory once again, but this time enhancing it with the notion of 'logic' and presenting the structure in which the argument of this investigation will take form in the following chapters. Laclau proposes a method to understand what populism is and how to categorize a 'political movement' as populist with three theoretical prepositions: (1) 'The specificity of populism requires starting the analysis from units smaller than the group';[109] (2) It is an ontological and not an ontic category. For instance, its meaning cannot be understood by simply observing the 'political or ideological content' practiced by a particular group. Instead, we must examine 'a particular mode of articulation of whatever social, political or ideological contents';[110] (3) This 'articulating form, apart from its contents, produces structuring effects which primarily manifest themselves at the levels of the modes of representation'.[111] In other words, what Laclau argues is that we must analyze the way in which different demands are articulated and how a sense of a common identity is constituted.

This analysis starts by postulating 'an asymmetry between the community as a whole ("society") and whatever social actor operates with it'.[112] That is to say, 'there is no social agent whose will coincides with the actual workings of society conceived as a totality'.[113] The attempts to bridge a chasm between political will and communitarian space cannot succeed unless that 'bridge specifically defines the political articulation of social identities'.[114] Social actors have their own individualistic approaches, but this approach is 'entirely holistic, with the only qualification that the promise of fullness contained in the notion of an entirely self-determined social whole is unachievable'.[115] 'Individuals are not coherent totalities but merely referential identities split into a series of localized subject positions'.[116]

To analyze smaller units, Laclau uses the category of 'demand', which can be a request, or in more active terms, '*imposing* a request—a claim—on somebody else (as in "demanding an explanation")'.[117]

28 *Populism in Venezuela*

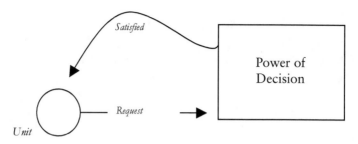

Diagram 1.1 A request is satisfied.

In this diagram, a neighborhood (unit) makes a request to the locus of power and this demand, which is punctually satisfied, does not construct any chasm or frontier within the social. The key is that 'nobody puts into question the right to present the request or the right of the decisory to take the decision'.[118] In this context 'social logics are operating this institutionalized, differential model, called *logics of difference*'.[119] This is a 'legitimate demand satisfied in a non-antagonistic administrative way'.[120] In this case, Laclau classifies how a unit, which is the term he uses as a component of social logics, has a request which is effectively dealt with by the 'power of decision'. The power of decision represents any governmental form within the institutional structure.

Now, let us suppose that one request is rejected. Only one such demand will not alter the situation substantially. But, if we have a variety of unsatisfied demands, this can create 'multiple frustrations' and 'trigger social logics of an entirely different kind [see Diagram 1.2]'.[121]

For a popular subjectivity to emerge, the equivalential moment must be constituted out of those diverse demands. They need to be made equivalent to one another in order to constitute the popular will. This is constructed by shadowing their particular demands (categorized as the *logic of difference*) and 'reaggregat[ing] themselves' in order to form what Laclau calls 'an *equivalential chain*'.[122] This can be understood by conceptualizing

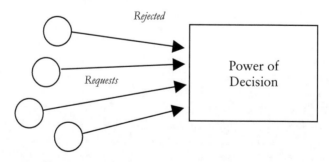

Diagram 1.2 Multiple requests are rejected.

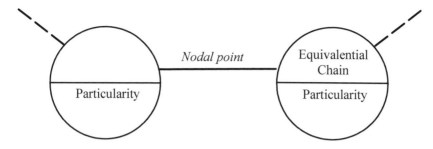

Diagram 1.3 A nodal point arrests the flow of differences in an equivalential chain.

these particular demands as 'different from all others ... this particularity is shown in the lower semicircle in the representation of each of them [see Diagram 1.1]'.[123] The fundamental popular formation is the upper circle representing the notion of being 'equivalent to each other in their common opposition to the oppressive regime'.[124] Another vital feature of Laclau's theory is the *nodal point*. The task of the nodal point is to 'arrest the flow of difference' and provide a partial fixation that plays the centered role signifying the meaning of the units' equivalence.[125] These characteristics are illustrated in Diagram 1.3.

This new social articulation begins to take on strength when the units realize that their neighbors or other sectors (other units) are equally dissatisfied (for different reasons). Thus, some kind of solidarity between them emerges because they share the negative dimension that their demands remain unsatisfied. This is the first precondition of political articulation, which Laclau calls 'populism'. This is exactly the meaning of the *logic of equivalence*, and regardless of their differential character, these demands 'tend to re-aggregate themselves to form an *equivalential chain*'.[126]

The subject put forward is now different. This begins to be a universalized demand, showing the construction of the fragmented community joining forces against the power of decisions (the institution). Diagram 1.1 (differential particularity) represents a subject whose demands are punctually dealt with, which Laclau calls the *democratic subject*. But, the second case, with a wider subject structured from the equivalential aggregation of a plurality of democratic demands, is called the *popular subject*. We must recognize that there is no emergence of a popular subjectivity without the creation of an internal frontier. The equivalences are only such in terms of a lack pervading them all, which requires the identification of the source of social negativity. 'Equivalential popular discourses divide, in this way, the social into two camps: power and the underdog'.[127] Therefore, we are no longer dealing with requests but a fighting demand. With 'equivalences, popular subjectivity, dichotomic construction of the social around an internal frontier, we have all the structural features to define populism'.[128]

30 Populism in Venezuela

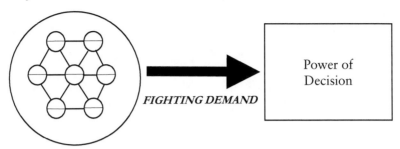

Diagram 1.4   A fighting demand against a common enemy.

The purpose of creating an internal frontier and the equivalential chain by a variety of unfulfilled demands is to recognize 'an anti-institutional character' made possible by subverting the 'particularistic, differential character of the demands'. This can take effect by formulating a totality demand. These wider 'equivalential demands confront us immediately with the problem of the representation of the specifically equivalential moment'.[129] We have to realize that particular demands don't disappear, and the 'more universal dimension' of the equivalence recognizes its inability to provide 'any direct . . . mode of representation'.[130] The prime feature of the equivalential chain is to create a 'frontier within the social and it is necessary to represent the other side of the frontier'. In other words, the two sides of this frontier constitute an 'us-them' axis. Laclau believes that 'there is no populism without discursive construction of an enemy: the *ancient regime*, the oligarchy, the establishment or whatever'.[131] This is precisely what he means as the other side of the frontier: an enemy oppressor, a regime held responsible for their misfortunes. Accepting that the notion of representation of their particular demands cannot be entirely materialized temporarily solves this problem. Nonetheless, the particularity of their demands doesn't have to be abandoned but can be formulated in the new role of 'functioning as a signifier representing the chain as a totality'.[132] Thus, by accepting a degree of subornation of their own particular demands and supporting this new popular arrangement, 'a particular demand represents the equivalential, which is called *hegemony*'.[133]

Nonetheless, Laclau notes that the more 'the chain of equivalences is extended, the weaker will be its connection with the particularistic demands which assume the function of universal representation'.[134] Articulating 'a popular subjectivity' decisive enough to impose a fighting demand to a regime 'is possible only on the basis of discursively producing *tendentially empty signifiers*'.[135] For instance, Laclau describes it by using 'poverty' as a populist symbol. Its objective is to politically 'bring to equivalential homogeneity a highly heterogeneous reality, and this can only do so by reducing to a minimum their particular content'.[136] In other words, there is the construction of an antagonistic pole that is against a common enemy—the

Populism, Theories, and Logics 31

oppressive power. He elaborates his theoretical argument by stating that 'this process reaches a point where the homogenizing function is carried out by a pure name: the name of the leader'.[137] What is interesting about Laclau's theoretical framework is that, only at this point, he presents the notion of the leader as a way to satisfactorily signify all the demands as one. The timing of his argument explains the type of necessary conditions that need to emerge before the logic of leadership can successfully satisfy a variety of particular demands.

We must recognize that before a leader is named, successful bonds (nodal points/empty signifiers) must be established among miscellaneous unsatisfied social units (e.g. civic centers, communal organizations, etc.) in the equivalential chain, and a new discourse from this social turmoil (logic) in that society must invest in a political platform. We can classify this as the political logic. Its objective is to somehow represent the demands of all participants regardless of their differences, by unifying them and politically constructing them as 'one' force. This is what Laclau means by hegemony: the embodiment of a universal demand. So far, there has been a discussion about the relevance of social logics to Laclau's theory of populism. But, there is another important logic, which is political logics.

1.2.4 Political Logics

Earlier, I addressed the conception of the social and how it interlaces with Laclau's theoretical approach to populism. However, this schema also requires another critical conception, which is the political articulation. The category of 'political logics' helps us contextualize the terms and conditions from which a political project emerges and from which it is constructed and crystallized.

According to Glynos and Howarth, 'political logics aim to capture those processes of collective mobilization precipitated by the emergence of the political dimension of social relations, such as the construction, defense, and naturalization of new frontiers'.[138] The co-authors highlight the emergence and mobilization of unsatisfied and underprivileged (for different reasons) sectors of a society. These social sectors subvert their differences and a new political project mobilizes them as a collective force. These are vital components for the emergence of a new populist platform representing a political frontier against a common enemy: the oppressive regime. They further explain that the category of political logics can also 'include processes which seek to interrupt or break up this process of drawing frontiers'.[139] Howarth described this aspect with the 'logic of apartheid', which had the purpose of avoiding the emergence of a resistance against the regime. Glynos and Howarth's theoretical stand is based on the following remarks of Laclau: '"social logics consist in rule-following, political logics are related to the *institution* of the social"'.[140] From this perspective, the process of institution '"proceeds out of social demands" rather than an "arbitrary fiat" and is "inherent to any process of social change"'.[141]

32 *Populism in Venezuela*

Glynos and Howarth explain the meaning and usefulness of Laclau's passage. Their viewpoint is that 'if political logics are concerned with the *institution* of the social, they are also related to its possible *de-institution* or *contestation*'.[142] With these perspectives, they draw attention to the notion that the 'very institution of a new regime or social practice presupposes the possibility that a previous social order is successfully displaced from its hegemonic position and thus de-instituted'. In other words, they argue that 'political logics are integral to the processes of contestation and institution of social practices and regimes'.[143] This means that two camps can use political logics: one camp represents the social order of a new political project; the other defends or attempts to reconstitute its displaced institutional structure. Glynos and Howarth's outlook on Laclau's remarks indicate that the 'contestation of a hegemonic discursive formation and the possible institution—or failed institution—of a new one via political logics can never be totally external, and thus arbitrary, in relation to the social formation itself'. They re-emphasize this key theoretical aspect by stating that 'the radical institution of the social emerges from concrete empirical demands within a particular order'.[144]

Thus, the importance of political logics is that it helps us harmonize 'our understanding of the ways in which dislocation is discursively articulated or symbolized'.[145] This can be accomplished, for instance, by carefully analyzing the socio-cultural significance of political articulations like Venezuela's Bolivarian project. This political project has used the symbol of the Liberator Simon Bolívar as a nodal point to subvert/arrest differences among social sectors in order to construct an equivalential political platform. It is important to be aware that the situations in which the political dimension of social relations develops have a sense of 'collective mobilization' and thus could be categorized as 'political logics'. Glynos and Howarth stress that this type of construction works because it aims to simplify and politicize 'the entire national social space by transforming it into two camps'. This configuration can only be successful when 'social logics are supplemented by political logics'.[146]

This contextual connection of the logics is very useful because political logics can 'provide a conceptual vocabulary to show how these limits are constituted, transformed, and absorbed, and they do so by focusing on the way the logic of equivalence comes to predominate over the logic of difference, and vice versa'. Glynos and Howarth summarize this connection by stating that 'if the logic of equivalence involves the simplification of signifying space, the logic of difference involves the expansion and complexification [of signifying space]'.[147]

Glynos and Howarth's methodological model develops from the logics of equivalence and difference. They argue that when there is a terrain where there is a 'dimension of equivalence' that 'captures the *substitutive* aspect of the relation by making reference to an "us-them" axis . . . two or more elements can be substituted for each other with reference to a

Populism, Theories, and Logics   33

common relation or threat'.[148] To re-confirm the meaning of Laclau's theoretical approach, they state that 'they are equivalent not insofar as they share a positive property (though empirically they may have something in common), but, crucially, insofar as they have a common enemy'.[149] Thus, political logics of equivalence and difference are analytical instruments that contain 'a descriptive framing device which is derived from a particular understanding of discourse and the importance accorded to the processes of signification'.[150] These logics within the spectrum of political logics have the useful features of classifying the interests of various units, hence helping us refine 'our approach to social science explanation by furnishing a conceptual grammar with which to account for the dynamics of social change'.[151] With this organizational method as a focal point we could better analyze 'how social practices and regimes are contested, transformed, and instituted, thereby extending our grammar beyond social logics'.[152]

So far, the notion of 'logic' has been the subject matter on the methodological front, with Laclau's populist theoretical approach as a parallel structure furnishing the theoretical schema for this investigation. Social logics categorize sedimentation. Political logics activate the key elements that shape the process of a new hegemonic discursive formation. This is precisely the moment when there is a clear scope of contestation against a repressive institution. But there is still another category missing, which will be discussed next. The third category is called fantasmatic logics, and it functions as the tightening element that consolidates, or bonds together, social and political logics.

1.2.5   Fantasmatic Logics

Glynos and Howarth present fantasmatic logics as the 'critical layer to the process of accounting for change or continuity'.[153] They rightly point out an essential feature of populist practices I have observed, which is precisely the continuous search for a better future for the excluded population. The co-authors state that if political logics 'provide a politically-inflected signifying frame within which to show how social practices come into being or are transformed',[154] fantasmatic logics provide a method to understand 'why specific practices and regimes "grip" subjects'.[155] What I particularly find important is how they put emphasis on the meaning-dimension of gripping together a variety of different subjects in order to consolidate some form of unity of subjects despite their differences. Again, Laclau's analysis is used by stating that 'if political logics concern signifying operations, fantasmatic logics concern the force behind those operations'.[156]

This analytical relationship between fantasmatic logics and social practices demonstrates that even though 'social practices are punctuated by mishaps, tragedies and contingencies of everyday life, social relations are experienced and understood in this mode of activity as an accepted way of life'.[157] They argue that within this context, the role of fantasy is not to

34 *Populism in Venezuela*

'set up an illusion that provides a subject with a false picture of the world, but to ensure that the political dimension of a practice remains in the background'.[158] We can outline this component as an objective/aim for the people to 'invest in' because it manages to deliver, in one way or another, the assurance that some kind of wholeness or fullness redressing their lack will materialize.

Fantasmatic logics operate as the key reminder for the 'social dimension of practices' of that fundamental lack that manages to keep the need for a struggle worth fighting for. In other words, 'logics of fantasy have a key role to play in "filling up" or "completing" the void in the subject and the structure of social relations by bringing about closure'.[159] A crucial force in the populist project I narrate and analyze in the following chapters is the provision of a satisfactory notion of fullness that responds to a variety of missing factors (e.g. healthcare, water, food, work, education, housing, etc.) in the underprivileged population. This is what 'filling up' or 'completing' implies.

Glynos and Howarth state that fantasmatic logics relate to political practice because 'political logics are linked to moments of contestation and institution'. These circumstances 'presuppose contingency ... [and] involve the attempt to defend or challenge existing social relations through the construction of social antagonisms'.[160] They highlight that although 'social antagonisms indicate the limits of social reality by disclosing the points at which "the impossibility of society"' becomes evident, they argue that 'social antagonisms are still forms of social construction, as they furnish the subject with a way of politicizing the lack of the structure'.[161] This can be interpreted that the notion of lack, a sense of emptiness or unfulfilled components of a polarized society, demands a way to materialize those missing elements. Political logics organize and represent those sectors that support the new antagonistic social force and provide a vision that satisfies them with a transitory fulfillment. The meaning and importance of the articulation of fantasy in social practices can be understood by realizing that its attempt is to 'implicitly reinforce the "natural" character of their elements or to actively prevent the emergence of the political dimension'.[162] The word 'prevent' in this context was earlier described in Howarth's explanation of the institutional efforts to maintain the logic of apartheid in South Africa. 'The function of fantasy in political practices is to give them *direction* and *energy*'. This is what Glynos and Howarth refer to as the 'vector'.[163]

What does '*direction* and *energy*' mean? I understand these terms as referring to a vision/trajectory for underprivileged social sectors/units that arises because the authorities repeatedly reject their requests. The only way to change their antagonistic position is by supporting and investing in the construction and galvanization of a radical political movement. This radical mobilization is effective because it has an element of popular appeal that shows a sense of belonging and carries a

Populism, Theories, and Logics   35

magnitude of different supporters sharing a common conviction, which is change. The political articulation has a clear objective and this affirmative endeavor is the 'direction' it follows, like a 'better future ahead'. In terms of 'energy', once this political movement is fully fledged and its existence shows a prominent degree of socio-political power at various levels, the sense of 'energy' that moved this political project from one phase to another was created by symbols of radicalism and plans to reach fulfillment. There are several aspects involved in the process of emerging, organizing, and consolidating a political project. Social involvement (that of people) is perhaps the most important. The desires of underprivileged sectors to displace an institution and create a popular and fair institutional structure that defends and works for the well-being of the people are critical in this process. I view this as the 'vector' Glynos and Howarth discuss.

The articulation of fantasy and the political dimension varies because we have to determine whether there are 'the equivalential or differential aspects of a discursive construction predominate' in the latter.[164] For instance, if the logic of equivalence is predominant, the 'articulation of political discourse is dominated by a logic of substitution that links different demands together, harbors the possibility of a more *populist* or *revolutionary* politics'. Glynos and Howarth argue that in conditions amenable to populist politics, 'fantasmatic logics may take the form of a narrative in which an internal obstacle (or "enemy within") is deemed responsible for the blockage of identity, while promising a fullness or harmony to come'.[165] Their diagnosis re-affirms my interpretation of 'direction', 'energy', and 'vector'.

If the logic of difference predominates in a political practice; this means that 'the articulation of discourse is dominated by a logic of combination that decouples demands and addresses them in a punctual fashion by channeling them into the existing system of rule'.[166] This is totally the opposite of the former and 'harbors the possibility of a more *institutionalist* or *reformist* politics'.[167] If I observe this kind of practice in Venezuelan politics, I cannot claim that the Bolivarian project is populist. Glynos and Howarth state that political logics can be analyzed 'into two main components—the logics of equivalence and differences'. But, the logic of fantasy 'is defined solely by the function of closure'. This means, 'in concealing—suturing or closing off—the contingency of social relations, fantasy structures the subject's mode of enjoyment in a particular way', which the co-authors call the "enjoyment of closure"'.[168]

Thus, it could be said that there is degree of enjoyment in gathering with others that share the same struggle, hence subordinating particular differences. The emergence of ways to nurture that affective bond/comradeship creates a sense of enjoyment. Also, the process of deciding on and bringing about demonstrations as tactics to end their underdog position, or as reminders of a traumatic past, can subconsciously

36 *Populism in Venezuela*

be a very enjoyable experience. The logic of fantasy links a range of emotional elements triggered by a political context that joins together a variety of social grievances. The opportunity to speak as 'one voice' is critical to the excluded population. Furthermore, it creates a high degree of collective joy.

Glynos and Howarth stress that 'political logics are used to explain the discursive shifts in the wake of a dislocatory moment'. And, 'fantasmatic logics describe and account for the *vector*' (the magnitude and direction to follow) 'and *modality* of those discursive shifts'.[169] This effectively captures 'the way in which the subject *deals* with the radical contingency of social relations as a subject of enjoyment'.[170]

Before concluding the section on fantasmatic logics, it is vital to further discuss what Glynos and Howarth mean with the notion of the '*modality* of those discursive shifts'. During moments of social contestation, we must pay attention to the role of ethics for the people during periods of dislocation. They argue that 'the space of the ethical—like the political, social, and ideological—is understood in relation to the radical contingency of social relations and the way in which the subject "responds" to this ontological lack'.[171] In other words, it is understood in relation to what 'we', the excluded, are missing. The concept of ethics, unlike issues such as 'right conduct' or 'our proper obligations to others', 'is not reducible or equivalent to questions about normativity—at least not in any straightforward way'. Neither is 'the construction of binding norms that may or may not be agreed upon by all affected social agents'. Their 'concept of the ethical is not to be understood in terms of the inculcation of an appropriate set of virtues or dispositions that enables human agents to live the good life, though the concern with issues about "ethos" move in the direction we want to go'.[172] On the whole, Glynos and Howarth are not interested in the general meaning of ethics. Thus, we question, what do ethics mean to them?

The co-authors perceive ethics (and ideology) as a pivotal element in 'the *mode* of the subject's engagement'. They draw attention to 'Althusser's suggestion of the subject which is "the constitutive category of all ideology" marked by a fundamental misrecognition that can never be transcended'.[173] Therefore, 'the subject is no more than a void in the symbolic order whose identity and character is determined only by its identifications and mode of enjoyment'.[174] Glynos and Howarth state that it is important to 'address issues that arise from the different modalities of subjectivity in relation to the ultimate contingency of social existence'.[175]

There are critical issues that must be considered in order to crystallize those elements that attempt to constitute a new mode of ethics. For instance, we must address the following questions: 'how does a subject relate to the contingency of social life that is disclosed in dislocatory events? How does it identify anew? How does it translate its "radical

Populism, Theories, and Logics 37

investments" into social and political practices? How does a subject relate to its identification and consequently to its own contingency?'.[176] These questions raise important abstract issues that need empirical explanations. Glynos and Howarth emphasize 'that these modes of subjectivity could not be understood in cognitivist or intellectualist terms'. They are trying to underline that 'the categories of ideology and ethics has nothing whatsoever to do with the idea that someone can apprehend and even consciously affirm a particular ontological schema rooted in the radical contingency of social relations'. Moreover, they argue that 'modes of subjectivity are also modes of *enjoyment,* and modes of enjoyment are always *embodied* in material practices and thus not completely reducible to conscious apprehension'.[177]

Thus, observing political engagement from this angle, they argue that 'one should approach the question of subjectivity and identification. For example, does the mode of identification privilege the moment of closure and concealment (ideological dimension), or does it keep open the contingency of social relations (ethical dimension)?'.[178] Glynos and Howarth go on to state that these 'two ontological dimensions' are elaborated in their 'logic of fantasy'.[179] The role of ethics and/or change of ethics during moments of dislocation can reveal vital aspects of the need of subjects from excluded sectors in a dichotomized society to set out new rules of 'popular' ethics and can reveal how this is politically furnished and crystallized in populist practices. Thus, fantasmatic logics identify the importance of these elements in a democratic political articulation where 'radical investment' is pivotal.

The concept of populism is indeed 'awkward' and 'slippery' (quoting Taggart's view). The logics approach can shed light on those slippery and awkward elements of populist practices. In the following chapters, social, political, and fantasmatic logics will be employed to address the Venezuelan case. Apart from explaining the populist 'drive' behind the Bolivarian project, I aim to articulate these logics in order to unpack those invisible, 'awkward', and 'slippery' elements of populist practices in general.

The second question raised in the introduction of this section inquires if there is a methodological model in the literature that could help us conceptualize the socio-political phenomenon in Venezuela and that could underpin a theoretical framework to categorize vital populist elements in this case study. The methodological and theoretical literature discussed so far provides a systematic theoretical method for this investigation.[180] The third question asks how to conceptualize and organize this method, and how the method is discursively related with populist practices.

As Glynos and Howarth point out, 'the function of logics in social scientific analysis is not only to make social processes more intelligible, but in the process of *describing* and *explaining* it should also furnish the possibility of a critical engagement with the practices and processes under investigation'.[181] I find this model useful because they confirm that *'all logics carve out a space for a critical conception of explanation because they all presuppose the non-necessary character of social relations'*.[182] What is critical to this schema is its ability to connect the three logics together. Glynos and Howarth verify this by stating that 'social, political, and fantasmatic logics are articulated together in an overarching explanatory logic that combines descriptive, explanatory, and critical aspects'.[183] Thus, this methodological model can help us descriptively unpack and analyze key elements to explain the conditions and practices in a populist case study. However, before addressing how I'll articulate a post-structuralist analysis in this investigation, I need to conceptualize my own understanding of the three logics and how they inter-relate with each other.

The diagram below, which I name 'methodological framework', explains the articulation between the three logics. Fantasmatic logics form a sense of an affective union between social and political logics. Fantasmatic logics keep together social elements involved within the political context and create a sense of constant mutation in order to keep its appeal/popularity active. Social logics are the nucleus of political contingency. Political logics institute the social (agents/units) by re-constituting the origins of their political platform, which is a form of 'radical change' against a timeless oppressive enemy. A populist project needs to keep that sense of 'radical change' alive in search for 'eternal fulfillment' to the popular masses. This is achieved by developing a 'gripping' symbol-scheme that tightly packs together all the subjects and reacts with some form of alertness against the external camp without losing the core value of their objectives. Without this discursive mechanism, an organic crisis would eventually dismantle that political project. This continuous symbolic political revival can be done 'through metaphoric and metonymic processes articulated around Lacanian master signifiers', depending '"on fantasy in order to constitute itself"'.[184] This is how the three logics articulate with each other and craft a 'methodological framework'. Fantasmatic logics are fundamental components that package together various subjects as one political force. Political practices are structured upon the logic of equivalence by concretely articulating a variety of social practices against a common enemy.

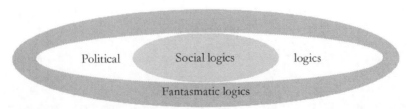

Diagram 1.5 Methodological framework.

1.2.6 Research Strategy

So far, I have addressed several discourse methodological categories compatible with Laclau's theoretical framework. Nevertheless, a research strategy that is able to contextualize relevant material has not been discussed. In his article 'Applying Discourse Theory: The Method of Articulation', Howarth explains that an 'appropriate *research strategy*' must have the ability to generate empirical data and methods to analyze texts. It is important to be aware that the notion of analyzing any form of 'text' can be understood as discourse. Thus, the methods already elucidated, such as the logics in this case, are the underlying principles to depend on. 'This depends on the kind and quality of available data and the depth of analysis required. . . . Whether these are targeting the rhetorical or narrative structures of texts—or both—is relative to the kinds of research questions' asked.[185] These points aim to 'establish the proper limits of the employment' and the qualifications of 'research strategies in discourse theory'.[186]

The strategy to generate data for this in-depth investigation of populist practices in Venezuela consists of collecting information from a wide range of sources. An extensive amount of information has been collected from newspaper reports available online from *El Universal* since 1996, and to a lesser extent, from another prominent daily broadsheet newspaper called *El Nacional*. Other online Venezuelan newspapers such as *Noticias 24* and *Tal Cual* have also provided textual news reports for this analysis. Newspaper reports of vital dislocatory events prior to 1996 (not available online)—i.e. from 1989 until 1996—were read during fieldwork visits in the microfilm archives stored at Venezuela's National Library (*Biblioteca Nacional*) in Caracas, Venezuela. Also, a wide selection of video clips available on a video-sharing website called *YouTube* have been used in this investigation. These clips include, for example, Chávez's inaugural speech in January 2007, his views on the first government electoral defeat in the constitutional referendum in December 2007, General Raúl Baduel's involvement and decision to campaign against Chávez's political agenda in the 2007 constitutional referendum (see pages 83–87 in Chapter 3), the discourse of anti-government student demonstrations in 2007, Chávez's announcement of his cancer diagnosis from Havana on June 30, 2011 (see pages 139–40 in Chapter 6), and so on. Furthermore, video documentaries produced by English speaking producers and commentators have also provided key 'live coverage' material, showing the discourse both camps articulate and the settings in relation to the events that led to the failed April 2002 coup d'état and its aftermath. I translated into English all the information written and spoken in Spanish.

Election results, poll forecasts, and surveys are used throughout the chapters as supplementary information to enhance and discursively recap some of the social and political dynamics practiced in Venezuela. Four fieldwork visits were conducted from December 2007 until December 2011. Most of

40 Populism in Venezuela

the data in Chapters 4 and 5 was collected during the second visit, which was in March–April 2009. For Chapter 5, eight Cuban medics stationed in three states were interviewed, as well as patients, nurses, chauffeurs, secretaries, and Venezuelan medical students in the healthcare centers visited. Ethnographic observations from these visits form part of the overall analysis of this free healthcare program. Cuban medics requested to be anonymous. Regarding the anti-Bolivarian student movement presented, non-participant observations and interviews took place in January 2008, and thorough interviews with former students in Caracas and San Cristobal, state of Táchira, were conducted in March 2009. Some of the information a student mentioned during an interview (as requested) has not been disclosed in this analysis. Other informal conversations with the general public during fieldwork visits have helped me contextualize other perspectives about people's daily problems and overall perceptions of this populist Bolivarian project.

Interviews with senior political leaders have also been conducted. Interviews with Luis Miquilena, President Chávez's former political mentor and strategist, uncover vital elements of the construction and sedimentation of this new wave of populist political practices in Venezuela. Also, interviews with Felipe Mújica, the president of *Movimiento Al Socialismo* (MAS—an important political party that has played a prominent role in organizing regional popular support during elections in the last twenty years), provide valuable information about internal party-affairs, and the decision of MAS to end its political alliance with Chavista factions in the government in January 2002 and join the opposition camp. Furthermore, an interview in December 2011 with Leopoldo López, the great, great, great, great, great nephew of Simon Bolívar, enriches this investigation. López represents a new generation of opposition political leadership. As a descendant of Bolívar, his view about the use of Bolívar's name in Venezuelan politics gives us another insight into Chávez's populist discourse. Another potentially important interview, with General Raúl Baduel, which was organized to take place in Maracay on April 8, 2009, didn't materialize because he was arrested and imprisoned on April 3, 2009.[187]

The rich source of textual, rhetorical, ethnographical, and numerical data, as well as of official documents, make this in-depth investigation well substantiated. A key objective of this data collection strategy has been to gather information from a wide range of sources, and carefully select what empirical information, coupled with the theoretical and methodological tools, can help explain the drive and direction of this populist project, and the social and political forces behind these operations. Returning to Howarth's recommendations for a research strategy in discourse analysis, he points out that research questions are crucial components for a research strategy. There are two research questions in this investigation, which are as follows:

1. I shall employ Laclau's theoretical approach to populism and determine to what degree the case of Venezuela constitutes instances of

Populism, Theories, and Logics 41

populist politics. I intend to use this case study in order to provide a fuller and more general understanding of the phenomenon of populism. Here I will be concerned to investigate the key factors that account for the emergence and reproduction of populism, and to differentiate between populism as a mode of opposition and populism as a mode of governance.

Earlier, I mentioned that if I cannot observe an articulation of political discourse dominated by a logic of substitution that links different demands together, therefore developing the necessary conditions for populist or revolutionary politics to emerge, the degree of populist practices in this case is insignificant. That is to say, I will analyze whether the logic of equivalence, as defined by Laclau's theoretical approach, predominates instead of difference. In terms of classifying the degree of populist politics in the Venezuelan context, this can be examined by analyzing the periods in which new populist politics emerged, and the formation of an internal frontier with a wide range of social demands that consequently articulated a new equivalential chain. I will also evaluate its ability to successfully mutate its political stance once instituted and to maintain/increase the popular support received during opposition. In other words, I will analyze whether there has been a shift between equivalential and differential articulations during different periods.

2. I am concerned to explore whether or not a more general account of populism can be applied to this case and be used to evaluate existing theories of populism, e.g. those proposed by Canovan or Taggart.

My objective is to provide a fuller theoretical framework using Venezuela as a case study. This research is constructed on Laclau's theoretical approach and Glynos and Howarth's methodological schema. Laclau's theoretical elements, such as the logic of difference and equivalence, provide the mechanism for this in-depth analysis. This investigation might be labeled as testing and/or re-affirming the accuracy of Laclau's theory. Even though his theory is helpful, there are still many issues Laclau does not address. Theoretical refinement can be a more suitable term for this investigation of populist practices. For instance, Laclau does not provide a theoretical discussion regarding the points mentioned in the first research question. Laclau's concepts of 'organic crisis' and 'floating signifiers' don't explain how a populist project operates within a democratic context.

CONCLUSION

In the first section of this chapter theoretical approaches and understandings of populism were addressed. In the second section, three questions

42 *Populism in Venezuela*

were raised and answered by assembling a model where key theoretical and methodological aspects can be carefully employed with the empirical material I address and analyze in the following chapters. The category of 'logics', which is divided into three sub-categories—social, political, and fantasmatic logics—constitutes the methodological framework required. With Howarth's paper 'Applying Discourse Theory: The Method of Articulation', Glynos and Howarth's *Logics of Critical Explanation in Social and Political Theory*—intertwined with Laclau's *On Populist Reason* and 'Populism: What's in a Name?' and Laclau and Mouffe's *Hegemony and Socialist Strategy*—we have a conceptualized method/theoretical schema to classify and analyze the selected empirical data and contextualize populist practices in Venezuela.

2 The Venezuelan State
Its Formation, Consolidation, and Decline

The first chapter of this book draws on interpretations and theories of populism in the literature, and Laclau's populist theoretical approach coupled with Glynos and Howarth's methodological schema. This chapter seeks to present the genealogical basis of this investigation. The first section presents a genealogical review of Venezuela since its independence from Spain in 1821 until the first moment of popular dislocation on February 27, 1989. The second section contextualizes the degree of social inequality in the country, and how neoliberal reforms in the 1990s further 'excluded' a great proportion of the population. This chapter describes the conditions that made Lieutenant Colonel Hugo Chávez organize a coup d'état in 1992, and the unprecedented popular support this radical attempt received from Venezuela's poor and underprivileged population. This moment of dislocation laid the foundations for a collective social uproar against a common enemy: an 'us-them' axis. Chávez's 'on air' speech requesting other coup plotters in the country to surrender had unprecedented effects upon the popular mass. His presence and the discursive meaning of Chávez's '*Por ahora*' became an empty signifier that fulfilled that sense of lack to people living in marginalized areas in Venezuela.

A focal point in this chapter is to narrate and thus analyze the context upon which small/medium political parties and social/business groups constructed a new political platform that promised to challenge and displace the institutional structure. I'll describe how institutional breakdown gave Chávez the terrain to construct a socio-political project that helped him win the 1998 presidential elections. This is a post-structuralist analysis (using Laclau's theoretical approach), contextualizing how different subjects, elements, and practices managed to constitute a radical opposition populist force that demanded the end of a corrupt and elitist institutional system. Glynos and Howarth's 'logics approach' methodological schema provides the tools to understand the social, political, and emotional/fullness-to-come (fantasmatic) practices that changed Venezuela's institutional system.

44 Populism in Venezuela

2.1 HISTORICAL CONTEXT

Venezuela was a Spanish colony until 1821. Simón Bolívar, also known as the Liberator, defeated Spanish forces in Venezuela and five other Latin American nations. Bolívar's struggle for independence is a symbol of emancipation and national identity in Venezuela. Until 1908, Venezuela experienced political struggles of continuous civil wars ruled by *caudillos*. Dictator Juan Vicente Gómez finally managed to consolidate territorial control due to the funds invested in the military from a new source of revenue to the state: oil. Prior to the emergence of oil, Venezuela's economy was fundamentally based on agriculture and most of the population depended on agricultural activities. A new period began when foreign oil companies were granted concessions to explore, produce, and refine oil in the 1910s. The local oil workforce soon represented Venezuela's emerging working class, and a new generation of educated and politically driven movements started to challenge the dictatorial regime for democratic practices.

Social conflict burst out in February 1928, when leaders of a student political movement known as the '*Generación 28*'[1] organized a mass demonstration in Caracas. The regime ordered the police to suppress the revolt. Demonstrators were killed. This dislocatory event forced the dictatorial regime to recognize that Venezuela wanted radical institutional change. This was 'the first large project of reform of the modern state in Venezuela'.[2] Student leaders of *Generación 28* began to form a new political articulation that transformed from its initial student setting into a wider national configuration. According to Fernando Coronil, in response to 'criticisms produced within civil society, the state neutralised its opposition but also legitimated a reformist discourse which intensified the social pressure to democratise the polity'.[3] Rómulo Bentancourt, a key *Generación 28* leader, was the main founder of the political party '*Acción Democrática*' (AD) and a crucial figure in Venezuela's democratization process.

The struggle for democracy in Venezuela was finally achieved when the first open presidential election took place in 1947. Rómulo Gallegos of AD won the elections and took office in February 1948. However, months later, a coup d'état seized power until 1958. The return of a dictatorial system harshly repressed and tortured those that challenged the regime. This period ended when a faction in the military overthrew the regime and organized an interim civic-military government. In December 1958, Venezuelans democratically elected Rómulo Betancourt to the presidency. In 1958, the framework for this new democratic institutional system was laid down in a sharing accord named the '*Punto Fijo*' Pact—agreed upon by three key political leaders.[4] The pact strongly rejected events such as a coup d'état, and aimed to establish political accords to assure the development of democratic practices (e.g. respect for electoral results). The political arrangements in the *Punto Fijo* Pact were vital in the constitution written

The Venezuelan State 45

and approved in 1961. It articulated a symbolic order that followed principles of political agonism.

In the 1960s two AD administrations were elected; and in 1968, Rafael Caldera of COPEI (*Comité de Organización Política Electoral Independiente*) was elected with a narrow margin. Henceforth, a bipartite system controlled the political structure in Venezuela. *Unión Republicana Democrática* (URD) lost its influence in the *Punto Fijo* Pact power-sharing accord. Caldera's administration managed to fully integrate a wider agonistic frontier by successfully persuading and incorporating (via a process of pacification-amnesty) the Left[5] into the democratic structure. The Left agreed to express its ideological views peacefully and end their guerrilla activities. At this stage, the Venezuelan polity had fully incorporated all political camps under the same umbrella.

Venezuela started to experience a joyful period driven by oil revenues in the 1970s. This element of abundance, linked with a flourishing democratic system, significantly transformed the socio-political structure of the nation.[6] In retrospect, this oil windfall had a detrimental effect on Venezuela's young democracy. Oil revenues aplenty promoted political patronage, clientelism, and corruption. The emerging middle class started to experience and benefit from a period of bonanza. Most sectors of this society naively believed that the oil bonanza would continue promising endless enrichment to everyone. In the December 1973 presidential election, Carlos Andrés Pérez of AD won. Pérez benefited greatly from oil embargoes and conflict in the Middle East. The nationalization of the Venezuelan oil industry in 1976 further enhanced government control. Government revenues increased to a staggering estimate of 170 percent.[7]

This petrodollar boom helped to ease international credit opportunities and a massive expansion of the state budget took place. The government increased employment opportunities and extended the network of subsidies. 'A public spending increase of 96.9 percent between 1973 and 1978 allowed public services and extensive job opportunities. By 1978, 10 percent of the population lived in general poverty, and of this population just 2 percent lived in extreme poverty'.[8] Venezuela's middle class evolved from the oil revenues. A new generation of educated professionals started to establish their social status. Networks of political clientelism articulated the social fabric by infusing it with 'universal fullness' to come. There was a collective perception that this mode of good living was infinite. Naively, the administration splashed the country with petrodollars. By 1979, Venezuela's foreign debt was U.S. $9 billion.

The next administration was of Luis Herrera Campins from COPEI. Herrera started with firm neoliberal principles and tried to encourage a sense of political awareness. However, these concerns were soon abandoned because oil revenues continued to rise during the early years of Herrera's presidency.[9] He spent heavily on striking public works projects, and channeled funds into agricultural and industrial projects, paying generous

46   Populism in Venezuela

subsidies. This administration continued Pérez's policy of borrowing on a world market awash with petrodollars. By the early 1980s Venezuela owed the banks nearly U.S. \$24 billion. When oil revenues began to decline crisis was inevitable. On February 18, 1983, the government was forced to devalue the local currency 'Bolívar' (bs.), a day known as Venezuela's '*el Viernes Negro*' (Black Friday). From a fixed bs. 4.3 for 1 U.S. dollar, the currency floated to 12–15 by the end of Herrera's term. Days of shopping in Miami or Aruba for the Caracas middle class were over.

After *el Viernes Negro*, a wide range of socio-political groups blamed corrupt politicians directing benefits to their business cronies and ruining the country. The next administration paid little attention to the growth of social discontent with the establishment.[10] Instead, policies benefited a minority: 'the elites'. Jaime Lusinchi of AD (1984–89) was elected president and promised to pay back every last cent of the debt. However, the International Monetary Fund (IMF) advised Lusinchi to implement reforms in order to contain inflation. Moisés Naím states that institutional devastation of the public organization responsible for social services caused public utilities and services to plummet. 'Water, sanitation, telephone, electricity, transportation, and the police, together with persistent price increases . . . are stark realities for very large segments of society'.[11] Coronil describes Lusinchi's administration as a 'myth of progress' that soon failed to deliver. The president 'courted local sectors by maintaining a modified version of the protectionist and distributionist system he inherited, but also responded to international pressures by implementing some IMF stabilisation measures'.[12]

During Lusinchi's administration, the debt service reached U.S. \$30 billion, consuming almost 50 percent of the nation's foreign exchange; yet the debt only decreased from \$35 to \$32 billion. 'The real debt, although it remained largely invisible until the next administration, was higher yet, for the "floating debt" raised the debt to nearly \$43 billion . . . international reserves were practically depleted to \$200 million'.[13] The political system was so corrupt that it opted to bleed out the nation rather than build one. Underprivileged sectors were the most affected. Even 'soldiers had to live with inadequate supply of boots, uniforms, housing, and implements to cover their basic needs . . . the salaries of junior officers eroded to such a degree that they could no longer afford a car or even adequate housing'.[14]

Sectors of the armed forces were also struggling. This explains why in 1982, mid-ranking officers like Hugo Chávez and his compatriots in the Military Academy founded a clandestine 'Revolutionary Bolivarian Movement' named *Movimiento Bolivariano Revolucionario* (MBR 200).[15] The MBR 200's objective was to overthrow a corrupt government (in 2007, Raul Baduel, a key founder, opposed Chávez in Government. I'll present this episode in Chapter 3). This resentment was against anyone involved in the *Punto Fijo* bipartite system that signified political clientelism and corrupt practices. This included senior officers in the armed forces, responsible for the deterioration of living conditions for less privileged sectors in the armed forces. Even in this 'unit' (using Laclau's term: see pages 27–29 in Chapter 1), antagonism emerged and was felt as a 'common' consensus with other (different) excluded social sectors. Throughout the 1980s, political clientelism and economic paybacks to elite sectors became normal practices. Politicians preferred to extend an apparent period of socio-economic stability, keep social unrest to a minimum, and let another administration decide the best way to implement economic measures.

Carlos Andrés Pérez, with an anti-neoliberal campaign, was re-elected in December 1988. Most people voted for Pérez hoping to revive the good times many enjoyed in the 1970s. There was a fantasy that Pérez could create another oil bonanza. However, shortly after taking office, Pérez borrowed U.S. $4.5 billion as a way to boost necessary measures for the economic package ahead called the '*Gran Viraje*' or the U-turn package. The motives behind the package were of a neoliberal structure—exercising IMF recommendations. In other words, the package involved socio-economic adjustments designed to enhance the 'Washington Consensus' criteria. This economic program brought further hardship to the masses.

2.1.1 Backlash to Neoliberal Reforms— Institutional Fragmentation

On February 27, 1989, days after Pérez began the presidency, the popular mass, the mob to some, protested. This event, known as the '*Caracazo*', five days of looting and violent unrest in major cities, was a clear sign of social desperation. In Laclau's terms, this is a moment of social dislocation. What triggered this incident was an increase in public transport fares, which followed the 100 percent rise in domestic petrol prices.[16] These measures were part of an orthodox economic adjustment plan that was intended to be accompanied by market-oriented structural economic changes (e.g. liberalization of the exchange market, prices, interest rates, and trade, as well as a fiscal reform including privatizations). In Caracas alone, violence brought a death toll of nearly 300 people. The real number of casualties is thought to be 3,000.[17]

Teodoro Petkoff, the leader of *Movimiento al Socialismo* (MAS) viewed the revolt not as 'the Venezuela of workers organized in trade unions or associations. No, it was another Venezuela, it was the non-organized Venezuela, the Venezuela that has been piling up in . . . wretched poverty . . . [it was] the roar of the wounded animal'. For many of the rich it was an outburst of primitivism, animality, and barbarism.[18] The *Caracazo* was a spontaneous collective social response to the collapse of 'state-responsibility' with the 'people'. It was a natural social uproar that manifested with a discourse of demand against (despite their difference) a common enemy: the political institution that imposed neoliberal practices, stretching the excluded even further to conditions of poverty and antagonism. The *Punto*

48   *Populism in Venezuela*

Fijo Pact ignored Venezuela's excluded population. It seems that Pérez was forced to accept and implement a foreign neoliberal package and pressed even further those living in deprived conditions.

This protest uncovered a collective sense of popular dissatisfaction with an elitist institutional system. It became clear that *el pueblo* wanted radical institutional change. There was a pressing need for a new popular political project (political logic) representing Venezuela's poor. In other words, there was a need for a political force that could fully identify their requests and truly signify radical change with a new 'direction' by constructing (fantasmatic logics) a frontier that could emotionally fulfill (fullness to come) what they lacked: food, basic public services, education, water, electricity, employment, etc. Nonetheless, for this political platform to emerge and crystallize, an 'equivalential chain' needs to be constructed—linking together a variety of different entities in the social terrain. The flow of differences is arrested with a partial fixation that signifies radical change against a common enemy. This will be empirically explained later.

According to Janet Kelly and Pedro Palma, 'Pérez's program was an instant disaster that quickly turned into what looked like a success'. However, the damage was so great 'that the incipient signs of success were insufficient to undo the political harm'.[19] Venezuela was soon globally recognized as an economic miracle. That is to say, the country was an impressive neoliberal 'cheerleader' under the 'Washington Consensus' criteria. Its economy grew in 1991, which attracted investors and financiers at home and abroad. On February 2, 1992, Pérez boasted of his success at a meeting in the World Economic Forum in Davos, Switzerland. The president stated that 'the spirit of the reforms is no longer a subject of controversy'. However, when Pérez returned to Venezuela (on February 4), the Minister for Defense waited for him at the airport to inform him of a coup d'état in Caracas and warned Pérez not go to the Presidential Palace. This was the second dislocatory event that changed the course of Venezuela's history.

2.2   THE BOLIVARIAN COUP D'ÉTAT

Whilst Pérez was applauded abroad for his economic success, Venezuelans protested rising prices, falling wages, shoddy public services, and government corruption. In a poll conducted in November 1991, three months prior to the coup d'état, 68 percent of respondents regarded current conditions as poor. Social dislocation was spreading and an alarming degree of socio-political dichotomization further polarized this society. This military coup d'état that tried to unseat Pérez discursively articulated what the underprivileged, the excluded, the 'popular mob' wanted: radical change. At this stage, Venezuela's institutional system had little credibility with *el pueblo*. The coup plotters represented a symbol of a common collective

The Venezuelan State 49

popular demand that soon articulated a new antagonistic logic demanding an end to many years of political abuse.

The coup leader, Hugo Chávez Frías, a young 38-year-old mulato-mestizo mid-officer, became a fresh and convincing figure for many.[20] This surreptitious MBR 200 military movement branded itself with the name of the 'Liberator Simón Bolívar': a very affective national identity symbol representing independence, emancipation, equality, and so on. The failed coup d'état unraveled the dimension of antagonism in a country that seemed to be benefiting from an apparent economic growth. What shocked the regime was the popular support this military coup d'état received.

The COPEI offered explicit support to Pérez's government. However, Senator Rafael Caldera indirectly endorsed the coup d'état. The ex-president rhetorically stated in congress how concerned he was for the people because in the past 30 years the polity failed to serve and consolidate an institutional structure for the development of the country. The coup d'état was the result of Pérez's neoliberal reforms.[21] Caldera's discourse was indeed a key element that welcomed, despite its violent actions, the right of 'popular' sectors to rebel. As a result, the coup plotters automatically received a sense of legitimacy. Most politicians harshly criticized Caldera by endorsing a coup d'état in congress. He stated in response: 'this is the time for the President to listen to all the criticism and what I said in the congress is precisely what the "people" want to hear'.[22]

The conditions in Venezuela made it possible for populist practices to emerge. Temporarily, a social antagonistic force (spontaneously, different social sectors were united as 'one' to protest against a common enemy) rebelled in the February 1989 *Caracazo* revolt. The MBR 200 was also an excluded 'social unit' (part of the [at this stage] dispersed and unconstituted antagonistic force) that challenged the regime and tried to displace it with a coup d'état in February 1992. All these different sectors belonged to the same camp because they shared a common enemy: a corrupt institutional system. However, how could a political platform demanding that much-needed radical project desired by Venezuela's antagonized majority be constructed?

Even though Caldera was part of the institution, he tried to politically capitalize on this attempt to de-institute it. For a populist political platform to work, an equivalential chain built upon the construction of a dichotomic frontier is required. Caldera did not have the right social background or the political base to construct a populist framework. However, Chávez did have the right conditions to construct a populist project after a brief speech that quickly embodied the emotions of the popular mass. Apart from his attempt to overthrow the government, his physique, which much resembled the majority of common Venezuelans, played a key role in his instant popularity.

When the coup failed, Chávez, in the Presidential Palace, requested from the authorities national 'live' media coverage to inform other military

50 Populism in Venezuela

compatriots to lay down their arms in other key positions in the country. Whether this was Chávez's real intention or not, I can only speculate. Nonetheless, this gave him the stage to capture people's imagination during a critical occasion of public turmoil. Chávez quickly became a symbol of change to Venezuela's underprivileged population. That is, a symbol of hope appeared on television and filled up that missing element for those that felt excluded by spontaneously informing *el pueblo* that he was one of them. This short, yet direct and energetic rhetoric, was:

> First of all, good morning to the people of Venezuela. This a *Bolivarian message* for the brave soldiers who are presently at. . . . Unfortunately, for the moment—For now (*Por ahora*) the objectives we established in the capital were not achieved. That is, we here in Caracas have failed to seize power. You did an excellent job out there. However, this is time to reflect. New opportunities with better circumstances will arise again. Please, this is a time to re-consider because the country has to embark towards a better destiny. Listen to commander (*Comandante*) Chávez who kindly is asking you to reflect and lay down your weapons, because right now the planned-objectives nationwide are impossible to achieve at this moment. I sincerely appreciate your loyalty, courage, and willingness to fight against this system. And I confess to the country and comrades I take full responsibility for this Bolivarian military movement. Thank you very much.[23]

Let us discursively flesh out vital points (underlined) in Chávez's one-minute speech:

- First of all, Chávez defines this underground movement with Venezuela's independence liberator Simón Bolívar. This entails several key elements in the context of struggle/liberation and national consciousness. The role of Bolívar in Venezuela signifies more than the historical events of Venezuela's struggle for independence. Bolívar is a signifier of national identity and pride, and is an iconic symbol of emancipation, freedom, and equality. The process of articulating some form of resemblance with Bolívar captures social emotions that can easily transcend individual differences and become the 'vector' in a political project (see pages 34–36 in Chapter 1). These elements can effectively 'grip' an antagonized society, and the logic of equivalence can be constructed with a universal demand.
- Chávez's '*Por ahora*' soon became an influential socio-political catchphrase that strongly represented an imaginary better future for the 'people'. In other words, Chávez fills up a gap and truly promises change where there is lack (some form of fullness to come). In a sense, he conveyed to his compatriots and people in general a direction to follow. These were spontaneous political messages from Chávez that

opened a fresh/uncontaminated political discourse in a country tired of corruption, business elites benefiting from neoliberal reforms. '*Por ahora*' signified no surrender. These two words were later used as a gripping 'nodal point' to convey and remind social sectors of their struggle against a common enemy. In other words, the phrase became an 'empty signifier'[24] that effectively totalized all their differences (e.g. miscellaneous demands); it was constructed by labeling the outside as evil: a repressive regime.

- Third, the term '*Comandante*' had two key meanings in the speech. First, Chávez publicly 'labels himself' as the leader of the coup d'état. He was responsible for seizing power in the Presidential Palace because he had worked there and had knowledge of its surroundings. Second, in Venezuela, the meaning of 'commander' commonly indicates other elements apart from military status. It is a term—often used by Fidel Castro—that subconsciously links together emotions of trust, servility, and admiration. That was to be Chávez's nickname.

Chávez became a symbol of hope for many Venezuelans. The affective underdog radical position of the failed coup was the birth of a new political frontier. The coup crystallized the extent of dislocation in Venezuela and the terrain on which to construct a new political project demanding the end of a repressive institutional structure. This is precisely what Panizza points out; it is possible to interpret the leader's 'words as signifying a political relation in which private wants and needs were transformed into public demands by the leader's action of bringing them into public discourse'.[25] This dislocatory event ended with 14 dead and 51 injured. Also, 133 officers and 956 soldiers were detained for treason. '*Comandante*' Chávez was sent to the prison in Yare.[26]

That element of social exclusion in Venezuela began to be an institutional problem in the 1980s when various sectors protested, expecting a response to their needs. The problem lay with the decrease of the oil revenue, an institutional framework prioritizing political and economic clientelism, corruptive practices, excessive borrowing, and so on. The degree of frustration in these social sectors reached such a level that it triggered a spontaneous social uproar in February 1989 (the *Caracazo*). These sentiments were quickly subverted but reappeared when a Bolivarian coup led by Hugo Chávez challenged the government. In spite of its undemocratic and violent actions, it successfully 'gripped' that sense of social antagonism with the '*Por ahora*' discourse: an empty signifier discursively demanding 'radical institutional change' and a better future for the underprivileged/excluded population.

On November 27, 1992, another military insurrection took place (detached from Chávez's MBR 200), which was quickly controlled by Pérez. However, in March 1993, Pérez was impeached on corruption charges. He failed to complete his term in office. These were critical events that further

52 Populism in Venezuela

fragmented Venezuela's political institutional structure. The next presidential election was in December of that year, and Caldera (expelled from his party because he endorsed Chávez), with an alliance called 'El Chiripero'[27], narrowly won the elections. The MAS,[28] with its well-established regional base, played a key role in Caldera's re-election.

Caldera tried to be populist without the much-needed popular support. He was a devoted center-right Christian democrat with strong links with the church and business sectors. In a 1993 *Convergencia* television presidential campaign ad, Caldera said: "'El Chiripero" was a popular democratic movement of "trust" represented by the "people"'.[29] These were political attempts to convince the 'pre-Chavistas' that the meaning of his political project resembled the radical significance manifested in Chávez's failed coup.

However, in office Caldera failed to stop institutional deterioration. He was forced to re-implement the neoliberal 'Washington Consensus' model, and failed to stop the continuous decline of public sectors and people's living standards.[30] Furthermore, Caldera pardoned Chávez and let him out of jail with no restrictions whatsoever. This gave Chávez the platform to construct a radical political project that campaigned for the displacement of a discredited institutional structure and the formation of a popular institutional framework. To some extent, many anti-Chavistas accuse Caldera for the emergence and galvanization of the Chavista project. Caldera not only endorsed Chávez's military coup, but also gave him the freedom to construct a political platform and democratically de-institute the bipartite structure Caldera founded in the early 1960s. In four years, Chávez and his supporters successfully constructed the socio-political base for his return to the Presidential Palace as a democratically elected president. These points are discussed and analyzed in the following sub-sections.

2.2.1 The Emergence of the Bolivarian Project

After Chávez was pardoned on March 27, 1994, the MBR 200 was only a clandestine movement of antagonized mid-ranking officers with no political composition. However, MBR 200 soon developed by welcoming other social sectors that experienced similar antagonistic conditions. This was the base upon which a Bolivarian logic of equivalence was constructed. This new political project promised to de-institute a corrupt and elitist institutional structure and displace it with a popular hegemonic project working for the well-being of the underprivileged population.

When Caldera pardoned Chávez, he argued that it was a matter of national interest because Chávez was part of Venezuela's destiny, a factor that could not be ignored.[31] If Chávez was part of Venezuela's destiny, as Caldera noted, so was the de-institution of the *Punto Fijo* hegemonic structure. Popular sectors wanted change and drastic improvements to their living standards. Politically, Chávez had no political base or a discourse that could represent a wide range of (fundamentally excluded) social sectors throughout the nation. However, MBR 200 rapidly re-branded itself as a political project and expanded by welcoming antagonized organizations to join.[32]

Becoming an MBR 200 member involved a kind of ritual called the 'Bolivarian compromise', which consisted in a commitment to be honest, hard working, humble, and supportive. Militants formed the 'Bolivarian Circles' with branches across the country. Town council coordinators in Caracas, and regional coordinators in all the states of the country coordinated these circles.[33] According to Chávez, 'social and political groups were indispensable, so we recognized the need to establish alliances . . . we brought together several projects, which was the popular constitutional assembly; others included defending people's standards of living, defending national sovereignty . . . called the "organization of the popular movement"'.[34]

The MBR 200 became a socio-political movement practicing the 'Bolivarian compromise' discourse. 'Bolivarian Circles' promoted across the country a project explaining the need for *el pueblo* to collectively mobilize itself to construct a new socio-political frontier demanding change. This process articulated a forum where people expressed their problems and dissatisfaction with the government. From this platform, the Bolivarian internal frontier emerged. All social negativity evolved into an equivalential popular discourse. This new *popular subject* (I refer to Laclau's terminology: see page 29 in Chapter 1) demanded radical change and an end to oppressive regimes.

The MBR 200's discourse fundamentally stressed that 'Venezuela's structural crisis requires radical solutions'. Prior to the failed coup in 1992, the movement's strategy was to overthrow the president, parliamentarians, magistrates in the Supreme Court of Justice, and key members of the institutional structure—and, with a referendum, to summon a new constitutional assembly to construct a viable system for Venezuela's poor.[35] This strategy didn't change when MBR 200 welcomed non-military members; on the contrary, it strengthened its political position by incorporating antagonized social units and thus expanding its discursive formation into new non-military boundaries.

According to Margarita López Maya, there are many MBR 200 documents addressing the need for a constitutional assembly. These documents emphasize the need to transform 'all' structures of the society and construct an 'original' and 'united' society.[36] These documents also draw on the democratic character of the movement—'describing it as a profoundly dynamic organization with the participation of a variety of liberated forces'.[37] Liberated forces mean 'social/political' groups or organizations that joined and participated in MBR 200's development. Bolívar was the 'vector' in the MBR 200 project. To Bolívar, 'democracy is a governmental system that ought to create a high level of happiness, social security and preeminent political stability'.[38] Bolívar's interpretation of democracy discursively

54 *Populism in Venezuela*

fabricated a sense of 'fullness to come'—ensuring a better future with the radical solutions this political project promoted. The project proposed a 'popular' democracy underpinning *el pueblo* as fundamental protagonists in decision-making.[39] I descriptively address in detail what 'popular protagonist' means in Chapter 4.

MBR 200 militants had meetings and discussed ideological and political issues. López Maya notes that this is how the military articulated a horizontal common ground where a sense of transition subordinated the notion of military hierarchy. On a regular basis, municipal, state, and national representatives discussed a variety of issues, which helped to articulate and hence refine the 'Simón Bolívar National Project'. The MBR 200 participants López Maya interviewed said: 'this organizational approach formed a political base that attracted the participation of the masses'.[40] In 1996, it was difficult to measure how popular this political movement was. Chávez never had an opportunity to compete in an electoral process. Only polls and surveys provided a quantitative estimate of the popularity of this 'revolutionary' political project. However, López Maya argues that most of the results gathered were not based on suitable/objective questions.[41] I'll return to this pool-popularity aspect later and discuss how other political projects appeared to have better chances in winning the presidential elections in 1998.

According to Chávez, with this popular movement, 'we began filling in the content of each project: each one needed a motor to drive forward'.[42] This was the process where different groups in each project accepted a common 'nodal point' in order to 'arrest the flow of difference'.[43] This is how the Bolivarian internal frontier was constructing its 'logic of equivalence'. The '"civic-military MBR 200 movement" began to have formative experiences', Chávez said. This popular movement formed Bolivarian committees where members expressed their ideas/opinions for a new constitutional assembly.[44] In other words, social subjects directly described their needs (lack) and expectations for a new institutional (fullness-to-come) structure.

In April 1997, the MBR 200 requested to be officially accepted as a political party. This was rejected because the electoral council rejected the use of 'Bolívar' to name a political party; thus Chávez changed it to Movimiento V [quinta] República (MVR).[45] The MVR's political strategy was fundamentally constructed upon a discourse that contested the *Punto Fijo* institution, seeking to displace it with an institutional structure designed by/for the people. Its political campaign demanded a constitutional assembly, an end to corruption, improvements in social services, a general salary increase, and '*Gobierno Bolívariano Ahora*' (Bolivarian Government Now). Chávez changed his looks, dressing in a more casual Western manner; however, he made it clear that the military uniform was underneath—and that, if necessary, he would change and get ready for combat.[46] Chávez re-packaged his political stance with a more balanced type of discourse in order to expand his popularity and attract another class-based sector: the middle class.

A discursive element that fleshes out key points is the wording. When the MBR 200 requested that the electoral authorities recognize the movement as a political party, this was rejected because the use of Bolívar in the wording. Perhaps rejecting the use of Bolívar's name for political reasons was a method to block/delay the advancement of this anti-institutional political movement. However, the Bolivarians retaliated with MVR: a name that still managed to discursively include Bolívar as the 'vector' (e.g. independence, patriotism, emancipation, equality, anti-elitism, and so forth) of this new political party.

The MVR had a clear dichotomic message: anti-corruption, anti-poverty, anti-*Puntofijismo*, and a new constitution for the 'people'. The Bolivarian movement fully complied with institutional regulations and was eventually recognized as a political party. The next step was to expand and crystallize its political frontier and form a populist Bolivarian hegemony promising the displacement of a common enemy: the *Punto Fijo* institutional structure. Existing political parties joined the Bolivarian equivalential chain, incorporating their party national social-base with the Bolivarian 'us' (the underdog) against 'them' (the corrupt/oppressive regime).

Kenneth Roberts states that Chávez's 'Bolivarian movement was slow to catch on. . . . A year and a half before the election, Chávez had secured a base of support among the lower classes—12 percent of whom declared an intention to vote for him—but he could only claim 7 percent of the vote intention nationwide and a mere 2 percent among upper-class respondents'.[47] Irene Sáez, Venezuela's 1981 Miss Universe, was the front-runner with the 'support of 24 percent of the poor, 42 percent of the middle class and 33 percent of the upper-class'. The other independent, Enrique Salas Römer[48], 'had a profile that was opposite of Chávez's, with support from 20 percent of upper class respondents but only 8 percent of the poor'.[49]

Both of Chávez's political adversaries were independent presidential candidates with different political strategies—much aligned with the hegemonic practices that had governed Venezuela since 1958. By claiming to be 'independent', these candidates tried to remove any connections with the *Punto Fijo* structure—widely criticized as corrupt and responsible for Venezuela's dichotomous society. Sáez and Salas Römer were both political moderates who represented only a superficial change. Neither of these presidential candidates articulated a political platform that either contested the hegemonic order or offered something to improve the lives of the poor.

However, Chávez's discourse demanded radical change: de-institute the *Punto Fijo* structure and replace it with a popular institutional structure. Sáez and Salas Römer were part of that 'other' institution. The 'us-them' axis politically stabilized the Chavista camp and consolidated its equivalential chain. Political parties that recognized a sense of obligation with their communal and regional party-base decided to incorporate themselves into

56   Populism in Venezuela

the Bolivarian political alliance. This was the next phase, which galvanized the project by incorporating party-electoral machinery into this populist force. The following sub-sections conclude this chapter with a chronological discussion of the political events that led to Chávez's victory in the 1998 presidential election.

2.2.2   MVR & political alliances: *Polo Patriótico*

The first political party that recognized the need to form an alliance with the MVR was *Patria Para Todos* (PPT). The PPT was founded in September 1997 and joined '*Polo Patriótico*' in March 1998. The PPT was a faction of LCR (*La Causa Radical*)—a party that received 21.95 percent of the votes in the 1993 presidential election. The political alliance with the MVR gave Chávez one of the missing political elements to succeed in the December 1998 presidential election. He noted that after national campaign visits, he knew that more than 80 percent of PPT's platform wanted to support the Bolivarian project.[50] The next party that joined the Bolivarian 'equivalential chain' was the *Partido Comunista de Venezuela* (PCV), which announced: '"We support *Comandante* Chávez's candidacy"'.[51] Chávez said: 'we began to meet with groups and people, and that was when Luis Miquilena[52] got involved because he is skilled politically. He organized the meetings with sectors of the Left' such as 'Causa R [later named PPT], with sectors of the MAS, and with other smaller parties like the MEP [*Movimiento Electoral del Pueblo*]'.[53] From this political base, in search of party-alliances, Chávez said: 'we were able to form *Polo Patriótico* and Miquilena assumed a leadership role, showing great political skill, he earned a lot of respect among allies and potential allies alike'.[54]

According to Medófilo Medina, the *Polo Patriótico* alliance with the PPT onboard provided the Bolivarian camp an important electoral footing because the PPT had a strong regional base. The PPT represented various labor union sectors, which helped to divide (fleshing out the dichotomic terrain) the Bolivarian hegemony against the AD hegemony. Also, PPT's political work in shantytown '*barrios*' areas and in student organizations was vital for Chávez's victory.[55] The *Polo Patriótico* was a symbol of protest against those sectors in the country that benefited from economic reforms and the international programs that strangled Venezuela's economic and political development. Nonetheless, Pablo Medina (the PPT's secretary general) stressed the complexity of solving Venezuela's poverty problem and give underprivileged/excluded sectors some form of fulfillment to their basic needs.[56]

The PPT discursively articulated the *Polo Patriótico* as the underprivileged/underdog radical camp against years of government negligence. That is to say, it articulated an antagonized populist approach against the *Punto Fijo* camp, formed to fill up the popular void (fulfillment to come) by investing in Chávez's 1998 presidential campaign. In March 1998, after political

The Venezuelan State 57

differences regarding details on constitutional changes, the MVR received PPT's full participation in the Bolivarian hegemonic project.[57] In other words, the MVR subordinated the flow of differences with 'their' *nodal point*: a universal demand for radical change. On April 30 of the same year—seven months prior to election day—poll results began to change. The firm '*Datanalisis*' confirmed that Chávez had a popularity of 27 percent, Sáez 22 percent, Salas Römer 16 percent, and Claudio Fermín (the 1993 AD candidate—now running as an independent) 8 percent. It was the first time Sáez was not the front-runner.[58]

As Luis Uzcategui points out, the beauty image of Irene Sáez attracted various social sectors. Nevertheless, her popularity declined because social subjects needed a symbol that signified change and a break from the *Punto Fijo* apparatus of lies and promises. Sáez used for her presidential campaign the 'Barbie doll': an American product designed in the 1950s that constantly changes its beauty and physical appearance (e.g. dress, body configuration). This was the type of discourse she used to portray herself as a calm and compassionate woman, like Princess Diana from the United Kingdom.[59] However, the 'Sáez Barbie logic' had no political substance (only an aesthetic element) to represent the hardship endured by underprivileged Venezuelans. The discourse of *Comandante* Chávez represented universal radical change demanding a new constitution, no corruption, no poverty, and so on. The Chavista *popular subject* drew together key antagonistic issues within a plan of radical reform, to re-build Venezuela with a direct/participative democratic system for the people.

To get a glimpse of the Chavista 'equivalential articulation', social groups like *Independientes Para la Comunidad Nacional, Gente Emergente, Solidaridad Independiente*, and *Asociación Agropecuaria* invested in the Bolivarian hegemonic project. The Chavista 'logics of equivalence' was expanding not only with political parties but also with social organizations. Social involvement representing different community assemblies played a key role in the construction of an *internal frontier* demanding radicalization. The *Polo Patriótico* further galvanized its political position when *Movimiento al Socialismo* (MAS) joined the Bolivarian project.

2.2.3 MAS invests in the *Polo Patriótico*

In January 1998, MAS's political committee was divided over the selection of potential candidates to support: Sáez, Salas Römer, Claudio Fermín, and Carlos Tablante of MAS. Chávez was briefly mentioned but did not play an important role in MAS's internal (committee) differences.[60] However, in April Chávez was included in the list because a key committee member (after a dialogue with Chávez) recognized the need to consider his political program.[61] The MAS (the third biggest political party) was influential when the *Punto Fijo* bipartite (AD and COPEI) democratic system crumbled. In 1993, it played a key electoral role in Caldera's

58   Populism in Venezuela

'Chiripero'. A similar tactic informed MAS's decision to invest in *Polo Patriótico*—five and a half months prior to the December 6 election day. Chávez stated that he respected MAS's internal differences but asked for party unity. Chávez appreciated Felipe Mújica and Leopoldo Puchi's insistence on responding to party grassroots results from a survey done by a firm MAS contracted. Chávez also stated his gratitude to '"Masistas" political-base, for their moral and intellectual consciousness to lead the country in the "right direction"'.[62]

According to Felipe Mújica, the president of MAS, 'even though many committee members strongly disagreed with MAS's involvement in the *Polo Patriótico*, it was recognized that ignoring nationwide popular support at party regional branches would have been a serious political error'.[63] Social opinion in the survey results was clearly in favor of supporting Chávez with the MAS electoral ticket. Mújica stressed that 'if we decided to ignore these results, our political base would have gradually collapsed. The idea of MAS's national committee imposing their preferences against their own well-established support at different regional branches would have been the end of MAS'.[64] The participation of this influential party (with an established regional electoral machinery) consolidated the Chavista equivalential chain. Political alliances crystallized the 'us-them' axis terrain—providing Chávez the democratic mechanism to win the December 1998 presidential election. This is how I interpret the articulation of a populist *internal frontier* in the Venezuelan context.

With MAS's political apparatus investing in the Bolivarian project, Chávez galvanized his political credibility, thus opening frontiers in other class-based sectors. In September 1998, Chávez's popularity was 41.6 percent in the polls, in October it changed to 44.8 percent, and in November it increased to 49.6 percent. At this stage, the *Polo Patriótico* was successfully articulating a populist project demanding anti-corruption, anti-poverty, *anti-Puntofijismo*, and a new constitution for the 'people'. The Bolivarian project discursively accentuated the need to emancipate and construct a socio-political institutional structure to help the excluded, the poor, the working and middle classes, and any individual that wanted 'change'.

The results of the December 6, 1998 presidential elections rubber-stamped the success of the *Polo Patriótico* equivalential chain when Chávez won with 56.20 percent of the votes.[65] The support of MAS's political machinery was vital in Chávez's victory. Following this result, Chávez rhetorically claimed that the attempt to overthrow Pérez by force was historically a legitimate decision supported by the people. And he quoted Caldera's remarks shortly after the February 4, 1992, coup: 'the people cannot defend a democracy starving'.[66] Less than a year earlier, the 'Sáez Barbie logic' was the favorite candidate for the presidency. In the end, only 2.82 percent of voters supported Sáez. Salas Römer's political coalition got 39.97 percent.[67] If MAS had supported the 'other' camp instead, election results would have been:

The Venezuelan State   59

- Salas R.   + MAS: 2,613,161 (39.97%) + 588,643 (9.00%) = 3,201,804
- H. Chávez - MAS: 3,673,685 (56.20%) - 588,643 (9.00%) = 3,085,042

Vote-Difference: 116,762

When I discussed this point with Mújica (president of MAS), he said: 'politics doesn't work like that. Voters are not numbers; there is so much that needs unpacking in order to understand what makes "people" support a political project. If we decided to join Salas Römer not Chávez, traditional MAS grassroots supporters would have voted for Chávez on the MVR ticket, not MAS. The survey demonstrated what Masistas wanted; thus the Committee of MAS had to seriously consider what loyal "social" supporters expected from their political party'.[68] What I want to emphasize is that rational choice, behavioral-positivist (quantitative) analytical approaches fail to cast light on these type of elements in political practices. These are underprivileged sectors of a society driven by emotional circumstances in their search for a political discourse (e.g. socialist principles) that makes sense of their conditions and discursively represents (fullness to come) what they seek: 'radical change'. On February 2, 1999, in the inaugural speech, the newly elected President Chávez stated:

> I repeatedly expressed to the Venezuelan people—in many ways and in many places throughout the country . . . that with God's help . . . this particular day, me accepting the post for the Presidency, I shall begin the inaugural speech with the following phrase: bless the 'people' that have finally fought for their right to have national sovereignty and exercise with absolute power.[69]

No one else had the credentials to convey and articulate a *popular subjectivity* like *Comandante* Chávez did: claiming to be the 'true' representative of the 'people'. The 'Sáez Barbie' discourse had no social or political meaning for those that had struggled with years of social antagonism. Moreover, Salas Römer's business experience and hidden neoliberal ideology had no 'grip' signifying 'fulfillment to come' for the majority of Venezuelans. In other words, *el pueblo* demanded the 'radical change' the 'Chavista equivalential chain' promoted.

CONCLUSION

In this chapter, I have presented an overall summary of Venezuela since the early nineteenth century, periods of dictatorial regimes until 1958, the *Punto Fijo* Pact that instituted a democratic bipartite system, the oil bonanza of the 1970s, the decline of oil revenues, clientelism, and corrupt practices in the 1980s. The implementation of neoliberal reforms on February 27, 1989 caused spontaneous social unrest, an event known in

60 Populism in Venezuela

Venezuela as the *Caracazo*: the first dislocatory event that destabilized the institutional establishment. The second and fatal moment of dislocation that directly challenged and tried to displace the establishment was a coup d'état of mid-ranking officers led by Hugo Chávez on February 4, 1992.

The coup d'état failed; nonetheless, in a one-minute surrender speech, Chávez's *Por ahora* became an empty signifier that spontaneously captured the imagination and support of antagonized social sectors. After Chávez was released from jail in March 1994, the MBR 200 began to construct a new 'Bolivarian' political project that intended to shift its pre-coup ideological beliefs by welcoming the participation and involvement of popular sectors in the process. In a period of three years, this military movement was officially recognized as a political party and constructed a collective *popular subjectivity* demanding an end to poverty and corruption and a constitutional assembly for the people. This 'dichotomic construction' consolidated a clear 'us-them' axis (demarcating two divided political camps) in a deeply polarized society. The Chavista equivalential chain naturalized its *internal frontier* when *Polo Patriótico* was formed: an alliance of political parties and community organizations joining forces (and subordinating their differences) to contest and de-institute a corrupt/elitist (*Punto Fijo*) institutional structure.

This political strategy was fundamentally constructed upon 'social' antagonistic forces that felt excluded from a society that explicitly benefited 'others'. The Bolivarian revolutionary discourse articulated a new form of political significance that 'gripped' *el pueblo* (the underprivileged, the poor, the working class, and part of the middle class) by harvesting the possibility of an institutional structure that promised fullness or harmony to come by displacing a common enemy. Laclau argues that we cannot claim this is populism unless there is a 'discursive construction of an enemy: the *ancient regime*, the oligarchy, the establishment or whatever'.[70] I have descriptively presented and analyzed the Venezuelan context in order to address the conditions that articulated the construction of an enemy, the dislocatory moments that made Chávez and the Bolivarian hegemonic project a populist platform, representing *el pueblo* as a political force demanding 'radical change'—with the intention of displacing an unresponsive and repressive institution. The other presidential 'independent' candidates (Salas Römer and Sáez) indirectly represented the 'other' hegemonic position. The logics of Chavismo discursively articulated a *popular subjectivity* vis-à-vis an institution responsible for the mishaps and tragedies of social subjects. Chávez was elected to end these antagonistic conditions. This will be discussed in the next chapter.

3 The Process of Deinstitutionalizing the Power Structure and Institutionalizing Venezuela's Bolivarian Project

The previous chapter narrates the historical background in Venezuela to explain the socio-political conditions that made the creation of a new populist project possible. The *Polo Patriótico* political camp founded by several social and political groups promised to displace the fragmented and discredited institutional system and build a popular institutional framework to help the poor and excluded population. The first section of this chapter discusses how the *Punto Fijo* institutional system was de-institutionalized. It then considers the anti-Bolivarian attempts to re-institute its failed 'hegemonic position', temporarily removing Chávez from power. The third section addresses a second phase of institutional radicalism, in which popular social programs were designed to improve the lives of Venezuelans living in marginal areas. The concluding section discusses the emergence and impact of new opposition forces—detached from the displaced *Punto Fijo* political structure.

This chapter seeks to achieve three important objectives: first, to define how populist practices have shifted from the mode of opposition analyzed in Chapter 2 to a mode of governance; second, to examine the context in which the displaced hegemonic order attempted to re-institute itself and how anti-Bolivarian resistance has tried to obstruct the reproduction of populism; and third, to discuss how the advancement and sedimentation of institutional radicalism has worsened the level of dichotomization in a deeply polarized society. In this chapter, I employ Glynos and Howarth's logics critical explanation schema and Laclau's theoretical approach to furnish an appropriate context for the issues raised above.

3.1 DE-INSTITUTIONALIZING THE *PUNTO FIJO* ESTABLISHMENT

Chávez taking office in February 1999 was the beginning of a new political period in Venezuela. Years of power mismanagement/abuse in an oil-rich nation caused discomfort and high levels of antagonism for many people from less privileged sectors of society. From the early 1980s, living conditions for poor sectors and a share of the middle class deteriorated. In spite

62 *Populism in Venezuela*

of the displacement breakthrough in the December 1998 presidential election, when the majority of electorates voted for a candidate from a new political force, de-institutionalizing the *Punto Fijo* institutional structure was going to be a complex endeavor. Key power divisions such as ministerial and legislative divisions, state/county sectors, federations, national trade unions, business organizations, oil industry managerial schemes, and so on continue practicing the *Punto Fijo* hegemonic order.

On November 8, 1998—28 days prior to the presidential elections—governors (23 states/divisions nationwide) and the parliament (National Assembly legislature) were elected. The *Polo Patriótico* (PP) barely got one-third (eight governorships) of the regional political base. Legislatively, it failed to get the required two-thirds (less than 33 percent) of parliamentarian seats to pass any of the drastic constitutional reforms promised in the presidential campaign. Their first objective was to displace the *Punto Fijo* Constitution and replace it with a popular constitution written to serve the people. The Bolivarian project called upon *el pueblo* to electorally support, in the coming referendum and elections, the displacement of the 1961 Constitution and the construction of a 'radical Bolivarian Constitution' hegemonic order. From April 1999 until July 2000, this new political project further galvanized its objective to radically change the country. The majority of Venezuelans supported the change the Bolivarian project promised.

Political elites involved in the *Punto Fijo* apparatus feared the emergence of new social and political actors that wanted to transform, via democratic means, the institutional structure they created and abused.[1] A day before the referendum, Chávez emphasized during an eight-minute speech—televised on all stations nationwide—the significance of every common Venezuelan's support of the construction of a constitution written for the people. Discursively, the president underlines key 'us-them' populist elements, saying:

> Never before have the 'people' been consulted to decide such an important decision that shall guide the future of this nation. . . . To constitute a new assembly is a must . . . it is vital for the country; precisely because, in the last forty years the political system in Venezuela lost the democratic essence, legitimacy . . . And, it doesn't have the framework to drive the nation to act accordingly with critical issues. . . . Peacefully and democratically 'We' shall do it—not because a *caudillo*, an autocrat or elite sectors want to, but the sovereign 'Venezuelan People'.[2]

Rhetorically, Chávez accentuates the extent of division in Venezuela. Chávez emphasizes his role as the representative of Venezuela's 'underdog/underprivileged' sectors, explaining that radical change is needed to improve the lives of the people. Politically, to articulate the necessary changes in a democratic context, popular support was vital in the referendum. In other words, it was vital to ending a constitution that politically and economically benefited privileged sectors—exploiting *el pueblo* for

The Process of Deinstitutionalizing the Power Structure   63

many years. Voters overwhelmingly endorsed the referendum with 87 percent of the votes. However, turnout was less than 40 percent. The degree of social awareness and interest to support this political proposal appeared to be partial. This level of social apathy was the highest ever in this democratic system.

The second election was for a new constituent assembly (generally known as a 'constitutional convention'). Shortly before election day (on July 24, 1999),[3] Chávez makes a vital speech at one of the country's important monuments. The '*Panteón Nacional*' is a building in the northern part of Caracas, originally built as a church. The central nave is dedicated to Simón Bolívar, with the altar's place taken by the hero's bronze sarcophagus. Other lesser celebrities are relegated to the aisles. This building is a monument devoted to elements drawn from Bolívar's fight for independence in Venezuela, Colombia, Panama, Ecuador, Perú, and Bolivia. Chávez's speech and where it was delivered clearly reveals the significance (the vector: *direction and energy*) of Bolívar in this new Bolivarian Revolution:

> I have the great honor to unsheathe, thus shine with natural light the 'Sword' of Bolívar beside his mortal remains . . . which have not perished . . . because his ideas travel a Continent forming a world in itself. That never dies. . . . The Liberator never dies. . . . It is important to inform the Venezuelan 'people' that Bolívar's 'Sword' has been left and forgotten in a safe in the Central Bank of Venezuela. I decided to hold the Sword and unsheathe it to encourage Venezuelans to analyze and appreciate Bolívar's sense of wisdom and struggle for emancipation.[4]

In my view, Chávez wants to create a scene where Bolívar's '*Sword*' becomes a symbolic signifier of patriotism, of struggle against a repressive enemy, and of a demand for freedom. Discursively, the '*Sword*' is an object of struggle and unity, a symbol that signifies a sense of radical demand for a new constitution specifically written for the well-being of the common people. In their methodological schema, Glynos and Howarth state that fantasmatic logics provide a method to understand 'why specific practices and regimes "grip" subjects'.[5] The use of Bolívar's sword as a 'gripping' symbol helps this new hegemonic project link together a variety of different subjects and thus crystallize the equivalential chain. As Laclau notes, 'if political logics concern signifying operations, fantasmatic logics concern the force behind those operations'.[6] In this context, the Bolivarian symbol is used as the centre (Glynos and Howarth categorize it as 'vector') of the operational force in order to make this emancipatory populist project resonate with the struggle of independence and freedom Bolívar signifies in Venezuela and Latin America. In the previous chapter, I discussed how in the early 1980s sub-officers like Chávez founded an underground revolutionary movement within the armed forces (*Movimiento Bolivariano Revolucionario 200*) named after Simón Bolívar. This element of naming it '*Bolivariano*' gives

64 *Populism in Venezuela*

us a glimpse of the discursive significance of the Liberator in the political revolution Chávez leads.

Returning to the July 25, 1999 constituent assembly election, PP's equivalential chain got exceptional results. Out of 128 elected members, 120 (93.7 percent) were PP partisans.[7] A day after the election, Chávez, from the presidential balcony, stated to a multitude of supporters:

> This is the balcony of the People . . . I swear to God I won't let you down . . . be humble with this victory and I request you to respect the minority because we have to teach them how to construct a country . . . to those who in the last forty years worked to destroy it. . . . The Constituent Assembly is truly genuine because it has the backing of the people. . . . The people in the World can be assured that the constitutional process will be peaceful, respecting human rights, freedom of speech, and the opinion of others. . . . We have informed the World that we have inherited the glory of Simón Bolívar . . . please dedicate this triumph to our Liberator Simón Bolívar, also to the children of our land who shall enjoy the fruits of the New Republic.[8]

In the above speech, Chávez asks his supporters 'to respect the minority'. The meaning of 'minority' in this context implies that whoever decided not to vote for a new constitution (i.e. didn't vote or voted for a non-PP candidate) is part of the 'minority'. Chávez also re-emphasizes the notion of 'forty years'. In other words, anyone who disapproves of a constitutional change automatically belongs to the other camp. Another aspect is the importance of 'Bolívar' in the speech: the 'vector' in this period of radical transformation. My point is to emphasize the influence of the past in Chávez's populist discourse.

According to Marta Harnecker, Chávez noted that 'the process of framing the constitution was quite open . . . once the Constituent Assembly was installed, it wrote its own regulations and created a Participation Commission . . . whose task was to encourage participation, receive diverse proposal, and take them to the assembly'.[9] The degree of popular participation reached to such a level that 'toll-free telephone lines were opened, so people could provide their opinions'. Chávez points out that 'once or twice per week they went to the regions from which they were elected to organize assemblies, to talk, to explore ideas, to look for projects'.[10]

This social participative model encouraged people to express their views with political delegates and hence be part of the constitutional drafting process and the formation of a new popular institutional 'hegemonic order'. In the referendum, 71.78 percent of the voters said yes to the Bolivarian Constitution—with 28.22 percent against it.[11] An interesting element in the new constitution is the inclusion of Bolívar in its naming (*Constitución de la República de Bolivariana de Venezuela*). Discursively, this reinstates the importance of Bolívar (i.e. functioning as the 'vector' of the project) in the formation of the new republic this revolution was constructing.

The Process of Deinstitutionalizing the Power Structure 65

According to Luis Miquilena,[12] the president of the constituent assembly, during the drafting of the constitution, the name of the country was voted and agreed on as the 'Republic of Venezuela'. At that time, Chávez was abroad and called Miquilena from Russia and China. Chávez called to express his anger over the decision to name the country 'Republic of Venezuela'. Chávez strongly wanted to include '*Bolivariana*' (Bolivarian) in the constitution. Miquilena replied, 'well that's an adjective idea of no importance calling it Bolivarian Republic. We are all Bolivarians, no need to underline that element'. However, after a long discussion with Chávez, Miquilena accepted to add 'Bolivarian'. Miquilena stressed that the Left/Marxists have symbolized their movements with foreign personalities such as Marx, Lenin, and so on. Including Bolívar (national symbolic figure) in the name of the country, Chávez wanted to emphasize the importance of patriotic values in this new hegemonic project.[13]

Dedicating this new Republic to Bolivar is an attempt to emphasize the difference between previous governments (clientele attitudes, corruption, etc.), and the urgency of reconstructing something honorable for the nation. Miquilena agreed to add 'Bolivarian'; nonetheless, Miquilena warned Chávez, 'if we dare to declare our political project Bolivarian we have to have a decent and genuine government. As incumbents, it is our responsibility to defend our "Liberator" because many *caudillos* and corrupters have used the name Bolívar to hide their unscrupulous behavior. We cannot degrade Bolívar'.[14] I argue that Bolívar was and still is (following Glynos and Howarth's terminology) the 'vector' in this populist project.

The process of de-institutionalizing a system that started to show incurable signs of dislocation after the *Caracazo* revolt was coming to an end. Via referendums in 1999 a new constitutional framework was formed, and the *Punto Fijo* political representatives elected in November–December 1998 (following the displaced *Punto Fijo* Constitution) were no longer entitled to those public posts. A new 'hegemonic position' emerged. The 'Bolivarian' institutional formation started to have the platform to implement radical changes in Venezuela. The new constitution helped to consolidate its hegemonic political-base on July 30, 2000 with more elections: for the presidency, governors, and parliament.

There were three candidates for the presidency. Chávez comfortably won with 59.76 percent of the votes. The second nearest rival was Francisco Arias Cardenas (another officer involved in the February 1992 coup), who received 37.52 percent, and Claudio Fermín (see page 57 in Chapter 2) gathered 2.72 percent of the votes.[15] For the governorship in 23 states, 17 *Polo Patriótico* candidates were elected.[16] Of the 165 parliamentarian seats to be elected, 99 were *Polo Patriótico* candidates.[17] The Bolivarian hegemonic project was expanding further and consolidating a viable political alternative in Venezuela.

For this new institutional system to advance, Chávez was granted a ruling decree through an enabling law for one year. More radical and unpredictable constitutional changes triggered further political dichotomization.

66 Populism in Venezuela

On November 8, 2000, 108[18] of the 165 members in the parliament voted in favor of a presidential authorization to rule by Decree Laws in six areas: the economy, transport, and service infrastructure, science and technology, reorganization of government ministries, and crime.[19] According to Buxton, the 'delay of nearly a year in the formulation of these measures spurred the opposition, turning the administration into a day-to-day political conflict'. This 'sense of political risk that persisted throughout 2001 accelerated capital flight . . . [which] combined with a decline in oil prices had a negative impact on the economy.'[20] Felipe Mújica recollects, 'many influential media and economic sectors fully supported and invested in Chávez. However, when this new Enabling Laws phase appeared, and its substance was unknown, for the first time, it created a sense confrontation/conflict between the above sectors and institutional divisions. To the political party MAS (*Movimiento al Socialismo*), Chávez ignored basic democratic principles; he didn't want to have any form of dialogue with anyone'.[21]

The 'New Enabling Revolutionary Laws', 49 in total, were finally completed throughout the given period of one year. Chávez argued that 'these laws will improve social and economic circumstances in the country. . . . We have worked analyzing economic and political issues—taken into consideration internal and external factors in order to present a 2001–2007 Development Program including a variety of sectors in the country'. He stressed that some of the most important laws were related with land reform, fishing rights, hydrocarbons, and banking reform to improve access to credit for micro-entrepreneurs.[22]

According to Miquilena, 'instead of decreeing Laws through the parliament (as we had the majority) Chávez requested the power to decide. The opposition (seriously worn off—after 40 years of power and allegations of corrupt practices) with some influence still in the parliament failed to radically abrupt the Presidential Decree process. After the Laws were presented, there was no dialogue or debate whatsoever in the parliament (even among members of the Chavista camp) about substantial Laws related with Land Reform, Fishing Rights and Hydrocarbons'. This was the moment when moderates and radical Chavistas split in the cabinet and the parliament.[23]

Miquilena, the interior minister at that moment, strongly disapproved of Chávez's land reform: expropriate private land without legally negotiating with the landowner. He recalls, 'as the Interior Minister, I had to deal with the business sector strike organized by Fedecámaras [*Federación de Cámaras y Asociaciones de Comercio y Producción de Venezuela*][24] in December 2001. The strike ended after meetings I had with members of Fedecámaras, bankers, business groups, etc., acknowledging that the government (which Chávez eventually agreed upon that night) would take a reasonable position with business sectors'.[25] Miquilena narrates, 'a document was written soon after—for it to be signed the next day by business representatives and the president. However, early in the morning Chávez called saying that he changed his mind and decided not to sign it. The document wanted to initiate a process

The Process of Deinstitutionalizing the Power Structure   67

of dialogue, concessions and agreements with the business community (e.g. the Land Reform). This was my biggest clash with Chávez'.[26] In other words, Chávez's plan to implement radical institutional changes was unconditional. The strike organized by the business community failed to block these radical changes. The opposition had no other option but to reconsider its position and find other drastic measures to challenge and displace this new wave of 'radical hegemonic practices' and re-institute their 'hegemonic order'. This will be discussed next.

3.2   ANTI-BOLIVARIAN ATTEMPTS TO SEIZE POWER

In December 2001, the confrontation of two clearly divided camps crystallized when the Bolivarian Government contested strike allegations. The opposition alleged that the strike intended to express the impact of some of the 49 laws enacted under the Enabling Act: reforms of land, hydrocarbons, and fishing implemented by Chávez. The strike was organized by Fedecámaras and the AD-controlled labor union *Confederación de Trabajadores de Venezuela* (CTV), and began on December 10, 2001.[27]

Industry sectors, the church, political organizations, and various individuals demanded that the government, specifically Chávez, change his manners and political practices. Their main objective was to shorten in one way or another his term in power. Many organizations affected by the land reform requested some forms of negotiations and dialogue; private property was at stake with this controversial law.[28] The opposition disapproved of Chávez's schizophrenic discourse threatening the U.S. (e.g. criticizing the killing of civilians in Afghanistan after the 9/11 attacks): 'whilst misery increases . . . governance is getting out of his hands. Many shout: Get out now! [Chávez]'.[29]

This was the start of an anti-Bolivarian discourse platform determined to block the sedimentation of the Bolivarian hegemony. This new form of contestation claimed to be of commercial nature. Fedecámaras's objective was to demonstrate its rejection of the government's economic decisions. Discursively, however, this was a social and political strategy that aimed to block this new phase of 'radicalization' inducted with the enactment of the 49 Decree Laws. It clearly exposed the level of dichotomy in Venezuela. The Decree Laws openly excluded social and economic sectors that had participated in and enjoyed the recently de-instituted 'neoliberal' hegemonic order.

On December 10, 2001, during the presidential TV show '*Aló Presidente*' near Chávez's hometown in Barinas, launching the land reform, Chávez warned the 'oligarchs' that he would take 'harsh measures' if the 'privileged minority tries to obstruct this democratic process by organizing a strike against the enacted 49 Laws'. Chávez reiterated to Fedecámaras:

> The people of the Bolivarian Revolution are responding . . . don't get this wrong, be rational and calculate this carefully, overcome this hatred . . .

68 *Populism in Venezuela*

you are desperate to get the power back. . . . Many are helping to consolidate the power of the 'people' and defend this Revolution because '*el pueblo*' knows the truth and are aware that this is the way forward.

Chávez continued accusing Fedecámaras of being a partner of former Venezuelan presidents, who are:

[a]lcoholics, demagogues, corrupters, tyrants, repressors, murderers, and all of those sucked on that tit (*y ellos pegados allí, pegados a la teta*). . . .This is a Government with no compromise that doesn't subordinate [itself] to any faction regardless of their weight. . . . This is not about me but the country, of a democratic Revolution for the poor, underprivileged and middle classes. This shall not collapse.[30]

This is the form of rhetoric Chávez articulated in response to the strike Fedecámaras and CTV organized. Fedecámaras responded with a request for dialogue in the parliament, claiming that the 49 Decree Laws were unconstitutional.[31] In other words, Fedecámaras attempted to create some form of an agonistic proposal with 'revolutionary' parliamentarians and construct a relation that suited political and business interests (pact). The land reform was a key topic in the discussion. Nothing was agreed upon. Miquilena's attempt (earlier discussed) to form a dialogue and mutual accord was rejected by Chávez. Perhaps, the main objective was to start a form of negotiation (similar to the *Punto Fijo* Pact), gradually exclude Chávez from power, offer a wide range of incentives, and discreetly manage and change practices in this 'Bolivarian Constitution hegemonic project'. In other words, the objective was to develop a moderate Bolivarian Constitution without the 'hegemonic radicalism' Chávez and his radical factions wanted.

A clear sense of dichotomy in Venezuela was fully unpacked when the considerable radicalism of Chávez's Decree Laws was implemented. The opposition recognized the need to construct a viable anti-Bolivarian project when it became clear that this 'Bolivarian Revolution' was more than an electoral propaganda catchphrase. Since Chávez was elected in 1998, referendums and elections became a normal affair. However, several social and political sectors misunderstood what this 'democratic revolution' signified, and panicked when they realized that Chávez's populist 'us-them' axis was non-negotiable. As Laclau notes, 'there is no populism without discursive construction of an enemy: the *ancient regime*, the oligarchy, the establishment or whatever'.[32] The 'us-them' axis reference demarcates the other camp: the enemy. According to Miquilena, 'Chávez does not understand the difference between an "adversary" and an "enemy"'.[33] In other words, Chávez governs as the representative of 'antagonistic forces' with a firm radical direction of 'emancipation' for the excluded population. The president rejects any socio-political arrangements with anti-Bolivarian sectors where rules of 'agonism and pluralism' abide.

The Process of Deinstitutionalizing the Power Structure   69

A vital element to address is the involvement of external agents, the U.S. in particular, in the construction of an opposition force that sought to overthrow Chávez from power. According to Eva Golinger, in September 2001, the U.S. Embassy informed Washington that Pedro Carmona Estanga,[34] president of Fedecámaras, was the man to replace Chávez because 'change in government would soon be possible'. In November, the U.S. ambassador in Caracas stated that "'the Land Law is an attack on the right of private property"'.[35] Apparently, months later, 'Carmona and fellow CTV union leader Carlos Ortega took several trips to Washington accompanied by other prominent opposition leaders . . . and other NED [National Endowment for Democracy][36] grantees'.[37]

America's financial involvement promoting their interpretation of 'democracy' in Venezuela has been astonishing. Current literature meticulously fleshes out the channels used[38] in order to re-institute a government in Venezuela that complies with the 'U.S. hegemony'.[39] 'Revolutionists' label opposition sectors as 'oligarchs': sectors of a dichotomized society that identify with 'democratic neoliberalism' and fantasize of living an 'American Dream' in Venezuela. Nonetheless, this new phase of radicalization in the Enabling Laws and Chávez's uncompromising position also affected the Bolivarian 'equivalential chain'. Internal differences in the *Polo Patriótico* platform caused the desertion of key political forces.

3.2.1   Internal Fragmentation

By the end of 2001, fragmentation in the Bolivarian camp started to emerge. The MAS, a vital political force that crystallized the Chavista platform for the 1998 presidential election, decided to leave the equivalential chain in January 2002 and join the opposition. However, seven MAS parliamentarians opted to continue their support for the Chavista faction in the parliament. As a result, they were expelled from MAS.[40] Also, Miquilena, Chávez's mentor, a key architect of the Bolivarian political frontier (see page 56 in Chapter 2) rejected the way radical changes were contaminating the structure of the parliament. He stressed that the radicals of the Chavista faction (*Movimiento V [quinta] República*; MVR) overruled principles of political dialogue with the opposition. On January 8, 2002, Miquilena 'demanded the president to recognize and understand that . . . a pact, a process of dialogue with other political members, was vital for the government'.[41] Days later, Miquilena resigned. Chávez responded: 'I'll never say goodbye to Miquilena, I'll always have him in my heart . . . the manager, strategist, his good will'. Still, Chávez went ahead with the radical changes.[42]

If Chávez and radical political factions were to accept dialogue raised by the Chavista moderates, and therefore compromise on their differences with opposition forces, this phase of institutional radicalism would have taken a totally different direction. The dimension of equivalence 'us-them'

70 *Populism in Venezuela*

axis would have balanced its differences and the radical populist project would have been moderate or diminished altogether. *El pueblo* invested in and expected improvements to their living standards with the promised radical transformation Chávez offered and clearly stated in the Bolivarian Constitution. If Chavista moderates managed to subordinate the radicals, Venezuela's populist practices would have taken on a different nature altogether. In retrospect, Chávez was elected to employ drastic radical institutional changes. With the gradual abandonment of an 'us-them' axis position and acceptance of 'agonistic pluralism' and institutional compliance with U.S. hegemonic practices, Chávez's electoral-base would have decreased and the conditions of possibility for popular insurrection to occur would have increased.

On January 23, 2002, the opposition organized the first major demonstration, called 'Defending Democracy'. Between 170,000 and 200,000 people from the east of Caracas, various political groups, and Carmona Estanga, the president of Fedecámaras, joined the march. In the demonstration, a protester had a poster stating: 'Chávez, don't ruin my whisky'. When the march started the crowd chanted rhymed anti-Chávez messages labeling him as mad (*Al loco, al loco* [mad] *le queda poco* [soon will go]), push off (*Chávez pa'l carajo*), and so on.[43] These sectors of Venezuelan society detest Chávez and the type of discourse he uses. They dislike Chávez's blunt criticisms of U.S. hegemony and the use of vulgar and 'popular' language. It is very common to hear racially driven nicknames for Chávez and his cronies like *niches*, *zambos*, *monos*, and so on. This type of discourse describes the feelings of anti-Chavistas and their failure to accept an elected president who speaks and behaves like those who live in marginal areas (shanty towns). Thus, there is a degree of un-fulfillment (lacking desire) in not having a president that 'ethically' follows protocols of good manners like them. 'Chavistas' in general embarrass them and wrongly represent the country vis-à-vis 'their' superior Venezuelan conduct/identity.

Fernando Coronil and Julie Skurski rightly point out how the 'civilized' viewed *el pueblo* in the 1989 *Caracazo*: 'The uprising of the pueblo changed the anatomy of the nation. From the perspective of the elite, the masses now embodied the menace of barbarism surfacing anywhere in the body politic, not just at its frontiers'.[44] The difference now is that the elite, oligarchs, neoliberals, and so on are the opposition and strongly label *el pueblo* Chavista 'barbaric'. After January 23, 2002, this middle class–based support was a crucial mass for other anti-Bolivarian events. Months later, this middle class multitude was organized to overthrow the Bolivarian hegemonic project altogether.

3.2.2 The Anti-Bolivarian Coup d'état—April 11, 2002

Two days before April 11, 2002, workers began a strike. It escalated further when CTV and Fedecámaras converted it into an indefinite national

The Process of Deinstitutionalizing the Power Structure 71

strike. It appears that workers in the oil and aluminum industry wanted to prolong the strike. Ortega called supporters in the park 'Parque del Este' to join the march outside the '*Petróleos de Venezuela*' (PDVSA)-Chuao building. A politician said: 'this week smells of glory, we won't let them take democracy away from us. We'll go all the way till they crack'. A PDVSA employee added, 'we didn't lose this fight, PDVSA provided and Venezuela responded'.[45] In the 'east' of Caracas, the 'well-off' neighborhoods and commerce welcomed the strike, whereas in the 'centre and west' of the city the residents traded as usual. There were posters stating: 'Chávez anti-Christ, get out of Venezuela with your violence and hatred—Satan, Out!'.[46]

When the march gathered outside the PDVSA-Chuao building, 'spontaneously', it was decided that it would continue towards Miraflores, the Presidential Palace. The same day, aware of the strike in the east, thousands of Chávez supporters gathered outside Miraflores.[47] However, the opposition claimed that, on their way to the palace, Chávez ordered open fire on the protesters. The opposition's side of the story is that high-ranking officials disagreed with the president and demanded his resignation.

According to Janet Kelly, the rebellion against the government was based upon constitutional violations. The opposition claimed that Chávez (in particular), Chavistas in the parliament, the National Electoral Council, judges in the Supreme Court, state prosecutors, and ombudsmen pretended not to understand the constitutional attributes in terms of autonomy in each branch. They accused the government of ignoring the difference between governance, party politics, public and party funds, as well as personal and collective interests. 'They strongly criticized how other regimes commonly abused the system, but now in power, they repeat the same "Sin"'.[48] The opposition stressed that in article 350 of the new constitution, 'people' can overthrow a Government that violates institutional principles.[49] It is still not clear what happened that day; we can only speculate. Barry Cannon points out that sections of the military, business sectors, the media, and so on must have been involved in the preparation of this 'apparent spontaneous march' to Miraflores. Details of how to lead the march were carefully planned. 'Road blocks were set up on some of the motorways . . . snipers of opposition police forces stationed at key points near the Palace open[ed] fire on government supporters and demonstrators too'.[50]

The next day, the media stated that Chávez had resigned.[51] The Army Chief, Efraín Vásquez Velasco, addressed the nation after discussing the terms of the resignation. Chávez asked to leave the country, a request which was rejected. The armed forces strongly disagreed with his order to open fire on opposition protesters and thus felt obliged to defend *el pueblo* and apologize for this outrage.[52] Article 350 was fully implemented by the armed forces and, as Chávez agreed to resign, there was a 'constitutional power vacuum'. Thus, the armed forces decided to contact the president of Fedecámaras 'to fulfill the presidential role'. However, soon after taking the post, 'Carmona Estanga proceeded to break the constitutional

72   Populism in Venezuela

order by abolishing all the constitutional powers and appointing a new government'.[53] The opposition media claimed that Chávez resigned; however, in Bartley and O'Briain's documentary *The Revolution Will Not Be Televised*, with 'live' footage inside Miraflores (April 11–12, 2002), it seems that Chávez refused to resign but handed himself over to the generals in response to the threat of bombing the palace.[54]

By late evening on April 11, the Chavista camp had no 'media' means to inform the nation of their side of the story. The Cuban TV news stated that Maria Gabriela Chávez, daughter of President Chávez, called to spread the word that her kidnapped father didn't resign.[55] The opposition, controlling the 'media', wanted to portray a version of the opposition as 'victims'[56] and tried to subvert any forms of discourse that contradicted their claim that Chávez resigned. On April 12, Venezuela had a new government. That day, a meeting in Miraflores with various personalities celebrated the end of the 'Bolivarian hegemonic Revolution'. Carmona, the president of Fedecámaras, now (unconstitutionally) the new interim president of Venezuela, stated:

> I, Pedro Carmona Estanga, President of the Republic of Venezuela, swear before God, the Nation, and all Venezuelans to re-establish justice, equality, solidarity and social responsibility. . . . Thanks to this mandate which we received from the Venezuelan people, . . . a mandate more valuable than any referendum. . .with the support of all sectors of society, . . . we accept this responsibility.

Beside Carmona, the newly appointed attorney general informed the cheering crowd representing various sectors of the recently re-instituted hegemonic order:

> We hereby decree that a democratic transitional government shall be established in the following manner: We hereby dissolve the National Assembly (parliament). We also dissolve the Supreme Court. We dismiss the Attorney General, the head of the Central Bank, the Ombudsman, and the National Electoral Board. [57]

In other words, the objective was to overturn fundamental principles of Venezuelan democratic practices that succeeded in articulating a 'radical' institutional structure. Carmona's interim government ignored the vote of Venezuela's underprivileged population that supported the institutional 'change' the Bolivarian hegemonic project signified (e.g. emancipation, better living conditions). Carmona's political agenda was to urgently re-institute the 'neoliberal' structure and dismantle the recently constructed Bolivarian institutional framework. Ari Fleischer, spokesman for the White House in Washington, D.C., blamed the Chávez government for this political crisis and praised the police and military for disobeying orders to shoot at opposition protesters. Chávez resigned and dismissed the vice-president and Cabinet.

The Process of Deinstitutionalizing the Power Structure 73

'This is not a coup—the "people" spoke. Chávez tried to prevent independent "media" channels from broadcasting what happened', Fleischer said.[58]

However, whilst Carmona and his team were inside Miraflores addressing their governmental program, across Caracas the police were trying to repress spontaneous 'popular' rebellion (now informed that Chávez didn't resign) demanding the return of Chávez. The next day, the 'excluded' from the shanties went down the hills and gathered outside Miraflores, rhyming: 'People are with Chavez—We want Chávez—The People United shall never be defeated!!!'. Protesters anxiously shouted: 'we want Chávez NOW, we don't want a dictatorship . . . yesterday they betrayed Venezuela—they violated our constitution'. Inside the palace, Carmona's newly installed government panicked and soon realized that the uprising was uncontrollable, and so decided to leave Miraflores. Chávez's military guard was still in the palace, sympathizing with the protesters who decided to re-take the palace.[59]

Even inside the armed forces, internal discontent was tattering Carmona's 'Republic of Venezuela' ('Bolivarian' now excluded). 'General Baduel later admitted that nobody in the High Military Command seemed prepared to jump in and defend Chávez; however, as the conspirator's project began to reveal its arbitrary and totalitarian side, some military forces began to re-evaluate the situation'.[60] General Baduel, aware that Chávez was imprisoned in the Isle of Orchila, coordinated the rescue of the president.[61] In the meantime, Chávez's government returned to Miraflores. On April 14 (2:50 a.m.) Chávez was back. A multitude of thrilled popular supporters outside the palace welcomed Chávez's return, signing 'we love Chávez, he's back, back . . he's back' like a jingle. In the same palace ballroom where Carmona swore to God as president two days earlier, Chávez said:

> Firstly, I call for calm . . . today Sunday April 14. . . . Well, I've been incommunicado for the past few hours, I had no information and I was very worried. The most important thing I want to say to you Venezuelans is to go back to your homes, we need to be calm. Those of you, who oppose me, fine oppose me! I wish I could change your mind. But, you cannot oppose this constitution. This is the Peoples' book. It's like the "Popol Vuh", the book of the Mayas. The book of the community. You have to recognize this. But most importantly don't be poisoned. Don't let them poison you with their poison, with their lies.[62]

The opposition naively believed that a middle/upper class demonstration from the 'east' of Caracas marching to the Presidential Palace represented Venezuela's social fabric. This interpretation of the 'people' subconsciously excludes the reaction of 'other people' dwelling in poor and rural areas. Chávez was reinstated because people from the slums demanded the return of their democratically elected president. In Chapter 4, I carefully address how this popular reaction warned the government to initiate social programs in the slums and help people living in poor conditions. This attempt

74 *Populism in Venezuela*

to re-institute a neoliberal 'hegemonic structure' and de-institute the Bolivarian hegemonic project ignored constitutional and democratic rules/principles. This abrupt and ill-planned decision undermined the opposition's ethical credibility altogether. Nevertheless, in spite of these setbacks, months later, the anti-Bolivarian camp tried another route to contest and thus de-institute Chávez and his regime.

3.2.3 The Second Strike

After the April 11–14 incident, Chávez realized the need to engage in some form of dialogue with opposition sectors. The president changed the cabinet, particularly economic ministers, and ordered them to be receptive with opposition economic sectors. Chávez also invited American Organization States (AOS) and the 'Carter Center' to help as mediators in a phase of dialogue with the opposition.[63] However, the possibility for agonistic pluralism after that political crisis was unlikely, in spite of the involvement of international organizations. Carmona denied any knowledge of the preparation to oust Chávez. He claimed that after Chávez's resignation, high-ranking officials asked him to take the interim presidential post.[64] Also, Carmona's appointed Minister of Defense vice-admiral Hector Ramírez Perez insisted that Chávez resign and authorized his decision to be public.[65]

After the failed April 2002 coup, nine opposition political parties formed an anti-Bolivarian alliance called '*Coordinadora Democrática*' (CD).[66] The CD welcomed any social organization: the church, universities, the media, and any non-governmental community group—regardless of their ideological position.[67] Opposition political groups continued intense social mobilization on the streets. From April until December, on the 11th day of each month, the CD (a reminder of the coup d'état) organized a multitudinous march. The Bolivarian movement responded with another march on the 13th day of each month to interrupt and counterattack CD's attempts to challenge the Bolivarian project. Both sides used these events to show their forces and ability to mobilize supporters. These events fuelled more division and hatred among supporters. Violent confrontations were unavoidable.[68]

The next strike started on December 2, 2002. The key objective of all the key sectors that participated in this strike was to put pressure on Chávez and force him to resign. Not only commerce sectors and part of the industry such as the managerial branch of PDVSA joined, but also a notable part of logistical operations and captains of PDVSA's Merchant Navy. The strike soon became 'indefinite' with a discourse: 'until Chávez falls'. The government recognized that the oil industry was 'virtually paralyzed' and criticized the strike as a 'criminal sabotage'. This political row affected many commercial activities: supermarkets closed and banks stayed open only half time. Also, the operation of private and some state schools came to a halt.[69]

The Process of Deinstitutionalizing the Power Structure 75

As PDVSA participated in the strike, the supply of petrol in stations dropped substantially. This was a critical aspect of the opposition's strength, which was used to press the government and accept their demands. CD's political memorandum was for the resignation of Chávez followed with a constitutional transition in the parliament to name an interim president, and a call for elections.[70] According to López Maya, the CD said to anti-Bolivarians: 'without these sacrifices (no petrol, injuries and deaths in marches, abolished Christmas) there is no final victory'. Private TV channels continuously broadcasted a daily update of CD leaders informing the public of their success and strategies.[71]

On January 23, 2003, the government organized their march. By then, the opposition strike had run out of steam. The second attempt to contest the Bolivarian project with article 350 of the constitution[72] failed to get the social (*el pueblo*) support from the 'other' camp. Opposition forces miscalculated its political position; it failed to understand and thus convince Chávez's popular-base. Datanálisis argued that 60 percent of Venezuelans were dissatisfied with the president, and 75 percent wanted a recall referendum for a new president.[73] It appears that the CD was convinced that people from marginal areas would change sides and support them. Chavistas retaliated with a '"defense/offense" contingency plan in the "*barriadas*" [slums]. In the military, they re-enforced its base to act accordingly with any opposition attempts to oust the government. Another incident like the April 11, 2002 coup d'état will not hit us unprepared', says a 'compatriot Chavista'.[74]

Those employees in the oil industry that decided not to participate in the strike kept their jobs, as well as the pensioners that participated to keep the industry working. The government slowly recovered normal levels of production and its operational systems and restructured its processes. By mid-February the government had full control of the oil industry. Towards the end of March more than 18,000 managers and workers of PDVSA were fired for their involvement in the strike.[75] If anything, the strike further consolidated the 'Bolivarian project'. It gave them the oil industry and a motive to fire those who challenged Chávez's government.

PDVSA managers being fired was a hard blow to the opposition. This created a lot of internal friction among anti-Bolivarian sectors in the CD movement. The strike inflicted more damage to PDVSA and the private sector in general. It undermined the opposition's credibility with their supporters and bankrupted small and medium industries and companies.[76] The CD thought that the strike that never ended but slowly dismantled itself was the way to end the Bolivarian project. Far from it—finally, the oil industry fell into the hands of Chávez's political project. Political fatigue pushed the opposition to reflect again and re-consider how to get rid of Chávez and his regime. In the meantime, the Bolivarian Revolution (now controlling the finances of the oil industry) started a new phase of 'radicalism' with a variety of social-welfare programs for Venezuela's underprivileged population.

76 *Populism in Venezuela*

3.3 FURTHER RADICALIZATION

Poverty and equality reached alarming levels in an oil-rich country. The 'Bolivarian Revolution' was elected because it signified hope and radical governmental change to many ordinary Venezuelans. Many Venezuelans lack basic needs and live in appalling conditions. The Bolivarian project claims to defend the poor and excluded population and promises a better future and thus an end to their daily struggle in a deeply dichotomized society. According to Richard Gott, after the April 2002 coup an individual from the *barriadas* said:

> We have to defend this Government . . . defend Chávez because he's better than any President there has ever been. We think he's the product of our struggle. People recognize him as equal. Obviously he is Indian and black, and maybe a little white.

From a theoretical perspective, this is what Panizza refers to as the 'imaginary identification'. As Panizza points out, 'people identify with a leader chiefly through the stories he or she relates not only with words but more broadly, by the use of symbols, including the leader's own body and personal life'.[77] Gott continues, recognizing that 'not everyone in these hills supports the Bolivarian Revolution. In one small hut in a rancho in Catia', Gott found 'a self-employed plumber who expressed his disillusion with the government', saying:

> I voted for Chávez, but now I regret having done so. I was completely deceived. I've seen no improvement. I don't want conflict between rich and poor. Because if that happens where will I get work?

'The plumber depended for his livelihood on his clients in the upper class section of the city'.[78] The reason why I address these anecdotes is to assess to what extent people of the *barriadas* really support the Bolivarian hegemonic project. The idea that populism is a straightforward exchange formula of financial handouts to the poor for electoral support fails to unravel fundamental logics that are not simply articulated on monetary gifts. The racial element effectively 'grips' subjects (fundamentally living in 'excluded' sectors) that share similarities with Chávez's skin color. They share the same race (which also touches class in Venezuela); thus there is the impression that they both fully understand their daily 'struggle'.

Referring to the disappointed plumber, because he hasn't seen any changes, we should not categorize political support on geographical settings only. Progress can mean different things to the *pueblo de las barriadas*. In dealing with these unfulfilled promises, Bolivarian social welfare programs started after the indefinite opposition strike. They offered change and improvement in excluded sectors by providing assistance with some of those basic needs those sectors lacked. In less than a year, the 'Bolivarian Revolution' experienced a coup and an indefinite national strike that affected most of the

The Process of Deinstitutionalizing the Power Structure   77

oil structure, collapsing Venezuela's economic bloodline. However, with the recovery of the oil production along with an increase of the price of oil, these revenues helped the government introduce social welfare programs.[79]

At this stage, the Bolivarian hegemonic project finally succeeded in integrating the oil industry into its institutional structure. This critical division, previously managed by sectors affiliated with the de-instituted hegemony, blocked any Bolivarian incentives to use oil revenues for social programs. Attempts to displace a democratically elected president by using their control of the oil industry cost them dearly. They lost the most important sector in Venezuela, hence giving the Bolivarian project the resources to accelerate this revolution to the next phase. The programs I discuss below give us a glimpse of the socio-economic, educational, and cultural projects, called 'misiones' (missions), that the government formed.

3.3.1   Bolivarian Missions

The first missions introduced between 2003 and early 2004 were the community healthcare program 'Misión Barrio Adentro', the literacy training program 'Misión Robinson', the high school completion program 'Misión Ribas', the university scholarship program 'Misión Sucre', and the subsidized food market program 'Misión Mercal'.[80] By 2008, 26 missions were created. These missions have been constructed via 'popular' participative programs and developed in a variety of sectors. I address the mission 'Barrio Adentro' in Chapter 4, providing an in-depth analysis that gives us an insight into how Chávez attempts to institutionally incorporate this healthcare project with the existing structure. Also, it provides an account of the strengths and weaknesses of the Bolivarian project.

Another mission is 'Misión Guaicaipuro': a program that focuses on the past, present, and future of indigenous people in Venezuela. 'Misión Vuelvan Caras' promotes the participation and direct involvement of the 'people' in the development of services to eradicate depressed living conditions in excluded areas (this applies to all missions). Missions have been created in a variety of social programs.[81] The implementation of these social programs requires not only substantial finances but also social participation and political organization. The key incentive is to offer new institutional structures that guarantee basic needs in previously excluded areas and helps the populations trapped in atrocious conditions for many years. However, whilst the government was constructing these social programs with grassroots supporters, the opposition was coordinating another attempt to unseat Chávez from power.

3.3.2   Referendum to recall Chávez

The third opposition attempt to displace the Bolivarian Government rested on article 72 of the new constitution, which states that once half of the term

78   *Populism in Venezuela*

in office of an elected official elapses, with the signatures of a minimum of 20 percent of voters a petition calling for a referendum to revoke an official is formulated. The *Consejo Nacional Electoral* (CNE) approved it and ordered a presidential recall vote in 2004 if the opposition succeeded in collecting some 2.4 million signatures. In August 2003, '*Súmate*'[82] presented 3.2 million signatures. However, the CNE rejected these signatures because *Súmate* was not an institution responsible for electoral practices. For that reason, a system was implemented and a date set for the revocation referendum if sufficient signatures were collected.[83] Ismael Garcia, a former MAS parliamentarian who supported Chávez's 'radicalization', strongly criticized *Súmate* and labeled it as a politically driven organization set up by CD with a clear anti-Bolivarian discourse.[84] Chávez said: 'unfortunately, we are dealing with a demented opposition. Our "people" will not even go to the corner for them. "*Este pueblo*" has shown consciousness and great wisdom'.[85]

According to Golinger, '*Súmate* promptly launched a massive media and propaganda campaign in support of the petition drive.... Utilising NED [National Endowment for Democracy] and USAID funding, Súmate mass-produced anti-Chávez and pro-referendum materials, which were distributed nationwide'.[86] However, the CNE later determined that only 1.9 million signatures were valid, and nearly a million were set aside and questioned for fraud. 'More than 800,000 signature lines had been filled out with duplicate handwriting in violation of CNE regulations. The opposition reacted to the news with violence'.[87]

From February 27 until March 4, 2004, in urban areas in the country, mostly in middle and upper class neighborhoods, confrontational and violent protests occurred. The CD called for 'civil disobedience', rejecting CNE's decision and the legitimacy of that entity. The international observers 'American Organization States' (AOS) and 'Carter Center' endorsed CNE's decision but expressed disagreements with CNE's 'reparable' criteria and recommended the continuation of discussions with all parties involved.[88] Eventually, the opposition agreed to 'repair' the signatures on June 3, 2004. The CNE accepted that there were sufficient signatures and organized a presidential recall referendum on August 15, 2004.[89] The opposition believed they could democratically revoke Chávez's mandate. NO (don't revoke Chávez) won with 59.09 percent; YES got 40.63 percent. The results accepted by international observers regalvanized Chávez's control.[90]

In spite of all these electoral complications, it was evident that this 'Bolivarian Revolution' had the backing of *el pueblo*. The opposition camp confidently claimed that Chávez won the referendum due to electoral fraud. Since then, CNE's electoral results were regarded as illegitimate. With respect to the next election, which was for parliament, the opposition claimed that 'as there was no electoral transparency, they were not going to participate in this fraudulent election but to go to churches and pray for Venezuela's future democracy, and not to get sucked in the jaws of Venecuba'.[91] Chávez reacted to the opposition's decision not to participate, saying:

The Process of Deinstitutionalizing the Power Structure   79

> What the opposition has done is a new coup d'état, but this time, in an electoral sense. George Bush has changed orders to his pawns. . . . They have started a new plot. I don't blame the dogs but the owners of the dogs, the American Government. I pray to God so the church hierarchy doesn't get caught in this conspiracy of the Empire. Also, the private TV channels: RCTV (*Radio Caracas de Televisión*) and *Globovisión*. . . . Be careful, I'm not letting you get away with things . . . I haven't forgotten your call for destabilization in 2002.[92]

By not participating, the opposition gave Chávez 'full' control of the parliament. Also, domestic political affairs started to be directly linked with an external enemy: the U.S. It is difficult to unpack why President Chávez strongly labels the opposition with a discourse like 'pawns' and 'dogs' of the 'Empire'. Perhaps these accusations rest on the donations *Súmate* received from American semi-governmental organizations. But mostly, America's interest in keeping good relations with Venezuela's Government is due to America's dependence on Venezuelan oil. The de-institution of PDVSA's 'neoliberal hegemonic project' after the 2002–03 strike destabilized America's relation with a major oil producer. The opposition was unable to construct a social and political base to contest the Bolivarian project. It had neither a platform that could effectively unite different opposition sectors nor the electoral backing to challenge the government. However, for the 2006 presidential election, the opposition began to construct some form of a partially unified political platform to contest the Bolivarian project.

3.3.3   2006 Presidential Elections—New Bolivarian Discourse: 'Homeland Socialism or Death'

After the defeat of the recall referendum and much self-inflicted damage resulting from their boycott of the parliamentarian elections in December 2005, opposition sectors managed to re-define themselves and agree on a single candidate for the December 2006 presidential elections: Manuel Rosales.[93] The opposition, concerned that fraud would happen once again, forced the principal of the CNE to state that 'there are more procedures to follow compared with the 2004 referendum recall. If there are any irregularities that change the result, the country will know straight away'.[94] The results democratically reiterated the degree of popularity Chávez enjoyed. Chavez obtained 7.3 million votes (62.84 percent) compared with 4.3 million votes for Rosales.[95]

When the votes were counted, there was a degree of concern that electoral 'fraud' would happen. If the opposition claimed that the CNE's final results were rigged, possible civil unrest would have made things worse for everyone. Rosales accepted defeat, but emphasized that the margin of Chávez's victory was not as wide as it looked.[96] Now re-elected, in January 2007 Chávez addressed the next phase of the Bolivarian Revolution by adding its ideological position:

80 *Populism in Venezuela*

> I swear, to this wonderful constitution . . . God, my children, honor, life, the liberators, my 'People' and Homeland . . . I shall never rest . . . I'll devote my whole life constructing Socialism in Venezuela, the construction of a new political system, and a new social and new economic system. I swear to Christ, the greatest Socialist in history . . . the pain, love, hope of the People . . . to fulfill the principles of the constitution . . . 'Homeland, Socialism or Death . . . I swear!'. . . . With a new Decree Law . . . Revolutionary Laws and a new reformulation of the constitution we'll have a unified machinery . . . there are drafted laws that can only work after reforming parts of the constitution . . . I ask all Venezuela to respect each other . . . recognize our differences and to acknowledge the decision of the majority . . .

Furthermore, Chávez responded to the Church and J. M. Insulza, Secretary General of the AOS, who raised their concerns about his decision not to renew RCTV's (opposition TV channel) broadcasting license, stating:

> The state respects the Church, the Church must respect the State . . . I don't want to go back to a period of confrontation with Venezuelan Bishops . . . that's their decision not mine. I'm here ferociously defending the sovereignty of the Venezuelan 'People' . . .[97]

Chávez responded to the concerns of the Church and OAS's secretary general about the non-renewal of RCTV's broadcasting license, arguing that his decision defends the well-being of the Venezuelan people.[98] This kind of discourse re-affirms Chávez's populist 'us-them' axis position. 'People' in this context only represents those that support the Bolivarian hegemonic project; those that voted against him are not recognized as the 'people' of Venezuela. Also, in the inaugural speech, with the slogan 'Homeland, Socialism, or Death' (*Patria, Socialismo o Muerte*), Chávez is trying to discursively announce and hence incorporate Cuban ideological practices as the next phase of the Bolivarian project. Chávez has borrowed Fidel Castro's 1960s 'Homeland or Death, We Will Win' (*Patria o Muerte, Venceremos*)—a vital slogan in Cuba's Revolution. In other words, what Chávez lays out in his re-election speech is that socialist ideological principles will be the next step of the Venezuelan Revolution, making clear reference to Cuba's social and political practices. Next, I'll discuss how new opposition forces emerged when RCTV's broadcasting license expired at the end of May 2007, as well as why key members of the Bolivarian equivalential chain decided to leave Chávez and join the opposition.

3.4   NEW OPPOSITION FORCES

In this section, I'll describe the involvement of three new sectors that partially succeeded in constituting a formidable opposition force vis-à-vis other

The Process of Deinstitutionalizing the Power Structure   81

failed attempts: first, a student movement that challenged the government's decision not to renew RCTV's broadcast license; second, former MAS parliamentarians who decided in January 2002 to continue their alliance with the Bolivarian Revolution in the parliament (see page 124 in this chapter), disagreed with Chávez's new phase of radicalism, and therefore defected from the Bolivarian project; and finally, General Raúl Baduel, the officer who organized the return of Chávez to the presidency in April 2002 but who disapproved this new phase of institutional radicalism and personally challenged Chávez.

3.4.1   *Radio Caracas de Televisión* and the Student Movement

The confrontation between the Bolivarian Government and this private TV channel is fundamentally based on RCTV's incitement of the April 2002 coup d'état and its extensive broadcast of opposition updates during the December/January 2003 national-oil strike. The broadcasting license ended on May 27, 2007. The decision not to renew RCTV's broadcasting license re-affirmed the government's strategy to terminate the opposition's ability to broadcast their anti-Bolivarian discourse. This decision provoked a new form of outcry from the opposition. People organized street demonstrations demanding the renewal of RCTV's broadcasting license. Taking RCTV away from the 'people' (regardless of their political or ideological position in this dichotomized society) negatively affected the government. RCTV's anti-Bolivarian political platform didn't influence people's (from all classes) affection for this private TV channel. Its role in Venezuela's cultural fabric can be traced back to the 1950s. From Chávez's perspective, RCTV was nothing but a division of the already displaced institutional framework that used the media to undermine his revolutionary project. In hindsight, by not renewing RCTV's broadcasting license, the government would have been in a better position to control the discourse broadcasted in Venezuela and thus avoid another incident like the April 11, 2002 coup d'état.

The RCTV TV station network grew throughout the years and had a prominent role in Venezuela's past and cultural evolution. Even though, for the first time, political confrontation clearly unraveled the extent of social exclusion in Venezuela, many RCTV TV shows (e.g. soap operas, comedy shows) still entertained and informed Venezuelans from all social classes. RCTV's anti-Bolivarian position did not interfere with the entertainment these TV shows provided to the people. I argue that even *el pueblo* in the hills (*barrios*) felt disappointed with the government's decision to punish this anti-Bolivarian channel. RCTV was a 'popular' TV channel enjoyed by many despite the social and economic problems many Venezuelans face.

When Chávez threatened not to re-new RCTV's broadcasting license, university students (mainly from Caracas) organized themselves and formed a student movement called '*Generación 2007*' (Generation 2007). Their initial aim was to challenge the government and prevent the closure of RCTV. These students had no political affiliation with opposition parties. They

82 *Populism in Venezuela*

organized meetings among university representatives and intellectuals to coordinate a demonstration strategy and avoid the end of RCTV. They argued that 'the abduction of RCTV violates two human rights, freedom of speech and beliefs, in a country where on a daily basis thirty human rights acts are openly violated.'[99]

The students of two universities started to protest outside their university campuses days prior to the termination of RCTV's license (on May 27, 2007). Their demonstration aimed to publicly state: 'with no RCTV the population would no longer have the right to be objectively informed because most of the other private channels made a treaty with the government'.[100] Days later, universities in other cities protested against the closure of RCTV. Chavistas and the police injured 14 students. Also, in Caracas students from various universities were violently restrained by the police—injuring 17 students.[101]

The RCTV scenario opened a new anti-Bolivarian force not affiliated with *Súmate*, CD, or any political organization. This student movement was a fresh opposition project that seemed to constitute something that could seriously challenge the government, offering something new vis-à-vis other discredited opposition sectors. In Chapter 5, I provide an in-depth analysis of this anti-Bolivarian student movement, thoroughly contextualizing its socio-political position, objectives, successes, and flaws. The closure of RCTV also had negative implications for the government in the parliament.

3.4.2 A Chavista Party Joins the Opposition

This sense of social rejection in the decision not to renew RCTV's license also affected the Bolivarian 'chain of equivalence' in the parliament. Ismael García, the leader of the party *Podemos*, and Ricardo Gutierrez (both former MAS parliamentarians that opted to stay and support the Bolivarian project back in January 2002) argued in the parliament 'not to call Bolivarian supporters to take the streets and confront students protesting against the closure of RCTV'. Only one MVR parliamentarian agreed. Garcia said:

> There are moments in which you cannot quietly agree with things and this is one of them. . . . We cannot have a double discourse. . . . The student movement is on the streets . . . they even pushed away politicians that wanted to use their stage . . . four million Venezuelans are not oligarchs. . . . This is a very difficult moment, we must have a dialogue with them, enough of confrontation.

Garcia argued that the four million (4,292,466) Venezuelans that voted for the opposition are not oligarchs. In Chávez's populist discourse, 'oligarchs', a political signifier used to demonize the 'other' camp—enemies of the Bolivarian project—are a minority and are held responsible for 'people's' impoverished conditions (lack). Interestingly, Oscar Figuera, a PCV (Venezuela's communist party) parliamentarian, noted that:

The Process of Deinstitutionalizing the Power Structure   83

With moments like this we have to be more thorough compared with other incidents. . . . We have to understand that by not renewing RCTV's broadcasting license, it is not a simple termination of the TV channel. . . . There are historical and socio-cultural codes deeply rooted which have never been exposed before.[102]

This new phase of radicalism infringed the 'nodal point' that unified (equivalential chain) the parliamentarian political alliance in the parliament. García, the leader of *Podemos*, clearly argued that dialogue and re-examining what the RCTV closure signified had to be considered. In other words, he argued that it was necessary to construct an agonistic platform where both parties can express their differences and reach a mutual agreement. Withdrawing the decision not to renew RCTV's broadcasting license was an obstruction to Chávez's new 'socialist phase' addressed in his January 2007 speech. Chávez ignored these drawbacks and proceeded with the necessary changes to organize the constitutional reform referendum scheduled to take place in December 2007. This decision also generated another critical problem for Chávez when a former key military compatriot betrayed him and publicly contested Chávez's real motives in the presidency.

3.4.3   General Baduel—Constitutional Reform Referendum

First of all, the constitutional reform consisted of radical changes to the 1999 Bolivarian Constitution in order to provide a new 'socialist' constitutional framework. During the re-election inaugural speech in January 2007, Chávez briefly announced his intention to construct a socialist state. One of the unsettling events that spoiled what the Bolivarian project signified to *el pueblo* was General Raúl Baduel's[103] deep concerns with the constitutional changes Chávez wanted to implement. Baduel stressed that '"*el pueblo*" should ask: what is the future of Venezuela instead of believing in this unclear Socialist idea for Venezuela Chávez is promoting?'[104] Chávez responded, 'my companion beloved friend, almost forty years in this struggle . . . I'll always be here Raúl'.[105] Baduel was a symbol of loyalty to the 'revolution' in 2002 and a vital founder of the 'Bolivarian movement'. Baduel joining the anti-Bolivarians was a shock to Chávez, the government, and Chávez's popular-base.

The emergence of these new opposition forces weakened the incumbent's ability to win the constitutional reform referendum. *Podemos* (a faction of the fragmented MAS that contributed 6.53 percent of Chávez's 62.84 percent in the 2006 presidential victory) officially joined the opposition, promoting a NO vote in the constitutional reform referendum.[106] Another influential anti-Bolivarian element protesting against the reform and 'radical' discourse was the student movement, now campaigning against the constitutional reform Chávez promoted.[107]

Constitutional amendments were divided into 'five thematic axes: The Explosion of Popular Power, New Productive Socialist Model, New

84 *Populism in Venezuela*

Geometry of Power, Dignification of Work and Cultural Diversity and the Consolidation of a New State and a New Institutionality'.[108] It consisted of 69 articles in total for reform presented in two proposals. Proposal A included Chávez's initial 33 articles plus 13 others from the parliament. Proposal B consisted of 23 articles put forward by the parliament. However, in spite of all the time and plentiful resources the incumbent invested in the referendum campaign, the Bolivarian project lost by a narrow margin:

> *Proposal A* Yes: 4,379,392 (49.29 %). No: 4,504,354 (50.70 %).
> *Proposal B* Yes: 4,335,136 (48.94 %). No: 4,522,332 (51.05 %).[109]

How did Chávez accept his first electoral defeat? It appears that he overrated the degree of 'popular' approval of the 'radicalism' he wanted to sediment. The speech below fleshes out how Chávez reflected on this unexpected defeat:

> The proposal is still alive . . . this is a reflection we have to do. . . . Last year, 7,300,000 compatriots voted for me . . . well . . . for the opposition around 4,100,000 . . . the opposition increased by 400,000. . . . However, we were 3,000,000 short . . . these people didn't vote. Why? We'll have to evaluate this . . . I'm totally sure that they are still with 'US', they didn't vote for the NO. Maybe doubts, fears . . . not well explained . . . these are political elements we have to consider in order to continue this battle . . . this proposal offers Venezuelans a political strategy of advancement . . . widening our direction . . . horizon . . . the construction of a 'Socialist Venezuela'. . . . This is not closed, this is the way we have worked on for the last eight years . . . this constitution has politically, economically, socially . . . strengthened Venezuela. . . . To me, this is not a defeat, it is another '*Por ahora*' (for now) . . . that's how I see it . . . I hope sectors of the opposition that are nervous, thinking I would not accept this reality . . . relax be happy, respect the Bolivarian 'people'. . . . Our 'people'. The Bolivarian 'people' that didn't vote . . . abstention defeated us . . . something for us to learn . . . this Bolivarian Republic will keep strengthening, we bear in mind our Liberator . . . we accept difficult times, apparent defeats are moral victories that develop into political victories . . . I hope we can respect our differences, have dialogue, far from violence, conspiracy, plans subordinated to the American Empire . . .[110]

There are three key features in Chávez's speech. First of all, he tries to reconstruct the *Por ahora* empty signifier used in 1992 (see pages 50–51 in Chapter 2). However, circumstances in the 2007 referendum were different. The use of *Por ahora* in this context, in the hopes that it would 'grip'

The Process of Deinstitutionalizing the Power Structure   85

people as it did in 1992, is dubious. Second, Chávez examines the final results and recognizes that the radicalism he wants to implement fails to get the expected electoral support. In other words, the 'people' have either reconsidered what this referendum entails (i.e. rejecting a socialist Bolivarian Revolution) or no longer believe that this political project represents them and offers something constructive (fullness to come). And third, a new type of discourse is used to address the opposition—'respect our differences'—and the need for 'dialogue' is acknowledged (the emergence of agonism?). Nevertheless, Chávez still claims that the opposition is controlled by external forces (the American Empire) and pleads with them to detach themselves from those negative subjects and work directly with Venezuela's popular-base and domestic political structures.

General Baduel's remarks (the same day and time as Chávez's speech— early December 3, 2007) unfold his position and why he decided to challenge Chávez's constitutional referendum:

> . . . I congratulate the Venezuelan 'people' . . . civically and democratically attended and manifested their own will avoiding any confrontation using the only civic weapon we have: 'the vote'. . . . This is a very delicate moment for the country . . . nobody won, nobody lost. These results cannot be recognized as a victory. All of us must reflect on this. *El pueblo* was asked to agree with constitutional changes, and only *el pueblo* has the right to do these kind changes. Today, our country must accept the results as a lesson, the beginning . . . not allow being used for change to benefit any political camp . . . nobody in particular . . . nothing that is not to the interest for those who live in this country. . . . We should not waste this moment to recognize the importance of our constitution . . . and reflect on where we have failed. We have to recognize that a proportion of this society has supported the President. . . . From today, we have to realize that in our country there is unity regardless of its diversity. I call all my compatriots, all Venezuelans in good faith . . . to construct a true democracy, to see with clarity beyond this event and understand the collective language that today says a clear message . . . this is a valuable opportunity to recognize each other and reject the use of our vote to benefit some. . . . *El pueblo* keeps its constitutional right and is the only one that can change it. . . . The President wanted to force Venezuelans to accept a project that belongs to him . . . he wanted to impose his will by manipulating the sentiments of our 'people'. *El pueblo* had nothing to do with it. . . . We have defeated once again the ghost of the coup like we did in April 2002.[111]

Baduel articulates the significance of the constitution, stressing that only *el pueblo* has the right to make changes to such a vital institutional component constituting fundamental principles about the rules, norms, and practices of the nation. Baduel also recalls his role as a defender of key

86 *Populism in Venezuela*

democratic principles, stressing his rejection of the April 2002 coup d'état and hence his decision to restore President Chávez to his post in Miraflores. However, this time, Baduel rejects Chávez's attempt to impose a system that would primarily benefit him, not *el pueblo*. Discursively, the meaning of 'manipulating sentiments' may reflect Baduel's belief that Chávez tried to exercise the popularity achieved in the 2006 presidential election for a constitutional reform (i.e. indefinite re-election for the president). However, the rather neutral, and to some degree of respectful (agonistic), acceptance of the results in Chávez's latter speech changed drastically two days later:

> I'm very proud of the Venezuelan 'people' that accepted my call, some with pain, others with sadness . . . and others very happy . . . went to celebrate in the east of Caracas . . . there was no celebration anywhere else . . . the opposition had nothing to celebrate. We didn't lose anything . . . be careful, a new offensive is coming . . . that reform or a rephrased one . . . I'm sure of it. I have received comments from popular leaders thinking of getting signatures to resuscitate that referendum with different conditions and time . . . representatives of the opposition, you shouldn't claim victory. . . . Be careful, don't get involved with our armed forces. . . . If something, someone is there who should not be . . . a 'traitor' that left . . . like Christ, he had twelve apostles, one betrayed him . . . what can I expect, I'm a simple Colonel. . . . We have to get rid of those touts . . . the ex Minister of Defense sabotaged our military reserves. I told them to be quiet, time will tell . . . the Empire has done its work . . . playing with his 'ego' . . . there are two components there: 'blood and shit'. . . . You know, 'shit'. And, here there is dignity . . . leave quiet who is quiet, administer your victory but you are full of 'shit, a victory of shit' . . . and ours, call it 'defeat'; but is of courage, values . . . 'empire' coup me! . . . hmm, you haven't even moved us. We'll move forward . . . 'Homeland, Socialism or Death, we will win'.[112]

The Baduel element changing 'direction', endorsing the opposition camp, had unprecedented consequences for the Bolivarian project. It encouraged socio-political and military sectors and questioned the validity of what the Chavista camp promoted for the development of Venezuela's democracy: 'socialism'. In my view, these are the reasons why Chávez directly denounces a former friend and is subjected to a divisive language not seen in the speech two days earlier. The populist sense of dichotomy is fleshed out again in full form. Chávez uses geographical means and claims that celebration in Venezuela is only in one sector of Caracas. Also, he re-emphasizes the external factor (i.e. the empire) in his discourse, stressing that the opposition are actors of the American hegemony: the enemy. In addition, Chávez compares Baduel to Judas Iscariot: the apostle who betrayed Christ (Chávez also uses this religious signifier to capitalize his new form of political discourse in another speech: 'Christ, the greatest Socialist in

The Process of Deinstitutionalizing the Power Structure   87

history'—see page 80 in this chapter). And finally, Chávez concludes with a discourse that trademarks this new phase of the Bolivarian project: the Cuban socialist slogan slightly modified by adding 'socialism' into it.

As a result of the implementation of the plans Chávez announced after his re-election as the next phase of the Bolivarian project, unexpected new opposition forces emerged. In a short period of time, these three forces succeeded in challenging and defeating the government in the December 2007 constitutional reform referendum. However, that defeat did not keep Chávez from re-framing his political base and organizing a second referendum, which took place on February 15, 2009. This time, Chávez allowed all politicians, not just himself (i.e. all for one and one for all), to seek re-election indefinitely. The Bolivarian project won with 54.85 percent of the vote. It is obvious that all of the Bolivarian political machinery saw collective benefits this time and worked hard to win this referendum. As Panizza notes,using Claude Lefort's viewpoint, 'democracy power is an "empty place" that can only be provisionally occupied'. Problems appear when a political discourse doesn't want to respect that 'empty' element in democracy. In my view, the potential for this element of emptiness in democracy power to be filled temporarily is reflected in Baduel's argument, because Chávez wants to extend indefinitely his right to stay in power. Panizza claims that when this phenomenon happens 'extreme populism descends into totalitarianism'.[113]

CONCLUSION

This chapter empirically captures the various phases of the Bolivarian project with Hugo Chávez in the presidency, the role of populist discourse and practices in government, how opposition sectors (throughout the various phases) have resisted the sedimentation of the institutional changes the project has implemented, the discourse and tactics used to challenge the government with the aim of displacing a lousy anti-American/pro-Cuban populist institutional framework. Laclau's theoretical understanding of populism, which uses concepts like logics of differences and equivalence, combined with Glynos and Howarth's explanatory logics, has provided the interpretative methods to understand social, political, and fantasmatic issues raised in this 'thick descriptive' chapter. The process of de-institutionalizing the power system and institutionalizing Venezuela's Bolivarian Revolution addressed in this chapter attempts to present a thorough assessment of the conditions and moments of dislocation in this deeply divided society.

In this chapter, I described three phases of this Bolivarian project and what kind of discourse both camps articulated. In each phase, the populist government sought to implement more radical changes in the new institutional framework constructed after Chávez was elected president in February 1999. The first phase was in December 2001, when Chávez announced

88 *Populism in Venezuela*

the 49 'New Enabling Revolutionary Laws'. The second phase was the construction, starting in April 2003, of social, economic, educational, and cultural *'misiones'* (missions) programs seeking to help the previously excluded in poor and remote areas of Venezuela. The third phase was the construction of 'socialism' in Venezuela, announced in Chávez's re-election speech in January 2007. This 'socialist construction', so to speak, required radical changes to the constitution; thus a constitutional reform referendum was organized.

What is interesting is that in the first and third phase of this expansionary process, the Bolivarian project lost valuable assets. Political and military agents (i.e. Miquilena and Baduel) who were key players in the equivalential chain publicly disagreed with the radical changes Chávez and his faction wanted to implement. Also, influential political organizations (MAS and *Podemos*) rejected the extent of radicalism Chavistas were putting forward. They all left the project and joined the opposition. Attempts to further sediment revolutionary changes to this institutional framework had a negative impact on the Bolivarian project. It is possible that these events have weakened its popular electoral-base. Further analysis with recent empirical material is required to determine whether these elements have had an impact on Chávez's populist project.

The next two chapters are two in-depth case studies. Chapter 4 discusses a *misión* healthcare program, Chapter 5 an anti-Bolivarian student movement. These two cases were briefly addressed in two sections of this chapter. These in-depth case studies seek to flesh out, using thorough ethnographic fieldwork, the nature, practices, strengths, weaknesses, and overall opinion of individuals who have been somehow involved in these activities. An analysis of a case from each camp in a deeply polarized society can help us better understand key elements of the concerns, needs, and politics of *el pueblo* from both sides of the spectrum.

4   A Healthcare Program in Excluded Areas

A Community Participative Model Constructs Healthcare with Cuban Medics in Venezuela

In the previous chapter, the Bolivarian Government via referendums reaffirmed the 'popular will' to displace the *Punto Fijo*/bipartite[1] system. The sub-section 'Further radicalization' outlines how in 2003 the government began a new phase with social programs called '*Misiones*' (missions). Over a period of five years, 26 missions[2] were formed. This chapter provides an in-depth account explaining how the government constructed a free healthcare program for people living in poor and marginalized sectors. What is considered critical in this analysis is to illustrate the extent of community participation in the creation of this new social program, as well as to contextualize how basic public services (in the context of healthcare) deteriorated in the last two decades, and how the displaced institutional structure tries to contest the sedimentation of the Bolivarian institutional structure. This chapter maps out the discursive articulation that formed a new phase of the populist Bolivarian hegemonic project with direct grassroots popular participation. This analysis demonstrates the government's strategy to materialize, in a true sense, the radical change promised to their electorate popular-base during previous campaigns.

My objective is to descriptively address and contextualize elements of the formation and reproduction of Bolivarian populist practices by evaluating how the popular Mission '*Barrio Adentro*' healthcare program for the excluded emerged, the political contestation it created, and how it has managed to advance. This analysis seeks to achieve two important objectives. First, it will provide an in-depth account of one of the key planks of the Bolivarian project, providing insights into how Chávez set out to institutionally embed this program. Second, it will provide an account of the strengths and weaknesses of the Bolivarian project through an in-depth analysis of '*Barrio Adentro*' (BA). To obtain a better understanding of this health project the following points will be addressed in this chapter.

This chapter contextualizes the deterioration of public healthcare services in the last two decades, and how the displaced 'bipartite' institutional structure resists government attempts to change the healthcare system. It also describes and analyses the role of community participation in the creation of a new healthcare program in marginalized areas of the country. The expansion of this program and the problems it faces are carefully analyzed. I will

90 *Populism in Venezuela*

address the relevant literature about BA and, in particular, evaluate two different interpretations in one sub-section. I attempt to provide a 'thick descriptive' analysis of the BA program, examining the role of the 'people' forming BA, political reactions to institutional resistance, and the methods opposition healthcare sectors use to discredit this healthcare program. Furthermore, I'll reflect on how the BA program has been incorporated in rural and urban regions in Venezuela and to what extent there is 'social' satisfaction with this 'revolutionary' healthcare system. These observations are used as evidence for my overall argument reaffirming that BA has radically transformed healthcare for the previously excluded. First, I turn to the failure of the bipartite system in providing an adequate healthcare system.

4.1 THE OLD 'BIPARTITE' INSTITUTIONAL HEALTHCARE SYSTEM

The 'bipartite' 1961 Constitution acknowledged state obligations to guarantee a national healthcare system for the impoverished population. In practice, however, services fell far short of this ideal. Access to social programs belonged to certain groups: a given political party, an important workers' union, the armed forces, or the population of salaried employees. It also benefited those living in urban areas or near the public service network. Public investment in health services in rural and marginal areas began to decline in the 1960s as urban healthcare demands increased.[3] Private medical services expanded and private hospital services increased, whereas public hospital beds per population decreased.[4]

The bipartite system only worked to promote equitable distribution of oil income. When oil revenues fell, this institutional system began to crumble. Venezuela was driven to a socioeconomic crisis, with 54 percent of the population living in extreme and critical poverty conditions by the end of 1989.[5] President Pérez began his administration in February 1989 with a neoliberal program claiming to fight poverty. However, ordinary Venezuelans responded to this neoliberal package with a spontaneous social uproar (the *Caracazo*). This institutional system never recovered after this event. Public enterprises were privatized during Pérez's neoliberal program. In terms of healthcare, the neoliberal arrangement led to a decentralization of a broad network of existing public services, removing national control and handing it over to regional governments.[6] The main intention was to reduce state finances and obligations regarding social affairs. Medical services were privatized, fixed prices on basic products ended, foreign investment was welcomed, and a variety of transnational health/social insurance services appeared on the market.[7]

Decentralization and Delimitation Laws were approved, and regional governments assumed new roles. Decentralization led to a process of intensive privatization of this public service due to a dramatic budget deficit.[8] As national power decreased, local health services worsened, thus jeopardizing healthcare access for the people.[9] The population that (for socio-economic reasons) could not adapt to these new settings was simply excluded even further. By 1997, 73 percent of health expenditure was private.[10] Public health services fell and were replaced with a reform that imposed neoliberal policies on social affairs, in a country where two-thirds of the population were living in conditions of poverty.[11] Two-thirds of the population was forced to accept further deterioration of public services, including health services. These conditions were crucial for the populist practices that were to unfold, since a variety of unsatisfied social demands in the poorer sections of Venezuela's society called for a radical political project that demanded and promised a new and fair institutional structure.

Chávez began his administration by appointing health ministers to incorporate Latin American Social Medicine (LASM) principles into policies and practices.[12] However, these policies and practices were largely ineffectual in transforming the Ministry of Health and providing adequate healthcare for the 50 percent of Venezuelans living in poverty.[13] The LASM is a collective approach to healthcare, stressing the importance of political-economic and social determinants of disease-healthcare processes.[14] Several Latin American countries practice this approach to healthcare: they treat 'health as a social and human right and extend universal and equal healthcare, oppose the privatization of health . . . and advocate strengthening the state's role in guaranteeing access to health services'.[15]

However, efforts to challenge the national healthcare establishment proved to be a difficult task. The government recognized that any attempt to practice LASM principles first required a better strategy to challenge that complex structure within the healthcare system before any radical changes could take effect. As Charles Briggs and Clara Mantini-Briggs point out, a key influential healthcare body, '*Federación Medica Venezolana*' (Venezuelan Medical Federation; FMV), aligned with the bipartite institutional structure 'that lost power in the 1990s, and many members who worked in the private healthcare sector opposed Chávez's emphasis on reinvesting in public healthcare. The federation's hostility towards Chávez, an opposition-led coup (April 2002), and an oil strike (December 2002–January 2003) were important factors leading to the failure to implement LASM principles'.[16]

Policies were 'generated in the Ministry of Health in a top-down fashion rather than being worked out collaboratively with underserved (excluded) sectors'. There was little support from middle class medics—a sense of apathy to the poor.[17] There was no socio-economic or political interest in attending to patients who supported the radicalism the 'other' camp demanded. The opposition tried ferociously to displace the Bolivarian project in 2002 and early 2003. However, by 2003, conditions to implement a healthcare system in poor/rural areas changed drastically. The opposition's

92 *Populism in Venezuela*

attempts to oust Chávez from power gave Chávez the oil industry and thus the resources to crystallize his Bolivarian hegemony with Venezuela's previously excluded population.

4.2 CONSTRUCTING A NEW HEALTHCARE SYSTEM

During the coup on April 13, 2002, the people of the *barrios* took the streets to support the ousted President Chávez. People spontaneously mobilized themselves, demanding, outside the Presidential Palace, the return of their president. This is not the first time el *barrio* went down the hills (e.g. the *Caracazo*). Rubén Alayón Monserat[18] emphasizes the significance of what this entails—recognizing that these popular sectors could go down the hills again and challenge the government if they were ignored. Alayon points out that the government began to organize popular assemblies in the *barrios* and find ways to tackle the problems people faced in marginal areas of Caracas. With the participation of community representatives, social programs were created.[19]

Gregory Wilpert also refers to the February 1989 *Caracazo* social unrest to describe the formation of the popular mechanism he calls 'citizen assemblies'. Wilpert notes that 'the inspiration for citizen assemblies comes from a movement that emerged following the 1989 *Caracazo*, when citizens in the *barrios* got together'. Following the riots, 'these assemblies attempted to articulate the grievances of the people living in the *barrios*, and the general lack of attention from governmental authorities'. The Bolivarian institution activated these citizen assemblies to 'address the frustration of the *barrio* assemblies by giving citizens a forum in which such assemblies would be more effective than the *barrio* assemblies ever were'. Wilpert points out that community involvement 'helped shape the *Misión Barrio Adentro* program in the country's poorest neighborhoods'.[20]

Glynos and Howarth note that 'political logics aim to capture those processes of collective mobilization precipitated by the emergence of the political dimension of social relations, such as the construction, defense, and naturalization of new frontiers'.[21] What I discern in this case is that excluded social groups re-activated the rules practiced in other events (e.g. the *Caracazo* in 1989) and formed a popular mass that collectively mobilized in order to 'defend' the political platform they elected. Prior to the 2002 coup, this 'political dimension' didn't 'construct' a new frontier articulated through a process that required social relations. I find Glynos and Howarth's methodology useful, but in Alayón's description I find that the social (*el pueblo*) defended itself first. The Bolivarian political project realized the importance of constructing a new frontier that embedded the excluded into the Bolivarian process and delivered the promised radical change. A political project has to keep an active relation (grip) with its social popular-base in order to include them in the construction and consolidation of a new hegemonic project during periods of opposition and governance.

These new processes, encouraging people to participate and be protagonists, formed a new phase of populist practices in Venezuela. Before, only organizations from the armed forces and *Círculos Bolivarianos* (revolutionary grassroots circles) worked in the *barrios*. There were no direct projects designed to radically improve living conditions in underprivileged areas. Participation in the *barrios* was vital for the creation of a new healthcare program in the hills of Caracas. This participative model was later used to address other important issues: food, popular economy, consumer cooperatives and associations, cultural issues in communitarian radio reports, etc.[22] This new phase gave 'people' the power to make decisions. The Bolivarian political project recognized the significance of treating the 'poor/excluded' as key actors in this process. Giving them direct involvement in tackling problems of the 'people' living in the *barrios* was the way to fully incorporate popular sectors and activate a new phase of the Bolivarian political project. This model formed a sense of 'fullness to come' for Venezuela's previously excluded population.

Health committees (*Comités de Salud*) were organized in the communities and a health initiative program was formed in April 2003. '*Comités de Salud*' created a project called '*Casas de la Salud y la Vida*'. Its objective was to construct 734 life/health modules (houses) providing Integral Medicine to 250,000 families—approximately 1,250,000 people residing in the '*barriadas*' of Libertador municipality.[23] However, it became very difficult to find medics to work in the *barrios*. Prior to the arrival of Cuban medics in the *barrios*, the municipality invited medics to a public symposium; only 50 attended and only 20 (all specialists) showed interest in getting involved in the program. However, concerned about their personal safety, these 20 medics decided not to participate. Mayor Freddy Bernal of Libertador municipality had to explore other options, and the idea of incorporating Cuban medics in the program (based on an energetic economic and social pact Chávez signed with Fidel Castro in 2000) was agreed upon by both governments. In April 2003, 53 Cuban medics arrived. They were assigned to work in the health program in the *barrios* of Caracas.[24]

Community members were asked to offer shelter to Cuban medics in their homes, and a space to set up primary healthcare surgeries. The community overwhelmingly helped and their contribution is recognized as pivotal in the formation and success of this healthcare program.[25] To get a picture of the demand for this healthcare program, in 2003, 9,116,112 patients were attended and 4,143,067 health education interventions were conducted.[26] The importance of community involvement in this new phase of the revolution has been addressed. Next, a more in-depth analysis of the ins-and-outs (thick description) of these crucial social and political processes will

94   *Populism in Venezuela*

demonstrate how local and community practices work together to improve living conditions in this community.

4.2.1   Healthcare Program: '*Casas de la Salud y la Vida*'

Alayón claims that without the 'participative and protagonist democracy' model, this new healthcare program would never have materialized.[27] Alayón was involved in the communal debates where this new healthcare program took shape. This new democratic model consists of assembling sectarian organizations in a community, and with their active/direct participation, other Bolivarian '*Misiones*' programs have been developed. This model allows *el pueblo* to manage economic, social, and political programs in their communities. These popular sectors created a set of new managerial roles in the community. According to Alayon, 'community participation went beyond political expectations, to such a degree that social sectors much dominated decision-making processes in the program'.[28]

This prototype model started off with open forums where government officials and community representatives addressed their objectives in order to build a sense of trust, respect, and credibility. Available information on healthcare (e.g. census or institutional reports about healthcare in the community) was gathered and, through interviews and field-visits, a list describing the health conditions of the population in the *barrios* was made. The involvement of group organizations and local representatives made it possible for government officials to meet and propose a healthcare project to community members. Assemblies at different parishes organized public discussions, house-to-house visits, along with leaflets, posters, wall murals, portable megaphones, etc. The community was encouraged to participate and become protagonists in the making of this healthcare project.[29] Missions were successfully embedded in the *barrio* community because the community was part of them. Workshop dynamics were crucial in the crystallization of the program. The government provided the resources to cope with these problems, transforming the previously excluded into 'active agents' directly involved in the decision process.[30]

During my fieldwork visit in the *barrio* Carrasquelero in Calabozo Guárico state, Luis Lara, the elected president of the communal assembly, said: 'it is only now that "*el llanero del barrio*"[31] is fully involved with community affairs to improve the *barrio*'. According to Lara, they have a communal discussion every fortnight under a big mango tree in a communal park. There are 15 members in the assembly—each representing a sector of the *barrio*. Each member discusses concerns and needs and offers suggestions and plans related to that sector of the *barrio*. Anyone can join and speak during an assembly discussion. Before, 'there wasn't a communal assembly, any possibilities to have a dialogue with the authorities were beyond one's grasp'.[32]

A Healthcare Program in Excluded Areas   95

One of the topics discussed in the communal assembly was how to construct primary healthcare modules in the *barrio*.[33] 'The healthcare program has helped *el barrio* a lot. I've accompanied *"defensoras de la salud"* [nurses] doing house visits reviewing the health and living conditions of families in the *barrio*'. People appreciate the work of Cuban medics. It's done with a sense of ethics, and the medics are always willing to attend to patients. They work in spite of the unpleasant conditions in the *barrio*. 'They are here with us in the community', Lara says.[34] The 'participative and protagonist' model has been crucial for basic improvements in Carrasquelero. Plans to improve the supply of electricity, water, and wastewater and to improve new and old schools go ahead as planned.[35]

Another example gathered during fieldwork is from Caricuao, Libertador municipality, Caracas. Doña Nuñez, a local committee coordinator of a *barrio* health committee since its formation in 2003, said: 'the beginning of [the] program was very difficult. When the first Cuban medics arrived, social "participation" was essential [to] dealing with the shortcomings in the *barrio*. This is the first time "health" gets to the "people". The community now enjoys a broad healthcare system free of charge'.[36] This new healthcare program was inaugurated in April 2003 in the Libertador municipality. It was a primary healthcare prototype project that consisted of social and political involvement (Cuban medical assistance), later named Mission *Barrio Adentro* (BA).[37] Individuals like Doña Nuñez are examples that show how projects like BA have produced a sense of fulfillment with *el pueblo*. She showed me some of her posters: '*Barrio Socialismo Adentro*' (Socialism—Deep in the Slums) to celebrate six years of BA on April 6, 2009.[38] These are signs of discursive formation constructing an ideological symbol molded in BA. It slowly infuses the significance of socialist practices for 'popular sectors' in the Venezuelan context. This ideological theme in the healthcare context will be raised and analyzed later in this chapter.

To restate what this signifies to the people of the *barrios* in Libertador municipality, a health committee coordinator stated:

> It used to be that here they made all the decisions for us. We were like puppets. But that's not true any more. Now we are an organized health committee, which has had to pioneer everything. . . . We are going to be our own advocates in solving our problems. No one is going to come here and tell us what's going on. Here we are really going to be heard. The idea isn't to hand the responsibility over to the president and then attack him. It's the other way around: he is giving us the tools, and we have to learn how to use them successfully.[39]

The above cases are clear examples of what the 'participative and protagonist' model entails. The formation of community assemblies in an organized manner has created a new social platform where popular sectors—combined with political practices can construct new communal projects. This created

96   Populism in Venezuela

a new phase of Venezuela's popular democratic system—giving the 'previously excluded' in rural and urban areas the right to be central protagonists in the improvement of their living conditions. People elected Chávez hoping to get a sense of fulfillment and empowerment with the radicalization the Chavista political project promised. The de-institutionalization process of the bipartite system underwent a phase of referendums in order to democratically re-affirm popular support for a new constitution. However, these changes were not sufficient to fully displace a hegemonic order. In practice, the old bureaucratic institutional structure continues to work. As Laclau points out, 'political logics are related to the *institution* of the social'.[40] This is precisely what we see in the 'participative and protagonist democracy' model. The Bolivarian Revolution attempted to give popular subjects direct participation and power in community assemblies, and thus the ability to take part in the construction of a new institutional structure.

Dislocatory moments like *el Caracazo* and the Bolivarian coup d'état in February 1992 revealed how dichotomized Venezuela's society was and still is. These were moments for antagonized social sectors to express their rejection of governmental policies and a clear demand for institutional change. The privatization and decentralization of public healthcare services, discussed earlier, contextualizes the degree of popular dissatisfaction with the de-instituted system. The 'participative and protagonist' model was the structural forum where Venezuela's 'popular base' could collectively discuss and directly participate in new programs to improve their living conditions in the *barrios*. However, friction with public institutions began (the involvement of the old institutional structure was required), partly because their administrative apparatus was cumbersome or because that institutional structure opposed the changes dictated to them by this Bolivarian model.[41]

The above descriptions give us the background to comprehend the terrain that made social participation in the Bolivarian mission programs a success. Glynos and Howarth state that 'social actors in general can interpret new situations in a variety of ways, ranging from passive resignation, despair and alienation, to a mounting anger and outrage that leads to new grievances which can be articulated as claims and demands'. They argue that claims and demands 'may lead to the construction of new identities and subjectivities . . . linking various demands together into new political projects or social movements'. These sets of conditions can channel and reshape 'grievances into the existing institutions and structures of power'.[42] The Bolivarian Government was elected to assemble a new political system representing the 'popular' mass and deal with claims and demands rejected by previous governments. Mission programs were a direct response to people's claims and demands.

As Glynos and Howarth point out, 'political practices bring about a transformative effect on existing social practices . . . to the degree that such movements become hegemonic by managing to link various demands

A Healthcare Program in Excluded Areas   97

together across a variety of social spaces and sites of struggle, they can exercise a transformative effect on an entire regime of practices, resulting in the institution and sedimentation of a new regime and the social practices that comprise it'.[43] In Venezuela, this is precisely what we see in the Bolivarian mission programs; political practices aim to transform the conditions where a variety of social demands emerged. This new set of practices requires the participation of social actors in 'excluded' communities in order to construct new social and political mechanisms within existing social practices. In other words, the Bolivarian political platform was opening a new terrain where subjects from underprivileged sectors of a dichotomic society could be protagonists in the formation of a new hegemonic structure and a popular institutional system.

These anecdotes convey the flavor of the circumstances and practices of various social and political actors who put together a new healthcare program in poor areas. This description does not pretend to give any final answers. Nonetheless, this assessment provides an overall picture of how actors from popular sectors have directly participated in communitarian projects and taken key organizational and managerial roles in the construction and crystallization of these social programs. Next, I'll discuss how Chávez's hegemonic order expanded from a pilot healthcare project in the *barrios* of Caracas to other regions of Venezuela.

4.2.2   Primary healthcare program: *Barrio Adentro* (BA)

This healthcare program entered a new phase when Chávez informed the nation of plans to expand the pilot health project in the *barrios* of the Libertador municipality to other regions of the country, naming it *Misión Barrio Adentro*. On July 6, 2003, President Chávez stated in his '*N. 155 Aló Presidente*' program:

> *El pueblo* now has Mission *Barrio Adentro*: free integral medical healthcare for the excluded, the poor people. With Cuban medics and methods adapted to Venezuelan needs, hundreds of thousands of people start to fight against that battle against obscurity . . . in places where poverty is distressing and no government has ever tried to deal with their needs. That's our biggest compromise. The Bolivarian Revolution we'll go to the deepest end of the *barrios* . . . I call for Venezuelan medics and volunteers. Communitarian organizations have started thanks to massive participation from people in the *barrios* that ethically work bringing healthcare to everyone with no exception.[44]

The lack of healthcare services has been a national problem for many years. To deal with this crisis, in the first year of BA, 10,169 Cuban medics were stationed throughout the country. Another section of BA was formed that year called '*Dale un Sonrisa al Barrio*' (give a smile to the *Barrio*), a dental

98 *Populism in Venezuela*

care services program.[45] Also, ophthalmological centers began receiving patients and providing free glasses. Cuban personnel played a critical role in the implementation of these health operations.[46] In less than a year, this primary healthcare pilot project became a national mission. That initiative in the *barrios*, building a sense of communal unity combined with political initiatives in the municipality, formed a free national healthcare system.

In September 2003, the *Ministerio de Salud y Desarrollo Social* (MSDS) started to get involved in the development of BA. Shortly after this, a presidential commission was formed and the *Coordinación Nacional de Atención Primaria* (CNAP) of MSDS took on the ministerial role of developing BA in coordination with the Cuban Medical Mission. The CNAP's role was to coordinate, plan, and monitor personnel, land, construction of healthcare centers, and technical equipment.[47] However, this didn't work due to 'internal' problems with Cuban personnel. Cuban medics are managed under the Cuban Medical Mission with their 'own' national, regional, and communal coordinators. Assistance abroad reports only to the Medical Federation in Cuba.[48] As Thanali Patruyo points out, the 'Cuban Medical Mission's thriving autonomy has been a drawback to the mission right from the start. This has seriously obstructed the dynamics of the program, in terms of influx information and plans to create health clinics'.[49] The CNAP intended to have a leading role in the development of BA; but it seems that the Cuban Medical Mission did not want to be part of Venezuela's ministerial/governmental political machinery. They expected full control and the power to implement what they thought necessary for the expansion of a Cuban healthcare system in Venezuela.

The BA program was officially rubber-stamped when a national decree (*Gaceta Oficial*—Official Gazette) was put into effect on January 24, 2004. A presidential committee was established to implement and institutionally coordinate Mission *Barrio Adentro* as the integral primary healthcare system. The objective was for BA to thrive and become the new management structure with the coordination, cooperation, and active participation of protagonist-organized communities.[50] Throughout the year, the program embarked on the development of new specialized health segments serving the population in areas with low density of services. However, political resistance to these changes in the institutional healthcare structure delayed the development of BA. Before analyzing political and institutional resistance, I'll explain how BA expanded.

4.2.3 BA—Further Development

Chávez recognized that if the BA primary healthcare project was going to be a national health program, as he stated in his 'N. *155 Aló Presidente*' of July 6, 2003, officially ratified on January 26, 2004, the government had to comply with the criteria for expansion (BA II, III, and IV) the Cuban Medical Mission proposed. In January 2005 Chávez announced that BA II

A Healthcare Program in Excluded Areas   99

would be the next stage of the healthcare service, covering a wider range of medical services. I start by describing the four divisions of BA II.

BA II

(1) *Centro Medico de Diagnostico Integral* (CDI): BA I offers preventive and curative care in the majority of cases; however, many patients required para-clinical diagnostic examinations or more complex procedures. By the end of 2006, there were 300 centers providing a 24-hour emergency service with (on average) three intensive care beds and one in every CDI with an area for emergency surgical operations.[51] (2) *Salas de Rehabilitación Integral* (SRI): these centers provide treatments like electrotherapy, ultrasound laser therapy, and speech therapy.[52] (3) *Centros de Alta Tecnología* (CAT): these are diagnostic support services, performing nuclear magnetic resonance, and more clinical laboratory tests.[53] (4) *Clínicas Populares*: these are small hospitals for elective surgical interventions, maternal and pediatric care, and other medical specialties.[54] BA III was the next step in this period of expansion.

BA III

Chávez announced the BA III plan in *Aló Presidente* (N. 232) on August 28, 2005. With an extraordinary budget, BA III consisted of recovering and modernizing 299 existing public hospitals managed by MSDS, governorships, IVSS, and armed forces.[55] Muntaner et al. state that 'BA III includes integration of the 300 existing public hospitals in the country. It began in 2006 and was re-formulated in 2007. The focus of this phase of the project is on improvement in infrastructure, equipment, and personnel training'.[56] I'll discuss what this expansion entailed in the next sub-section. The next expansionary move of this new healthcare system is known as BA IV.

BA IV

The final expansionary phase was formalized in December 2006.[57] This new segment was structured in two stages: the construction of six centers in 2009 and nine more in 2010.[58] In December 2011, of the sixteen hospitals (centers) being constructed, eight were in the final phase.[59] According to Muntaner et al., 'BA IV involves the construction of a dozen new general hospitals, each with a specific area of hyper-specialization', and 'broadening general hospital coverage (particularly in areas with low beds-per-population ratios)'.[60]

Above, I only characterize the services offered by BA II, III, and IV. Nonetheless, apart from describing the expansion of BA; analyzing diverging interpretations of this healthcare program in the literature can reveal more information about this mission program. Muntaner et al. and Patruyo

100　*Populism in Venezuela*

rest their arguments on a number of contradictory descriptive interpretations of BA's development. I view this divergence of viewpoints interesting therefore worth addressing in this investigation of BA.

4.2.4　Different Empirical Interpretations of The Development of BA

These two interpretations appear to diverge on insignificant issues regarding the development of BA; however, when these interpretations are put into context, these differences are remarkable. According to Muntaner et al., 'community participation has been an important element in constructing, equipping and opening of the various types of establishments for BA II'.[61] With a structure of communitarian health committees, community participation was encouraged in the national press and television. 'Health committee members met with building and equipment installation contractors, representatives of the Ministry of Health and the Cuban Medical Mission'.[62] However, Patruyo has a different interpretation. When Chávez inaugurated BA II,[63] more centers would be opened in 2005, constructed by the Ministry of Housing and Habitat (*Ministerio de Vivienda y Hábitat*) with Cuban medical personnel involvement and equipment from Cuba.[64] 'Community participation', crucial in Muntaner et al.'s account, is not mentioned in Patruyo's side of the story. Also, the Ministry of Housing and Habitat, not of Health, was responsible (combined with Cuban personnel) for the construction of new centers.

Patruyo claims that the expansion of primary healthcare created the need for a new segment of BA to attend to patients with specialized health concerns. By mid-2004, the government invested in a plan to remodel and equip the primary healthcare centers and hospitals of *Instituto Venezolano de Seguro Social* (IVSS) and the Ministry of Health, converting them into subsidiaries of the 'popular clinic' structure. The strategy was to rehabilitate and equip 151 urban healthcare centers and hospitals. However, only 12 clinics were built and the plan collapsed. The Medical Federation of IVSS disagreed with the way personnel were contracted.[65] As a result, Chávez turned to Cuba for help. Beginning in January 2005 extraordinary funds were used to construct and equip new centers.[66]

Patruyo puts the emphasis on political factors, hence fleshing out critical points for this analysis. That is, Patruyo focuses on political resistance to the changes the government was trying to implement, showing that the attempt to use the existing health infrastructure managed by anti-Chavista medical institutes/federations was a direct political attack on one of the last areas the opposition camp still controlled. This created a sense of 'institutional inertia' in the development of this new healthcare system, forcing the government to turn to another method: a request for more Cuban expertise for the formation of a new healthcare structure.

Regarding BA III, I also observe different interpretations. Patruyo highlights an interesting detail, which is the management setting of these public

A Healthcare Program in Excluded Areas   101

hospitals. Earlier I mentioned how in the 1990s decentralization gave governors control of public healthcare services. Governmental incentives to get involved in regional healthcare services managed by autonomous opposition sectors were bound to be treated as a political tactic. Also, the government's strategy of re-modeling and outfitting IVSS centers and hospitals for BA II didn't go far because the Medical Federation of IVSS disapproved of personnel contractual procedures, as the Cuban Medical Mission managed all aspects of the program. These points reveal how the two political camps confronted each other instead of reaching a pluralist common ground for a unified national healthcare system. However, regarding BA III, Muntaner et al. only mention 'integration' of 300 existing public hospitals in the country, and a 're-formulated' plan in 2007. Why did it have to be re-formulated?

According to Patruyo, the first step of this plan was modernizing the medical equipment of 43 hospitals managed by MSDS and IVSS and of military health centers. However, as most of these hospitals were used for university medical training, these changes were regarded as 'extremely complicated'. The second step consisted of modernizing 57 hospitals—a process categorized as 'complicated'. And, 150 hospitals (rather indispensable units) were considered 'less complicated'.[67] In February 2006, Chávez approved a budget of almost U.S. $500 million to purchase new medical equipment.[68]

The next stage consisted of a form (from the Ministry of Health) given to the directors of all 'units' (e.g. hospitals) to lay out what equipment needed replacing, and to agree on where specialized diagnostic exams, laboratory hubs, and other medical centers could be situated. However, that attempt to incorporate a structure of public hospitals into the domain of BA III worried several institutions—particularly those that maintained a degree of autonomy. Many of them viewed this health plan as a concealed 're-centralization' strategy of 'all' health services.[69] This resistance to the process of re-conditioning the system explains why in 2006, only 5 of 43 selected hospitals carried out the plan. This 'hospital recovery strategy' was a setback to the government, and institutional inertia obstructed the advancement of BA. Thus, it was decided that an entirely new infrastructure would be constructed[70]—that is, Muntaner et al.'s 2007 're-formulation': BA IV.

Both accounts describe BA IV as a plan to construct new specialized centers/hospitals throughout the country. Nevertheless, I see critical differences in these two interpretations. Patruyo argues that this is the cause of the government's failure in using existing healthcare infrastructure for BA III. However, Muntaner et al. only names it 're-formulation'. I view Patruyo's side of the story as more convincing, as it clearly reflects the conditions under which there is a degree of contestation and reprisal between two hegemonic healthcare positions. Muntaner et al. use the term 're-formulation' without explaining what this entails.

This healthcare program called *Barrio Adentro* is a discourse that has broadened to levels where that element of health has discursively shifted,

102 *Populism in Venezuela*

being articulated as a key theme of the revolutionary Bolivarian political project. I have tried to contextualize the grounds upon which the development of BA has been obstructed with political resistance in key divisions of the health institutional configuration. Presidential accords with Cuba's Medical Mission are problematic for Venezuela's existing medical establishment. The presence of an unrestricted external medical force operating freely, fully financed and legitimized by the government, seriously threatens one of the few strongholds the opposition still operates. This has shaped healthcare as a political subject, thus creating an institutional inertia blocking the development of BA. Next, I'll address how 'resistance' discourse is articulated and describe the grounds the opposition camp uses.

4.3 RESISTANCE TO BA—INSTITUTIONAL INERTIA

In this section, I aim to contextualize the discourse the FMV articulates to contest the Bolivarian attempts to de-institute their hegemonic position in healthcare. They claim that their 'know how' and pathological expertise in Venezuela are vital for the construction of a viable national healthcare program. They strongly reject the involvement of Cuban medical practices and power to construct a healthcare structure with no understanding of the pathology of Venezuela's healthcare problems. They also condemn the government's antagonistic position towards Venezuelan medics practicing in the public sector, forcing them to find work elsewhere.

To understand what resistance discourse entails, genealogical conditions help us unravel vital points. Briggs and Mantini-Briggs mention that 'gains achieved' in the public health sector were 'eroded in the 1980s and 1990s'. The gross domestic product spent on health fell substantially.[71] This refers to the neoliberal policies implemented during this period: decentralization and privatization. 'The majority of health expenditures were transferred to the private sector . . . the poor . . . faced large fees for many health services and medications'.[72] 'By the late 1990s, class-based disparities were enormous and much of the population effectively lacked access to healthcare'.[73]

Chávez's intention to merge BA with Venezuela's healthcare institutional structure didn't materialize. Only with Chávez's government-to-government relations with Cuba, the oil industry with its finances—in conjunction with community participation—was this healthcare program for the excluded population constructed. 'From the start, BA was a major focus of criticism from those opposing the Chávez Government's pro-poor policies. To get a glimpse of opposition discourse, the FMV claims that Cubans were not medics and that they "prescribed dangerous, outdated medicines"'.[74]

Let us review Laclau's theoretical approach within the Venezuelan healthcare context. As mentioned earlier, '"political logics are related to the *institution* of the social", where the process of institution "proceeds out social demands" rather than "arbitrary fiat" and is "inherent to any process

A Healthcare Program in Excluded Areas   103

of social change"'.[75] Glynos and Howarth suggest that, 'if political logics are concerned with the institution of the social, they are also related to its possible *de-institution* or *contestation*'.[76] That is precisely what we see in the subject of *Misiones*: social 'participation' constructs a new institution. Furthermore, the articulation of BA not only responded to social demands, but also contested the power of the anti-Chavista medical establishment and threatened to de-institutionalize it with an institution conveyed by the 'people' (the social).

Glynos and Howarth note that 'the institution of a new regime or social practice presupposes the possibility that a previous social order is successfully displaced from its hegemonic position and thus de-instituted'.[77] I define the displaced 'social order' as the 'medical community' that benefited from its hegemonic position within an institutional structure that is now contested because it fails to represent and provide a healthcare system to Venezuela's poor. A way to illustrate my point is the action the FMV president took in 2007; he advocated all kinds of actions against the regime from medics working in public health sectors. León Natera said: 'Salaries are dreadful (approx. U.S.\$120 per month), Venezuelan medics are discriminated [against] in their own country. For the last nine years, the government has harassed us; we cannot keep on accepting this. There are 30,000 Cuban medics in the country; they are not medics, they illegally practice medicine here, causing a serious health problem. They disclaim Venezuela's tropical pathology and have no plans to control infectious-contagious diseases'.[78]

The FMV states that 'during Chávez's Government, around 30,000 medics working in the public sector emigrated, putting hospitals with an estimate of 42 percent short of qualified medics. This is the result of government's discrimination against the 'Medical Union' and the healthcare sector in general. Miserable salaries, difficult working conditions in healthcare public centers (e.g. insecurity, no medical equipment and basic appliances) and government's antagonizing discourse forces many to practice privately or search for better conditions abroad. In the last 29 months [from August 2007 to February 2009), 2,400 medics have left the country requiring for medical certification from the FMV. There are many who leave Venezuela without requesting the certificates'.[79] This is clear evidence that a previous social order is contested and to some extent displaced from its hegemonic position.

A useful theoretical annotation relating to 'institution' is Glynos and Howarth's interpretation of Laclau's passage earlier presented. To them, 'Laclau's remarks imply that the contestation of a hegemonic discursive formation and the possible institution—or failed institution—of a new one via political logics can never be totally external, and thus arbitrary, in relation to the social formation itself. Instead, the radical institution of the social emerges from concrete empirical demands within a particular order'.[80] Before the emergence of BA, the Bolivarian Government lacked 'concrete demands' in healthcare. Without these demands the government couldn't contest the hegemonic position of those that operated the bureaucratic

104 *Populism in Venezuela*

structure in the Health Ministry (e.g. the FMV). However, as Alayón narrates, soon after the coup in April 2002, *el pueblo* went down the hills with a more general demand: the return of Chávez to the presidency. Subsequently, with a 'participative and protagonist' model the government organized the people to construct (in response to their demands) a healthcare program in the *barrios*. In this context, processes to challenge and partly de-institute the 'other' hegemonic order is crystallized and displaced with a radical institutional framework constructed and mobilized with concrete healthcare demands by previously excluded sectors.

Theoretical discourse can unravel what is at stake to all those involved, rather than viewing information as a mere description of events related to healthcare in Venezuela. For example, analyzing what 'de-institution' and 'institution' entails in this context unpacks a new insight about the meaning of social and political practices amid a process of radical change. These are populist practices constructing a 'radical institution' by contesting what is left of a wider institution that failed to keep its hegemonic position when Chávez was elected president in December 1998. Attempts to transform the Ministry of Health with LASM principles into policies and practices failed. Resistance to radical change in healthcare blocked any efforts for the formation of a new institutional framework. Conditions changed in 2003 when the BA program was constructed. This is the background against which institutional inertia is set. A new institution has discursively formed the conditions to contest the hegemony of key organisms like FMV. Thus, we have two opposed healthcare systems in Venezuela: the traditional system versus BA (coordinated by the Cuban Medical Mission). Healthcare has become another political terrain (at the expense of people) where the camps contest and challenge each other.

Criticisms from the anti-Chavista medical establishment are primarily based on their claims that illegal Cuban personnel in Venezuela practice inappropriate medical methods. Indeed, BA fundamentally depends upon Cuban medical personnel, with a variety of health policies, methods, and practices solely coordinated by Cubans. In the subsequent sections of this chapter I'll address the following points. First, I'll evaluate whether this new radical healthcare system can sustain itself on a medium/long term basis as demands for BA services increase. Second, I'll determine whether BA is effectively providing a satisfactory national healthcare system to the previously excluded.

4.4 BA: ITS DEPENDENCE ON CUBAN MEDICAL PRACTICES—VENEZUELANS REPLACING CUBAN MEDICS AND PEOPLE'S OPINION OF THE MISSION

This section examines BA by addressing the literature that draws on its dependence on Cuban medical practices in a wider context, and on the

A Healthcare Program in Excluded Areas   105

importance of incorporating Venezuelans into the program. Also, I attempt to uncover the level of Venezuelan medical personnel in BA, and the discourse of medical students studying 'Integrated General Medicine'. Furthermore, I discuss what can be learned from the experience and reflection of Cuban medics practicing healthcare at BA in various regions of Venezuela, and my overall impression of the BA modules/centers visited. To conclude, I'll address patients' views about the service BA provides.

Yolanda D'Elia and Luis Francisco Cabezas's article raises some interesting points about Cuban medical practices in BA. They mention that in 2004 the Ombudsman Office stressed that Cuban medics ought to be trained by Venezuelan therapeutic specialists and that more Venezuelan medical personnel should be employed at primary healthcare centers. However, after five years, less than two percent are Venezuelans. National academic authorities cannot certify Cuban health practices because the Cuban Medical Mission overturns the healthcare regulations practiced in Venezuela.[81] In other words, Venezuela's health ruling body (FMV) couldn't assess, approve, and coordinate national health policies due to the inclusion of a new foreign health entity that ignores FMV's authority.

These quotes give us a picture of the discourse anti-Chavistas use to discredit the BA program. The presence of uncertified and unregulated Cuban medics in Venezuela is a clear contestation of the hegemonic position of the ruling medical regulatory system. For example, the Ombudsman Office stating that 'Cuban medics ought to be trained by Venezuelan therapeutic specialists' is simply an institutional attempt to defend their 'hegemonic position', implying that the Cuban Medical Mission must follow domestic healthcare regulations and follow Venezuela's medical practices. If those practices are ignored, which is the case, this could explain why Cuban medics and healthcare practices are categorized as illegal and dangerous. To conclude that this form of discourse is mainly politically driven, not medical, further observations and analysis are required.

As D'Elia and Cabezas put it, after five years, less than two percent are Venezuelans. That is to say, more than 98 percent are Cubans. This implies that BA fully depends on Cuban personnel. These are signs of dependence on Cuban involvement in healthcare. Part of the agreement between the governments is that Cuba receives 100,000 barrels of Venezuelan oil per day, which is primarily paid for with medical services.[82] Venezuelan dependence on Cuban healthcare benefits Cuba's interests, hence jeopardizing the future of BA. Nonetheless, there are programs training Venezuelans to replace Cuban medical personnel practicing in Venezuela.

In 2005, it was announced that 20,000 young Venezuelans would be recruited for a three-year integral medical course taught by Cubans—and would join the program by early 2010. However, as there were not enough places and equipment to train them, the target of one medic for every 250 families was unrealistic. In order to solve this problem, Venezuela and Cuba agreed in 2007 to construct Cuban medical schools in Venezuela. Official

106 *Populism in Venezuela*

figures show there has been a 20 percent reduction in Cuban personnel—from 15,000 in 2005 to 12,000 in 2007.[83] The strategy is to train 'locals' in Cuban health practices and thus replace Cuban personnel.

Since the inauguration of BA in 2003, this healthcare program has expanded significantly, offering a wide range of free medical services to the population. In March–April 2009, I interviewed eight BA Cuban medics working at three different states in Venezuela. All of them mentioned that there are 30,000 Cuban medics working in the country. Nevertheless, I got the impression that there is a shortage of personnel. In rural areas, I observed that 'BA I' primary healthcare and dental modules were closed. This is because the allocated Cuban medics were on holiday (after three months of work, a medic can return to Cuba and rest for 20 days). My observation correlates with Patruyo's account.[84] Personnel shortage can also be the result of BA's enlargement: shifting medics to work in other BA centers without adequate substitution. Figures for 2007 show that, in communities with BA modules, 'residents' go on a regular basis to public hospitals for checkups and consultations with medical specialists. Furthermore, personnel in BA I and II centers have expressed concerns because shortages in space, input, and human resources keep them from doing their jobs properly.[85]

My view is that the construction of a healthcare system modeled on the Cuban system is still in a process of sedimentation. If this dichotomic configuration in Venezuela's healthcare system continues, 'health' will gradually be another component of populist practices infused with socialist doctrinarian principles against the 'others': oligarchs, enemies of the Venezuelan people. Also, it is rather premature to conclude that 'dependence' on Cuban medical personnel is the appropriate term. This topic needs further investigation, to determine whether young Venezuelan medics who graduated from or were trained at Cuban medical schools in Venezuela have gradually replaced Cuban medical personnel in BA.

During fieldwork visits I observed the integration of Venezuelan medical personnel and students into BA's apparatus. In a run-down area of Calabozo, I visited a module of BA I managed by a Venezuelan medic and nurses called '*Defensores de la Salud*'. The nurses studied at a local branch of the Romulo Gallegos University, where the government incorporated a faculty of medicine to train locals. Also, the medic was a qualified nurse and, with grants offered by the government, she graduated in 'Integrated General Medicine'.[86] The second case is about students in Caricuao. Arranging a visit to meet a Cuban medic in the *barrio*, to my luck, she organized a forum with seven of her students in the module.[87] Delgado, I.—a student in Caricuao—said: 'BA has evolved in stages; we are now beginning a new one. When Cuban medics came here, "people" in general rejected them. Medical institutions tried to collapse the program. Now, people from both political camps visit BA, respecting and supporting BA's healthcare system'. Horopesa, J.—another student

A Healthcare Program in Excluded Areas   107

in Caricuao—stressed that 'the medics from the traditional system only attend patients if they have money. We are trained to take care of the "people". We have to work in dreadful *barrios*; many Venezuelans forget that these places exist'.[88]

What I want to emphasize by presenting the above anecdotes is that the government is making efforts to incorporate Venezuelans into the BA program. There are new training initiatives and programs to replace BA Cuban medical personnel. In both cases, located at different regions of the country, I found interesting comments about the significance of BA to them. The medic in Carrasquelero explained that after years of nursing school and lack of funds for further development, the revolution helped her study and graduate. Also, my fieldwork revealed how a new generation of Venezuelan medical students view the way BA has evolved—from initial criticism and resistance to Cuban medics to a phase of objective/non–politically driven perceptions of the program. Furthermore, it revealed their role in a new healthcare system for the 'people' vis-à-vis the 'others': practicing class-based medicine.

Another important element that needs to be addressed is the experience and reflection of Cuban medics practicing healthcare in BA at various regions of Venezuela.[89] A Cuban medic working in an SRI in the village of Cordero, Táchira, mentioned that when she started to work people didn't trust Cuban pathology. She said: 'people were very skeptical. Opposition propaganda spoke very ill of Cuban medical services and personnel. Fortunately, that has gradually changed. Most of my patients are opposition supporters. Now, they realize we're not part of a political agenda [and] hence appreciate our service'.[90] Another BA I Cuban medic in San Cristobal, Táchira, said: 'don't ask any questions of political nature. I only attend ill people and help with preventive medicine. During the four years working in this community, crime is an issue. One Cuban medic was killed in the street—this is a difficult place. There are things I cannot discuss, this is a pact of two nations, I attend patients only'.[91] In a well-equipped BA I module of primary healthcare and a dental surgery in Calabozo, a Cuban dentist described her experience with the locals, who are mostly baffled to receive this service 'free' of charge. A BA I Cuban medic in Caricuao, Caracas, stressed that 'often a patient needs "attention", someone to talk to, a bit affection and a good listener. I do a check-up whilst they tell me their problems'.[92] This kind of discourse reveals what Cuban medics experience and deal with in a society that is socially and politically divided.

In the five BA I primary modules/centers I visited (in three different regions of the country), the medical equipment I saw was the same. There is a sense of uniformity in the primary healthcare service, and it extends to medications: all are produced in Cuba. Also, in two SRI (BA II) centers, several pieces of physical therapy equipment were identical. It is obvious that the program is standardized and provides an organized

108   *Populism in Venezuela*

national service. Finally, of the four CDI (BA II) centers I visited, one had a big picture of 'Che Guevara' in a boardroom,[93] and an impressive intensive care unit with brand-new equipment.[94] Interestingly, in January 2009, before this fieldwork visit, Chávez inaugurated this CDI and stated:

> We have managed to build 465 CDIs, 540 SRIs and 21 CATs BA II centers as well as more than 3,000 BA I popular modules in five years. . . . In the last three years most of the work has been done. During the first two years we struggled against the oligarchs who tried to prohibit Cuban medics working here; they said they were witches! This is Socialism at work.[95]

Chávez's speech lists how many modules/centers have been constructed; stressing that most of the work has been done in the last three years. Furthermore, it discursively reflects what I call 'institutional inertia' and its implications for the development of BA. Also, socialism is a signifier that 'grips' agents and the political project together in order to collectively mobilize 'people' against the oligarchs. Discursively, Chávez tries to highlight how the opposition (FMV) labels Cuban medics as 'witches' (i.e. unqualified Cubans practicing dangerous medical practices).

What do patients think of BA? A patient in a SRI in Calabozo said: 'I'm very happy with the service. I came here with my grandson who had speech problems and much appreciate how Cuban medics have helped us with their techniques. He has started to speak now. Also, I fell six months ago and broke my ankle, I'm here doing therapy with all the equipment they have available'.[96] A patient in Carrasquelero told me how conscientious they are; he is attended with care and with clear knowledge of his health conditions.[97] Another patient in Caricuao, Caracas, listening to a discussion between seven students and me, said: 'the opposition doesn't care about our needs and problems. They are ignorant. They just don't know what BA means to us—thanks to the help of President Chávez'.[98]

It is rather difficult to make a detailed and thorough assessment of people's opinions about a healthcare program in Venezuela's remote rural and urban areas. I reflect on patient's comments and my overall ethnographic observation by visiting BA modules/centers in three different regions. It is rather evident that there is a sense of gratitude to the service provided in all the BA modules/centers. It is contextualized by the people as a service designed to provide healthcare to the 'excluded' population. In spite of the obstacles BA has had to overcome, the program is successfully providing a service to the 'people' regardless of their political orientation. In 2003, BA was founded to provide a 'free' healthcare system in poor areas (*barrios* in Caracas) where these services were almost non-existent. Henceforth, we see a national and sophisticated

A Healthcare Program in Excluded Areas 109

Barrio Adentro—realistically radicalizing what 'free' healthcare means to 'people' in Venezuela.

4.5 REFLECTIONS ON BA

Even though BA has succeeded in providing healthcare in a society where inequality is widespread, there is a degree of internal conflict within the operational structure of this mission. To get a glimpse of the problem, in 2007, BA I, II, and III received a total of U.S. \$3.258 billion. In 2008, PDVSA (*Petróleos de Venezuela*)[99] reduced it to \$130 million.[100] This has seriously affected personnel working in the program. I met BA secretaries and drivers in Táchira complaining about months of salaries pending;[101] however, Cuban personnel have two salaries: one in Venezuela (U.S. \$120 per month) and a salary of the same figure in Cuba for family support. On July 17, 2009, a group of BA workers went to the parliament to give parliamentarians a document to be handed over to Chávez stressing a series of irregularities such as up to five years of unpaid salaries and the deterioration of the mission.[102] All the managerial sectors BA workers contacted ignored them. The workers point out that 'this affects 20,000 employees; in some regions BA coordinators overlook the *"Comités de Salud"*. We're trying to stop a "macabre operation" that could ruin the mission. We're Socialist workers; this undermines the principles of the Bolivarian Revolution'.[103]

BA workers' effort to discuss their concerns about a series of irregularities in BA was ignored by the management. These are signs of antagonism in BA. In other words, the 'nodal point' in the chain of equivalence has been broken—the 'internal frontier' is unbalanced. Differences and individual interests are weakening the trust of the social base and the political project in general. My intention is to put into context the way sectors within the BA structure operate and how grassroots BA workers try to inform Chávez of these problems. Particularistic interests are overshadowing the initial socio-political and emotional significance of BA: a popular healthcare system for the 'previously excluded'. People of the *barrios* were key protagonists in the construction of BA (e.g. the *Comités de Salud*: founders of the healthcare program *Casas de la Salud y la Vida* in April 2003). A clear popular objective (direction) has not been maintained because individual economic desires have prevailed (corruption), instead of a new set of ethics: to construct a new popular healthcare system for the previously excluded; the downfall of BA will be due to internal antagonism, not external pressure. Without the social fabric there is no revolution.

In this context, the Bolivarian Revolution loses its hegemonic position altogether (the social imaginary of fullness or harmony to come is broken) and fails to re-activate (grip) the collective mobilization it previously enjoyed. The 'participative and protagonist' model constructed in 2003 becomes obsolete. The relation between social and political sectors

110   *Populism in Venezuela*

collapses. Democratically, it'll lose its popularity due to a series of irregularities: corrupt practices. I refer to the previous comment regarding the 20,000 workers of BA trying to inform Chávez of managerial irregularities in BA and years of unpaid salaries. In other words, these corrupt practices repeat that 'ill' practice the Chavista platform so much demonized in times of opposition, and accountable for Venezuela's current class inequality.

I have to re-emphasize that the future of this healthcare program and how sustainable the BA program will be is unclear at this stage. Chávez's statement about the conditions of BA on September 20, 2009 unfolds the complexities this healthcare program struggles with:

> We have a social emergency: health. We must all declare a state of emergency. 2,000 BA modules are closed. We are all to blame. Fidel Castro sent me a letter [a] couple of days ago stating: 'I have a moral obligation with this problem in the healthcare service'. Thus, I'll deal with it. We had a meeting in Cuba and Fidel ordered an assessment of all the Cuban Missions. On October 8, 2009, a new lot of 1,111 Cuban Integral medics will join BA's popular consultancies and 213 Venezuelan medics graduated in Cuba. Furthermore, 500 Cuban medical students will be working at primary healthcare modules.[104]

As discussed earlier, on January 7, 2009, Chávez inaugurated a CDI in Caricuao, Caracas, proudly announcing the construction of 3,000 modules in the last three years. However, eight months later, the president acknowledged that 2,000 modules were closed due to their own negligence. Also, with the direct involvement of Castro (Chávez's mentor and ally), Chávez recognized the need to add more Cuban medics to the BA program, as well as 500 Cuban medical students. In order to deal with the shortage of medics, Chávez has been forced to increase the amount of Cubans medics working in BA, incorporate 213 Venezuelan medics who graduated in Cuba, plus 500 Cuban medical students. These statements raise several questions about the sedimentation of BA in Venezuela. The plan to train 20,000 Venezuelans and replace Cuban medics by 2010 was too ambitious.[105] This might resonate with the managerial problems raised by 20,000 revolutionary BA workers who tried to inform Chávez on July 17, 2009 of a 'macabre operation' that could potentially end the mission.

On November 24, 2009, Chávez announced that his personal budget increased by 638 percent to U.S. $1.504 billion—compared with the 2009 ($209 million) figure. He might intend to prevent the spread of 'macabre operations' in BA and other mission programs. José Vicente Carrasquero, a Venezuelan political analyst, argues that 'Chávez shows no trust with the ministerial structure responsible to administer health, education and cultural programs. Therefore, the president has decided to financially administer most Missions from the Presidential office'. Chávez stressed that 'we must win two-thirds of the parliamentarian seats in the September 2010

A *Healthcare Program in Excluded Areas* 111

parliamentarian elections to guarantee the advancement of the revolutionary process. An opposition majority would make laws to sabotage the government'. Chávez sought to 'ensure his electoral popular-base for Chavista candidates in the parliamentarian elections'.[106]

However, in spite of an increase of Chávez's 2010 personal budget and electoral tactics (changing constituency boundaries to benefit Chávez's candidates in the September 2010 parliamentarian elections), Chavistas failed to get the two-thirds majority (see the first section of Chapter 6). Furthermore, returning to the complaints BA workers raised to the president in July 2009, using the 'macabre operation' discourse to warn Chávez of the managerial problems in BA, on November 17, 2010, BA workers from 17 states protested outside Miraflores Presidential Palace. They demanded payment of unpaid salaries to medics and nurses, full-time contract employment, improvement of working standards, and justice for all the unfair dismissals of the cases taken to the employment tribunal. Daniel Padilla, BA workers' union spokesman, said that the military guard of the palace informed them that a representative from the vice-presidency office would arrange an appointment with them.[107] I think their objective was to present their grievances directly to Chávez, not a bureaucrat working in the palace.

The above newspaper reports cast light on a series of distressing internal problems in BA and mission programs in general. For example, 20,000 revolutionary BA workers attempted to inform Chávez in July 2009 of managerial incompetence and 'macabre operations' in the program, and Chávez recognized the need to contract more Cubans in September 2009 as 2,000 BA I modules were closed. Henceforth, Chávez increased his 2010 personal budget from U.S. $209 million to $1.504 billion to finance the missions from the presidency because ministerial/institutional structures were not delivering (i.e. corruption) and to secure a two-thirds majority in the September 2010 parliamentary elections. However, despite having the time and resources aplenty to deal with problems, like the ones presented by BA workers, and to secure a majority in the parliament, Chávez and his machinery fell short.

These are clear signs of fragmentation of sedimentary processes previously consolidated. Those vital periods, encouraging the previously excluded to participate and become 'active agents', are in crisis. That platform of credibility, trust, and honesty between people and political sectors that 'gripped' together 'all' sectors (by subverting their differences) and constructed a common equivalential platform seems to be weakening. If the populist position of the Bolivarian hegemonic project shifts, becoming a discourse that no longer has the ability to embody and fulfill the hopes for the future of Venezuela's poor/excluded people, the meaning of the term 'revolution' becomes redundant and loses all substance.

This article is very rich and complex. It addresses the old 'bipartite' healthcare system and its failure in providing free healthcare to the majority of the population. Laclau's theoretical approach to populism, combined

112 *Populism in Venezuela*

with Glynos and Howarth's methodological explanatory resources, helps us examine this in-depth analysis by sketching out the terrain to analyze a new radical healthcare project in popular areas, the position/role of social and political actors in this process, and ways to situate institutional practices, as well as to categorize hegemonic contestation, institutional displacement, and attempts to construct a new institutional framework.

What I intend to flesh out in this concluding section are the internal problems BA is facing. These types of difficulties can have a detrimental effect on the sedimentation of the Chavista equivalential chain in a wider context. BA has managed to develop and provide a successful healthcare system in remote, rural, and poor areas of Venezuela. This healthcare program is a discursive reflection clearly demonstrating what underprivileged 'people' need and expect from a conscientious and responsive government. Chávez is fully aware of the value and significance of these social programs in the political revolutionary/socialist project he advocates. Nonetheless, we see conditions of possible uncertainties for this populist political project to advance because the popular electoral approval Chávez previously enjoyed seems to be fading away (e.g. 'macabre operation' in the works). If *el pueblo* no longer feels the socialist Bolivarian Revolution signifies fulfillment to come to the popular mass, Chávez and the populist project collapses.

CONCLUSION

In this chapter I described public healthcare in a genealogical context and how this service went through a process of privatization and decentralization—limiting healthcare access for those who could not afford private healthcare. I explained how in 2003, a 'free' healthcare program for the 'excluded' population in Caracas was founded. Community involvement played a key role in the formation of this new healthcare program. This consisted of a 'participative and protagonist model', which was a discussion forum where members of the community, political representatives, and medical personnel met to construct a healthcare program in the *barrios*. This project, providing primary healthcare in impoverished urban and remote areas, proved to be a success. This pilot healthcare project was soon implemented nationwide. The name given to the program 'Deep in the Slums' (*Barrio Adentro*) demonstrates what this program aimed to provide: healthcare in rural and marginal areas for the underprivileged population. A big obstacle for the development of this healthcare project was the criticism and institutional obstructionism from Venezuela's medical authorities. The presence of Cuban medics freely practicing without the control and approval of Venezuela's medical regulatory system brought a sense of 'institutional inertia' in the healthcare system.

In the sections 'Different empirical interpretations of the development of BA' and 'Resistance to BA—institutional inertia', I put into context the

A Healthcare Program in Excluded Areas   113

'us-them' axis that aimed to challenge and displace the anti-Chavista 'hegemonic order' and hence integrate the existing public healthcare infrastructure into the domains of the new radical institutional healthcare system. I employed Glynos and Howarth's methodological critical explanation schema and Laclau's theoretical approach to illustrate the nature of institutional inertia with respect to healthcare practices. At present, this new radical healthcare institution, providing free healthcare for Venezuela's poor, fully depends on Cuba's expertise and medical personnel. In this chapter, I've tried to explain plans to replace Cuban personnel with newly trained Venezuelans graduated in 'Integral General Medicine'. At this stage, it is still difficult to say whether there will be long-term dependence on Cuban medical involvement, and further analysis will be required.

In spite of all these politically driven discourses and tactics to minimize what BA provides to the 'people', based on my own ethnographical observation in three regions of the country, I claim BA has radically transformed 'free' healthcare for Venezuela's underprivileged population. However, I also observed BA personnel complaining because they have not received their wages for months. These accounts relate to the BA workers' attempt in July 2009 to hand over a document to Chávez stressing a series of irregularities in BA which are harming the program and stressing that thousands of workers have not been paid. These committed 'socialist workers' for the revolutionary process are warning Chávez of a 'macabre operation' in BA that could end this healthcare program and the principles of the Bolivarian Revolution.

Chávez increased his 2010 presidential office budget to finance the missions from the presidential office to alleviate these types of obstacles in these popular social programs. But still, by the end of 2010, these BA workers changed their discourse from 'requests' to 'demands' (these anecdotes can be seen as the beginning of the end of the populist project that promised fulfillment to the previously excluded), protesting outside the Presidential Palace ('power of decisions'—referring to Laclau's terms; see pages 28–30 in Chapter 1). It appears their grievances have been ignored once again. In a sense, the results of the September 26, 2010 parliamentary elections can be a reflection of Chávez's popularity.

In the Venezuelan context, it is a big challenge to avoid misuse of funds in a program operating 3,000 BA I modules and 1,000 BA II centers. On September 20, 2009, Chávez announced that 2,000 BA I modules were closed. It further demonstrated the complexity of managing a program of this size effectively. Corruption is a longstanding socio-cultural problem in Venezuela. With a new set of agents/groups managing new institutional structures, it is foreseeable that that element of desire/unethical greed (power and money) would reappear, ignoring what revolutionary 'radical change' (fullness to come) signifies to the people.

5 The Anti-Bolivarian Student Movement

New Social Actors Challenge the Advancement of Venezuela's Bolivarian Radicalism

As discussed in the sub-section 'New Opposition Forces' (page 80) in Chapter 3, in May 2007, a student movement emerged and temporarily succeeded in challenging the Bolivarian project with a new form of opposition discourse until the end of 2007. Students from different universities organized and constructed a protest strategy that took the Bolivarian hegemonic project and opposition supporters by surprise. This movement of young university students claimed to have no political affiliation with opposition parties. Their initial aim was to challenge the government's decision not to renew the broadcasting license of the private TV channel *Radio Caracas Televisión* (RCTV).

We are looking at this movement because an in-depth analysis of this anti-Bolivarian group can help us comprehend what the opposition political machinery lacked, and how this new social sector added new discursive elements to the opposition camp in order to challenge the expansion and sedimentation of the Bolivarian hegemonic project. The previous chapter was an in-depth analysis of a new healthcare program seeking to provide a free healthcare system for the population living in marginal and rural areas of the country. This chapter analyses how an anti-Bolivarian movement was formed, its demands, and its methods of challenging the expansion of government control, and why this student movement failed to transform itself into a long-term opposition force. A 'thick descriptive' analysis of two opposed cases in a dichotomized society is a key component of this investigation as it provides an understanding of people's circumstances from both camps, and of how different elements of social practices are politically articulated.

This analysis seeks to achieve two important objectives. The first is to flesh out how elements of youth—new, fresh, apolitical, innocent, and so on—are employed to challenge the expansion of the Bolivarian hegemonic project. The second is to define the antagonistic nature of a new generation of anti-Bolivarians that sought to 'grip' people from other sectors in a deeply divided society. By conducting ethnographic fieldwork and interviews with student leaders in different regions of Venezuela, this analysis of this young student movement describes the nature of the movement and the discourse used to block the expansion and sedimentation of the Bolivarian socialist hegemonic project. The student movement, while it starts off with a lot of possibilities and optimism and seems to constitute a challenge to the new hegemonic project, ultimately failed and was absorbed into other opposition political parties. In this chapter I explain why this movement failed to crystallize its full potential to contest the Bolivarian project.

The first section of this chapter describes how this movement emerged, its formative process, and how media exposure helped this student protest position itself as a new opposition force in Venezuela. It also describes the events that crystallized this movement, its key leaders, and the discourse used to represent this non-partisan movement. The second section discusses the diverging interpretations of this anti-Bolivarian movement found in the literature. To conclude, by employing Glynos and Howarth's critical explanation and Laclau's theoretical approach, the flaws in the latter interpretations are addressed, followed by an analysis of the student movement's success and its failure to evolve and continue challenging the expansion of the Bolivarian hegemonic project.

5.1 DESCRIPTION OF THE STUDENT MOVEMENT AND ITS DISCOURSE

The student movement became a major opposition force in Venezuela when the government insisted on not renewing RCTV's broadcasting license on May 28, 2007. Days prior to the termination of RCTV's license, students from *Universidad Católica Andres Bello* (UCAB), *Universidad Simon Bolívar* (USB), and *Universidad Central de Venezuela* (UCV) started protesting outside their university campuses. They claimed that 'with no RCTV the population would no longer have the right to be objectively informed because most other private channels made a treaty with the government'.[1] On May 28, 2007, students from universities in Caracas joined the protest against the closure of RCTV, shouting rhythms like '"freedom of speech . . . this is our future". The police violently dispersed the students with teargas and blank rifle shots, injuring seventeen students'.[2] Student demonstrations also took place in other cities. 'Chavistas supporters responded by shooting students with live ammunition. Fourteen students were injured, one seriously'.[3]

The second phase, critical for the galvanization of this new student movement, was when parliamentarians of '*Podemos*' (a Bolivarian political party that had recently defected and joined the opposition; see pages 69 and 82 in Chapter 3) assured the students that they would do everything to allow student representatives to raise their concerns in the parliament. In the parliament, Ricardo Gutierrez of *Podemos* stated that 'parliamentarians must do all they can to open any forms of discussion and dialogue. We cannot sit here comfortably seeing our universities paralyzed, our youth on the streets taking unnecessary risks with the police and National Guard

116   *Populism in Venezuela*

shooting and bombing them with teargas'.[4] The parliamentary director-
ate accepted the students' request to raise their concerns about freedom of
speech and the closure of RCTV in the format of a debate.[5]

On June 7, 2007, anti-Bolivarian student representatives expressed their
views at the parliament, which was broadcasted live on television and radio.
After speaking, they left the parliament, refusing to be part of the debate
with invited Bolivarian students and parliamentarians.[6] In the parliament,
Douglas Barrios from *Universidad Metropolitana* in Caracas stated:

> . . . [we] we are here in this rostrum to disseminate our rejection to
> the arbitrary closure of RCTV, the way our right to demonstrate was
> assaulted and the abuse inflicted upon the student movement. . . .
> Today, we don't come here to debate. . . but to reinstate civil liberties
> . . . we are not here to talk about our political leanings . . . we have ide-
> ological differences between us . . . we acknowledge the need to have a
> framework of pluralism where common ideas can be constructed. . . .
> Students are not socialists, we are social beings. We are not neoliberals,
> we are liberated beings. We are not the opposition; we are a proposi-
> tion. . . . Youth is not on the streets today fighting for business interests
> or political tendencies. We are on the streets making politics without
> traditional politicians, fighting for our nation, protecting the interests
> of our society . . . all Venezuelans should be treated the same, with
> no discrimination . . . we believe in equality. . . . We don't believe the
> hegemony of the minority nor the majority . . . we promote reconcilia-
> tion. . . . Our classrooms are on the streets, we don't ask, we demand
> the restoration of civil liberties . . . we are armed with consciousness,
> solidarity, optimism and modesty . . . a new generation that will fight
> today, tomorrow and forever to be free and genuine Humanists. Noth-
> ing else to say. . . . For now. [7]

Barrios's speech unfolds interesting elements about the student movement.
First, the closure of RCTV (the opposition TV channel) is no longer the
main reason why students are challenging the Bolivarian project. The
opportunity to address the nation with TV and 'live' radio coverage from a
center stage in parliament gave students the platform to shift their position
and expand into other contexts. Barrios recognizes ideological differences
amongst them; however, via pluralistic practices common ideas can be constructed. Their objective is to distance themselves from traditional opposition politics and represent a new socio-political frontier where differences
are respected and common interests agreed upon. Discursively, this is what
they want to convey by stating: 'we are not socialists . . . we are not neoliberals . . . we are a proposition'. Another interesting remark involves the use
of the term 'hegemony'. They don't accept a dominant hegemonic practice
that benefits neither the minority nor the majority of the population. It
appears that students think that via 'reconciliation', conflicts of interest in

this deeply polarized society can be resolved. Another new concept introduced in Barrios's speech is 'humanism'. I'll elaborate on the significance of this concept for this movement in the next section. And finally, in my view, there is the odd (to some extent plagiaristic) use of 'For now' (*Por ahora*), Chávez's catchphrase from his speech during the failed coup in February 1992 (see pages 50–51 in Chapter 2), in this anti-Chavista context. Discursively, the objective is to capitalize on its symbolic significance and get support from Bolivarian popular sectors.

Due to constant media coverage (i.e. *Globovisión*: the only opposition TV channel) of students demonstrating in Caracas and the 'live' broadcast in the parliament, there was a reason to believe this student movement was a national representation of anti-Chavista students. National media exposure provided the ideal platform for key university representatives who orally expressed their dissatisfaction with government decisions. The population assumed that the internal dynamics of this new student movement consisted of university representatives from various regions of the country, and that the student leaders seen and heard on TV were internally selected.[8] We question, how and in what context was this student movement formed?

According to Gustavo Tovar Arroyo (mentor, writer, and organizer of the student movement)[9], the student movement was formed after the failed coup in April 2002. It was founded by a new generation of young Venezuelans that shared a common concern about civil and human rights in Venezuela, a country divided by two political camps. Tovar Arroyo recounts that on April 11, 2002, the government and political opposition groups ordered '*el pueblo*' (people) to shoot each other. Students realized the need to call for dialogue instead of killing each other. Instead, the government encouraged more discrimination. 'None of our attempts to stop the government's misuse of power worked (strikes, referenda, using the judicial system); nonetheless, slowly and undetected by the authorities, a feeling of freedom emerged: the Venezuelan youth'.[10]

When Chávez announced his intention to close RCTV in December 2006, workshops on human rights principles with university and school students nationwide were organized. The closure of RCTV 'violated two human rights: freedom of expression and freedom of thought'.[11] Days before RCTV's closure, a nonviolent demonstration with representatives from various universities was organized. Students said: 'we shall not fight nor protest because of the closure of RCTV, but for human rights: freedom of expression and freedom of thought'. After their first march on May 28, 2007, 'more than eighty university representatives of the capital gathered to determine ways to expand this movement. They discussed their rights, politics, strategy, history, political organization and humanism'.[12]

Rayma López, a student leader who has been involved in student movements since 1998, gives us a different version of the emergence of the student movement. López points out that 'there was a student forum with student representatives from different regions of the country. However,

118 Populism in Venezuela

there was a degree of discontent from representatives not from Caracas because representatives from universities in the capital dominated the *Red Democrática Universitaria Estudiantil*. López claims that Tovar Arroyo's April 2002 version of the foundation of the student movement is incorrect. There were university groups already functioning. The *Red Democrática Universitaria Estudiantil* was a national student union federation founded in 2002. 'Student leaders met, but as the police intelligence harassed and prosecuted them, these meetings came to a halt'.[13]

Referring to Tovar Arroyo's account regarding the expansion of the student movement after May 28, 2007, López stressed that 'many universities with fewer students were simply excluded from the committee Tovar Arroyo mentions. Universities outside the capital were regarded as irrelevant'. López represented the state-run pedagogical universities nationwide, and struggled to persuade the 'group' to select her. She said: 'with all the pedagogical campuses across the country, we are the largest in Venezuela. I demanded our presence; otherwise, I was going to speak to the "media" as it violates the human rights principles they are advocating'.[14] Thus, I gather that the student movement Tovar Arroyo describes was mainly formed by representatives from universities in Caracas.

This implies that the student representatives seen and heard in the media in this period were from universities in Caracas. In his book, Tovar Arroyo states that during discussion meetings there were up to 127 student representatives. It was impossible to form a consensus among so many participants, so the movement decided to form what was called the G-8: student representatives from eight universities in Caracas. Twenty-five representatives formed the committee of which student representatives like Alexis Cabrera, Stalin Gonzales, Fabricio Briceño, Ricardo Sánchez, Rayma López, Yon Goicoechea, and Freddy Guevara were members.[15] These were the students who played a key leadership role in the 2007 student movement. This section describes how the student movement benefitted from media coverage—i.e. protesting against the closure of RCTV at the end of May 2007, its opportunity to publicize itself by speaking in the parliament, internal dynamics, and so on. However, the discourse used to represent this anti-Bolivarian student project and its socio-political significance in Venezuela's deeply polarized society has not been addressed yet.

5.1.1 Student discourse: '*Resistencia* & *Manos Blancas*'

The discourses that were to signify this anti-Bolivarian student movement were '*Resistencia*' (resistance) and '*Manos Blancas*' (white hands). Students created these symbols after contesting the government's decision not to renew RCTV's broadcasting license at the end of May 2007. *Resistencia* was the term chosen to contest the constitutional amendments presented in the December 2007 referendum.[16] Discursively, however, the meaning of 'resistance' as an anti-Bolivarian symbolic signifier was rather limited. It only put across an

The Anti-Bolivarian Student Movement 119

ordinary political message that didn't capitalize on the movements' attributes, such as youth, students, a new generation, non-partisanship, and so on. The discursive impact of *Manos Blancas* was more productive in challenging the expansion of the Bolivarian hegemonic project.

López recollects that in a meeting, various university representatives discussed their ideas about a symbol for the movement. 'There were many ideas . . . a white pigeon, a globe . . . until a student who was making a poster raised her hands "painted in white" to tell everyone to stop! because so many of them were talking at the same time about their symbol/icon ideas. When everyone looked at her with her white hands, quickly they realized that "white hands" was by far the best idea'. This meeting was after the May 28, 2007 RCTV closure demonstration.[17]

After the RCTV closure, *Manos Blancas* became a new form of opposition discourse detached from conventional politics. *Manos Blancas* was an anti-Chavista symbol used in demonstration banners, pamphlets, posters, and t-shirts, and an identity-code commonly used by painting palms of hands in white. For example, days after the closure of RCTV on May 28, 2007, a student clearly stated the significance of *Manos Blancas* to this new movement:

> Students are tired of a Venezuela divided by colors (political ideology/ affiliation) . . . we rest upon on reconciliation. Our movement has no political aspirations despite our firm call to the government for justice and respect. The only color we represent is ours: '*Manos Blancas*', a symbol of freedom. These hands shall stand to change our lives and mould our history. . . . Venezuela, we promise, we shall continue our peaceful demand for freedom and respect to our rights. . . . Enough of spectators! We are tired of division and polarization! Enough of labeling us with colors! [18]

This brief speech gives us a glimpse of what *Manos Blancas* signifies to the student movement. They stress their detachment from the opposition political apparatus by articulating the meaning of 'color' in political discourse, implying that their color is *Manos Blancas*—a logo signifying reconciliation, peace, respect, nonviolence, freedom, freshness, etc. In other words, it is a simple logo/symbol that aimed to get (grip) the support of people from both camps.

This symbol's apparent detachment from contaminated political sectors, associated with the de-instituted institutional system, helped the students open a new frontier that could have gradually developed into a new political project. The strategy to contest the Bolivarian hegemonic order with nonviolence and agonistic reconciliation had the potential to displace the government and re-institute another form of fulfillment to the people. According to Rayma López, *Manos Blancas* is an iconic symbol that provided a variety of groups with a unifying identity. Nonetheless, many viewed it as a rather powerless 'nonviolence' symbol. A better symbol for students in other regions

120 Populism in Venezuela

of the country was 'Manos Negras' (black hands). For students that burn tires, painting their hands 'white' was out of context; they didn't have the media coverage vis-à-vis those in Caracas. They had to resort to conventional demonstration methods to repel police attacks.[19]

From a post-structuralist perspective, the symbol Manos Blancas became an 'empty signifier' representing the underdog against an unresponsive and repressive decision-making power. For example, if we go back to Chapter 2 (pages 50–51), the 'Por ahora' in Chávez's 1992 brief televised speech—informing other coup plotters to surrender—'gripped' a variety of dissatisfied social sectors that energetically welcomed what the Bolivarian movement intended to do, in spite of its undemocratic method of overthrowing a government. The Manos Blancas symbol was also a 'gripping' signifier centered on what the opposition 'lacked' (e.g. reduction of freedom of speech by not renewing RCTV's broadcasting license, new opposition representatives, right for peaceful demonstrations, etc.) and bypassed the political machinery, which had little credibility to the anti-Chavista social camp. Chávez's 'Por ahora' was a signifier that was socially and politically galvanizing. However, the creators/actors of the Manos Blancas signifier failed to fully comprehend both its social meaning beyond its nonviolence context and the possibilities of transforming the student movement into an equivalential political project (by subordinating differences among opposition political parties) that would challenge the Bolivarian hegemonic order. I'll elaborate on these points in the last section of this chapter.

The student movement played a key role in the December 2007 referendum (see pages 83–87 in Chapter 3). Nonetheless, I argue that students' involvement in Venezuela's socio-political turmoil quickly changed. Perhaps as a result of manipulation by opposition political parties, the movement started to adopt political strategies rather than keeping its 'reconciliation, nonviolence, and non-partisan' (Manos Blancas) principles. These non-political planks were, perhaps unconsciously, brushed aside when the students campaigned against the constitutional amendment referendum at the end of May 2007 (months after the closure of RCTV). Alvarez rightly includes participants in the student movement as new political agents that helped to defeat Chávez in the December 2007 referendum.[20] I find diverging interpretations of the student movement in the literature. In my view, addressing them could give us different perspectives on the student movement and provide us with a fuller picture of its strengths and weaknesses. Furthermore, what the literature fails to address will be fleshed out and analyzed in the last section of this chapter.

5.2 Diverging Interpretations of the Anti-Bolivarian Student Movement

In this section, I discuss three diverging interpretations of the student movement. The first case is from Tovar Arroyo, addressing what he claims to be

The Anti-Bolivarian Student Movement 121

the movement's ideological plank and strategic methods. The second analysis is of a case from Ramon Casanova, an academic researcher at UCV who argues that this movement primarily consists of students that enjoy and promote neoliberal practices, and feel threatened by the institutional changes this new hegemonic order wants to expand and consolidate. The last paper is a critique written by members of a newly formed Bolivarian educational institution called '*Universidad Socialista del Pueblo*' (People's Socialist University). They argue that this *Manos Blancas* student movement is not what it claims to be.

5.2.1 The Student Movement:
Humanism, Reconciliation, and Nonviolent Action

According Tovar Arroyo, the movement follows the principles of 'humanism' (a concept I categorize as ideological); 'these principles are clearly stated in the Universal Declaration of Human Rights'.[21] Humanism is strongly connected to 30 human rights principles. The movement highlights the importance of understanding and following these principles to the task of humanizing civilization. 'As Martin Luther King pointed out, this is not just a national issue but also a problem that crosses barriers and needs to be dealt with in other lands'.[22]

Tovar Arroyo claims that Chávez's '"Socialism or Death" discourse is an ideological persecution and a death threat to half of the country'. He questions: 'is it possible to distance ourselves from ideological prejudice and live together peacefully? If the incumbent imposes "Socialism or Death" in Venezuela, limiting people's freedom, there shall be no room for us to coexist'.[23] According to Tovar Arroyo, the humanist *Generación 2007* (the name given to the student movement, perhaps in an attempt to associate it with the famous student movement *Generación 28* in Venezuela's struggle for democracy—see page 44 in Chapter 2) was a movement that campaigned for human and civil rights and reconciliation. Comments like '"Socialism or Death" is a death threat to half of the country' discursively shows how anxious they are if this socialist project advances. The significance of socialism and the way Chávez articulated it as the next phase of the revolution after being re-elected in December 2006 alarmed many Venezuelans.

The *Generación 2007* tried to let society know that it was possible to improve relations among supporters from both camps via reconciliation and dialogue. Mahatma Ghandi's nonviolence methods were central strategic practices for the student movement. 'To Gandhi, the idea of nonviolence transforms the heart of the opponent, not break it.' Gene Sharp, a nonviolence theorist and methodologist inspired by Ghandi's struggle, outlines methods of articulating humanism with a nonviolence strategy. According to Tovar Arroyo, Sharp's theoretical contribution has furnished the students' nonviolence methods. Sharp discusses political power in his book

122   *Populism in Venezuela*

'"*La Lucha Política no Violenta*" [Politics of Nonviolent Action], describing 198 concepts and methods of nonviolent action'.[24]

Tovar Arroyo states that the first step for a nonviolence struggle was to inform people of the 30 human rights articles the 'dictator' (i.e. Chávez) violates, and to train them in nonviolence techniques such as disobedience and non-cooperation.[25] 'To be free, a citizen must control the power structure (and its emergence), consolidate its institutions and independent organizations (to counter-balance political power); in other words, promptly act when freedom is threatened. Citizens gave the "dictator" political power, not the other way round. The nonviolence strategy aims to convert every man (*al hombre*)—not enslave him/her'.[26] The students are discursively implying that a traumatized future of slavery, prohibition, and repression is ahead if the nonviolence strategy is not articulated.[27] From a post-structuralist perspective, their objective is to 'grip' the population, '"filling up" or "completing" the void in the subject and the structure of social relations by bringing about closure'.[28] Glynos and Howarth's logic of fantasy helps us explain how these practices discursively articulate a sense of fear and the horrific dimension if the 'dictator' is not contested. More crucially, the students try to imagine a future portraying themselves and those that reject the dictator as deficient human beings. This is the method that 'grips' and attempts to convince people in a dichotomized society of the threat the Chavista hegemonic order imposes upon them, and a sense of urgency to challenge this dictatorial regime.

This sub-section narrates Tovar Arroyo's account of the emergence of the student movement, its humanist perspective, its human rights and reconciliation discourse, and its use of Sharp's nonviolent action. The *Manos Blancas* symbol addressed in the previous section was the discourse students used to discursively signify these nonviolent and peaceful intentions Tovar Arroyo describes in his book. Next, I'll discuss an article titled 'The Revolt of the Venezuelan Students in 2007—The Political Emergence of a Generation (*La Revuelta de los Estudiantes Venezolanos del 2007—El Levantamiento Político de una Generación*)', written by Ramon Casanova. This analysis contextualizes the student movement from a completely different angle, thus teasing out interesting class-based elements of the students and the educational structure in Venezuela.

5.2.2   Students: Product of Neoliberal Practices

Ramon Casanova, a UCV research professor at *Centro de Estudios de Desarrollo* (CENDE), argues that we have to analyze the students' social fabric in order to understand what's behind this anti-Bolivarian movement. According to Casanova, the student movement that began in 2007 is a product of the global hegemonic neo-conservative cultural revolution (from the Thatcher and Reagan era) that has shifted cultural values in the last 30 years.[29]

The Anti-Bolivarian Student Movement 123

Casanova's arguments reflect the extent to which Bolivarian institutional changes challenge an educational structure designed to benefit individuals that support and enjoy neoliberal class-based values. In a broader context, the students participating in this movement reject this new political structure, what it signifies, and the threat it inflicts upon their own socio-economic conditions, which includes their educational system—and they do so in a way tailored to satisfy their own social agenda.[30] In the late 1980s and 1990s, neoliberal practices were introduced into education. Casanova states that by 1994 there were 32 universities: 17 state and 15 private. In 1999, the number increased to 40: 19 state (public) and 21 private. In other words, there were more private than state universities.[31] State universities were forced to comply with a set of neoliberal institutional changes. A new mode of experimental management courses was introduced and managers started to make decisions previously made by academics.[32]

The students that participate in this movement are a product of social adaptation to neoliberal economic practices.[33] These students welcome the ideology of neoliberal capitalism as a structure that promises an illusion of fulfillment in the future. They feel threatened by a daunting revolution that promises an unconvincing future to them. The students' aim is to protect social and educational differences to guarantee the reproduction of their technocratic-elitist position.[34] The closure of a private anti-Bolivarian TV channel (RCTV) signified the unavoidable end of the old institutional structure. Casanova claims that 'this is a class revolt against the new order, not the other way round'.[35]

Referring to Douglas Barrios's speech in the parliament on June 7, 2007 (discussed in the previous section), Casanova uses the discourse Barrios articulates as evidence to substantiate his claim that these students are a product of 1980s and 1990s neo-conservative values. For example, Barrios addresses political ideologies by stating: 'students are not socialists, we are social beings. We are not neoliberals, we are liberated beings. We are not the opposition; we are a proposition'. Casanova argues that Barrios's statement implies that students promote the values of pluralistic liberalism in a democratic context, and that liberty subverts equality.[36]

According to Casanova, this student movement is only an upper-middle class protest against new hegemonic practices. At home and in school, these students live in their own social micro-world, and what they hear from the media is a very negative interpretation of the Bolivarian project and what democratic socialism means. 'They are petrified of Socialism; they view it as the apocalypse. Liberal thinking provides the basic principles for freedom, individualism and private rights'.[37] In retrospect, Venezuelan students of the 1960s supported left-wing principles and protested for administrative changes in universities. However, this 2007 student movement was protesting to defend global conservatism.[38]

For example, Casanova characterizes Father Luis Ugalde, the rector of *Universidad Católica Andrés Bello* (an established private university in the

124 *Populism in Venezuela*

capital) as one of the most influential ideological figures of the movement, who describes the movement (in a hagiographic manner) as the savior of a fractured society by 'offering' a way out of the violence and harassment the authoritarian government imposes upon them.[39] In my view, Casanova's interpretation of the student movement only focuses on the events he observes in the UCV and universities in Caracas and on what is seen through the media. Casanova gives a lot of attention to Stalin Gonzales, president of UCV's student movement (who joined party politics after graduating), Ricardo Sánchez, who replaced Stalin Gonzales in the UCV leadership, and Yon Goicoechea, a prominent student leader from *Universidad Católica Andrés Bello* who much benefited from media coverage.[40]

Casanova describes the anti-Bolivarian student movement as a social product of global hegemonic neo-conservatism. Casanova's argument fundamentally rests on the impact the Bolivarian hegemonic project is having upon the educational structure, instituted to benefit the population with better socio-economic conditions vis-à-vis popular class-based sectors. The next interpretation is also a strong critique of the student movement. This paper claims that Sharp's nonviolence methodology as practiced by the students (discussed in Tovar Arroyo's interpretative sub-section) is ill founded. It also criticizes the apolitical, pure, and defenseless image this movement tries to portray with the *Manos Blancas* symbol, and the disguised connection student leaders have with opposition right-wing parties.

5.2.3 Bolivarian perception of the *Manos Blancas*' Student Movement

The paper '*El movimiento de las "Manos Blancas"*', published by the Analytical Strategy Center of the People's Socialist University founded in 2007, addresses interesting points. They argue that Sharp's theory of nonviolent 'resistance' in the book *From Dictatorship to Democracy* uses dubious cases and methods to describe what a dictatorship is without historically contextualizing these points. Conclusively, cases are categorized as free or not free in a rather law-like manner to suit their own schema. Sharp discusses 198 methods to oust dictatorships and dictators, which are somewhat obvious, with a protest and persuasion, no cooperation, and intervention layout.[41] 'In order to conduct this analysis we have to agree, without any doubt, that we are dealing with a dictatorial and despotic regime. Nationally and internationally, students claim that the "State" in Venezuela uses repressive, arbitrary and violent methods. They pretend to be innocent unarmed victims prosecuted by a "brutal and genocidal" government'.[42]

According to the authors from the *Universidad Socialista del Pueblo*, this sense of victimization (to a certain extent cynical) hides the true intentions of this movement. Student discourse seeks to portray them as spontaneous and open. These tactics have given them a lot of popularity. It isn't difficult to understand the meaning of the 'Open Hand' symbol. 'Subconsciously,

The Anti-Bolivarian Student Movement   125

it convinces people that the movement (mainly university students) has "good intentions"; that they are "genuine", "spontaneous"—almost infantile: everyone look: we are not armed, we don't hide anything![43] They point out that 'if we compare it with other "spontaneous" movements using the same symbol ("Open Hand"), inspired by Sharp's "nonviolence" theory, we see interesting affinities. For instance, 'the Open Hand gradually changed to be a Fist'.[44] That is precisely what's happened with *Manos Blancas*. The symbol has changed, discursively articulating 'resistance' with a 'Fist' symbol—'the same as the one used in Serbia to oust Milosevic in 2000'.[45] 'They've plagiarized Serbia's OTPOR! Fist'.[46] This interpretation of the origin of this *Manos Blancas* symbol differs from the one I described in the previous section.

The authors state that 'we cannot forget this movement—contextualized in various forms (e.g. changing names) pretends to be apolitical, pure—acting like humiliated victims. It is obvious that not all "*Manos Blancas*" students are aware how they are manipulated by foreign organizations'. Some are right-wing students that strategically distanced themselves from opposition parties. However, 'once they achieve their objectives, they join those parties. In spite of this, society still views them as spontaneous, "pure", even innocent'. They claim to be the underdog, victims of a government that wants to antagonize them.[47]

Authors of the *El movimiento de las 'Manos Blancas'* paper criticize Sharp's theoretical framework by arbitrating what dictatorship is. They also argue that the student movement wrongly accuses the Venezuelan Government of being 'brutal and genocidal'—and use Sharp's flawed and unfounded theoretical approach. Furthermore, they claim that students are connected with foreign and right-wing interests (it could be because Yon Goicoechea received a U.S. $500,000 prize from the 'Milton Friedman Prize for Advancing Liberty' in April 2008,[48] and his decision to join '*Primero de Justicia*': a centre-right party). However, such claims have not been substantiated in the paper. Opposition party politics and foreign engagement prior to the closure of RCTV on May 28, 2007 is doubtful. Nonetheless, Goicoechea accepting the prize and becoming an active member of the opposition has weakened that element of 'freshness-grip' the students enjoyed in 2007.

In this section, three descriptive interpretations of the student movement have been addressed. The first interpretation described the movement as a humanist one seeking reconciliation in a dichotomized society, and implementing Sharp's nonviolent action tactics to contest the next phase of the revolution. The second case described this movement as a product of neo-conservatism contesting the advancement of the Bolivarian hegemonic project. The third case criticized Sharp's methods of nonviolent action, and claims that the student movement pretends to be 'spontaneous, genuine, infantile, apolitical and pure'. My views of the narratives and claims these authors articulate are given in the next section. Based on

126 *Populism in Venezuela*

ethnographic fieldwork, I'll describe why these claims are believed to be inaccurate and/or misleading. The next section begins by analyzing Tovar Arroyo's account of the formation of the movement, its humanist stance, reconciliation strategy, and nonviolent action. Also, the flaws in Casanova's class-based critique of the movement will be fleshed out. Furthermore, the interpretations and arguments raised in the *El movimiento de las 'Manos Blancas'* paper will be addressed.

5.3 CRITIQUE OF THE THREE INTERPRETATIONS OF THE STUDENT MOVEMENT

Tovar Arroyo's book provides a genealogical, ideological, and strategic outlook on the *Generación 2007* student movement. However, based on interview sources, I find contradictions in Tovar Arroyo's claim regarding the formation of the student movement after the failed April 2002 coup. Rayma López states that there was a national student mechanism called *Red Democrática Universitaria Estudiantil* before the April 2002 version Tovar Arroyo mentions. His account that student discussion didn't occur prior to the April 2002 appears to be incorrect. There was a dialogue among students from different universities in the country before the latter date. Danny Ramírez, a student leader from the state Táchira (600 miles from Caracas), agrees with López's side of the story. I'll elaborate on Ramírez's involvement in student demonstrations later.

As Tovar Arroyo points out, the student movement promoted reconciliation through dialogue in a deeply fragmented society. However, the regular use of the term 'dictator/dictatorship' in his analysis—i.e. discourse that condemns Chávez and the regime before a dialogue for reconciliation occurs, does not lay the right foundations, as it were, for both camps to share some common ground and develop a reconciliation process. If anything, claiming that the president is a 'dictator' could have further consolidated the Bolivarian hegemonic project. These types of statements, trying to demonize Chávez and thus separate him from his deep popular support, in my view, only work with people that share similar class-based conditions. Venezuela's popular class, living with different socio-economic circumstances for many years, need something radical to happen, for them to change sides.

That attempt to break Chávez's symbolic power among with his grassroots supporters (*el pueblo*—the previously excluded) needs a radical social and political project that requires the participation of the 'people'. Only claiming that Chávez is a 'dictator' is not sufficient to break that social grip (fullness to come) Chávez still enjoys and politically nurtures. In my view, the only way to displace this revolutionary process is if a popular social movement forces Chávez to resign or vote for the opposition, because he and the Chavista political machinery have failed to deliver what they

The Anti-Bolivarian Student Movement   127

promised to the masses. Chavismo is deeply ingrained in Venezuela's social fabric. As Caldera pointed out when he pardoned Chávez in 1994, Chávez was part of Venezuela's destiny, a factor that could not be ignored (see page 52 in Chapter 2).

Furthermore, in practice, Tovar Arroyo's reconciliation account appears to be different. According to López, 'reconciliation was only mentioned when the media was there. Once, Chavista students went to one of our meetings; there was a very brief moment of dialogue that concluded with gunshots (the top tells them not to talk to us. They get a lot of benefits for their Bolivarian support)'. Sharp's 'nonviolent action', mentioned by Tovar Arroyo, 'was a discourse that helped to congregate students and civilians in the marches—reassuring them that the police would not attack them. However, the riot police didn't attack because the media (live) was reporting the event'.[49]

Jhonny Prada, a student leader in San Cristobal, Táchira, mentions: 'we never plan a violent march. However, when the authorities want to disperse us using pellet shots, we respond with stones. Injuries have been horrific'.[50] Prada notes that internal discussions and plans are agreed upon. However, 'discourse related with human rights, humanism, nonviolence and reconciliation as Tovar Arroyo claims—are not subjects of discussion in our meetings. The discussion/debate focuses on planning and thus reacting accordingly in the march'. It seems that we are dealing with different student movements altogether. 'Our difference with Caracas is that their media coverage guarantees a pacific march, but here in Táchira, we have no alternative but to burn'.[51] This is what López referred to earlier as the '*Manos Negras*' (black hands). In my view, Tovar Arroyo's *Generación 2007* only represents students from universities in Caracas. The student movement he describes was not a unified/equivalential student project incorporating students from different educational sectors of the country.

Regarding Casanova's description of the student movement, my main criticism of his claims is his deterministic view that these students are only a product of neoliberal practices (neo-conservatism is the term he uses). Also, in my view, he makes the mistake of categorizing the student movement seen through the media as a national student opposition movement, which is not the case. Class-based generalization in this context does not give us an accurate picture of the student movement he analyses. As a non-participant observer,[52] I attended a student documentary shooting on January 7, 2008, where 12 students expressed their views and recounted their experiences during the 2007 events. A student representing UCV's Social Studies School mentioned her humble background and family sympathy for socialist ideals. However, she strongly rejected this 'socialist version' the government was imposing upon the people.[53]

On June 3, 2007, Ricardo Sánchez, the UCV student president noted: 'Government discourse only promotes segregation and differences. I'm from Catia (a poor/underprivileged area in the west of Caracas), but there

128　*Populism in Venezuela*

are also students from Lagunita (a wealthy district with golf courses and affluent homes). The UCV is diverse (class) and is determined to fight for citizens' rights. We don't accept social polarization'.[54] I accept that a considerable proportion of the students that contest the expansion of the Bolivarian project have a middle class background. Nonetheless, to claim that the student movement is just a class revolt against the new hegemonic order, in my view, is an incomplete and misleading argument.

The *El movimiento de las 'Manos Blancas'* paper highlights important aspects of the student movement and its practices. Its critique of Sharp's nonviolent action theory is based on the authors' rejection of the movement's claim that the regime is 'dictatorial and despotic'. However, there is no doubt that heavy-handed police tactics used at demonstrations led to injuries and deaths. Also, there is no reference in the paper to sustain the link between Sharp's nonviolent action method and the student movement. I guess the authors refer to Tovar Arroyo's book. They don't seem to realize that the student movement in Caracas is different from the Táchira student movement, where Sharp's nonviolent actions are not followed. Furthermore, the discourse used to describe the students as 'innocent', 'pure', 'almost infantile' ('everyone look: we are not armed, we don't hide anything!'), and 'victims' does not objectively reflect what this movement proposes. This paper seeks to demean the *Manos Blancas* movement and its ability to challenge the expansion of the Bolivarian project.

Nonetheless, the paper provides helpful observations, claiming that the *Manos Blancas* symbol was plagiarized from the Serbian resistance movement in 1998. Also, it stresses the connection of key student leaders with right-wing opposition political parties and foreign organizations. However, there is no evidence to substantiate these claims. In the next sub-section I analyze why this anti-Bolivarian student project failed to advance and evolve effectively after the 2007 events. Along with Laclau's theoretical populist schema of logics of difference and equivalence, Glynos and Howarth's critical explanation will be used to furnish an analytical approach.

5.4　THE STUDENT SOVEMENT: ITS SUCCESS AND FAILURE

To comprehend why this radical populist Bolivarian project emerged and successfully finds ways to evolve, we have to put into context the socio-political and economic problems in Venezuela before the emergence of this Bolivarian populist phenomenon (discussed in Chapter 2). Social antagonism was the force that made possible the emergence of a new political project demanding radical change. Tovar Arroyo claims that the student movement aimed to construct a platform of 'reconciliation' between two polarized camps. In my view, there are no possibilities for a reconciliatory platform to materialize. This new generation never experienced and thus did not fully understand what the socio-political significance of the

The Anti-Bolivarian Student Movement 129

moments of dislocation in the 1980s and 1990s, nor what they entailed. These are fundamental standpoints that explain why there is dichotomization in Venezuela and the conditions that fragmented the institutional framework the students want to re-instate. If we think of similar circumstances: can a young South African fully understand what apartheid signifies to others without ever experiencing these struggles and traumas? Or for a young German to comprehend the conditions between the two Germanys before the Berlin Wall collapsed?

Those moments of dislocation gave Chávez the opportunity to articulate a populist project. To contest and displace the Bolivarian hegemony requires a new political frontier that grips popular grassroots supporters. Discursively, the '*Generación 2007*' represented something very different from the previously excluded '*pueblo*'; in spite of their discourse of human rights, reconciliation, freedom, and peace, the students represented neoliberalism. Most of the popular mass viewed the students as a movement that intended to defend their class-based ideology vis-à-vis the revolutionary Bolivarian hegemonic project designed to help the poor. As Tovar Arroyo points out, they don't explicitly aim to oust Chávez from power, whereas the discourse used by the conventional opposition political platform only refers to the removal of President Chávez from office. Students aimed to form a new platform that doesn't subvert the will of the 'people', but through persuasion, wins their support.[55]

However, I argue that if the Bolivarian hegemonic project were to accept a process of dialogue with the students, it would imply that the dichotomic construction that forms the basis of its internal frontier no longer works. This would mean an end to its equivalential popular discourse by respecting and giving power to social and political groups from the 'other' camp (logics of difference start to dominate). In other words, the populist project constructed and continuously reproduced to maintain itself in power would basically fall apart.

As Laclau points out, for populism to work, 'equivalences, popular subjectivity, dichotomic construction of the social around an internal frontier' are necessary.[56] If the Bolivarian Revolution accepts any form of dialogue with any movement or organization that is not part of its internal frontier (investing in the imaginary fullness to come, blaming the 'others' as responsible for their deficient being), the populist dimension collapses. As earlier discussed, the Bolivarian hegemonic project is constructed upon dislocatory moments that fully crystallized the degree of antagonism demanding radical institutional change. Considering a dialogue with a sector which is the offspring of that 'other' camp could ultimately lead to the disintegration of the significance and emotional value the Bolivarian Revolution has for its grassroots supporters.

Nonetheless, the youth element tried to offer a new frontier, detached from the intoxicated political structure that governed the country prior to the radicalization of the Bolivarian Revolution. It fleshes out, in spite of the student's

130 *Populism in Venezuela*

class-based differences, a degree of freshness and sincerity, thus uncovering new possibilities that could grip segments of the 'others' in this divided society. This resembles Glynos and Howarth's methodology of social logic; it helps us conceptualize what is at stake 'as it allows us to simultaneously hold on to the idea of a pattern and an open-endedness'.[57] The student movement was an attempt to symbolize a sense of open-endedness and to offer a discourse that tried to convince 'people' from both camps.

Nonetheless, in the literature, the descriptions and assessments of the student movement, its discourse and practices, only relate to the student movement seen in the media and demonstrations that took place in the capital. In my view, an analysis limited to one geographic setting does not give us the full picture of the movement. Conducting fieldwork research outside Caracas gave me an insight into the formation and practices of student demonstrations elsewhere. In 2001 there was already an anti-Chavista student movement in the states of Táchira and Mérida called '*Movimiento 13*', protesting for better transportation, not receiving educational funds, etc. Táchira student groups from different universities and 'youth' sectors in political parties also work together. Jhonny Prada says: 'there are more student leaders in Táchira than in Caracas . . . "media coverage" has been a key element in Caracas. Student leaders like Yon Goicoechea have benefited with the right platform/stage the media gave him. A great Tachirense orator leader like Danny Ramírez has not had that advantage'.[58]

According to Danny Ramírez, in 2001, when Chávez began a phase of radicalization (e.g. the 49 enabling laws), thus unfolding his 'true intentions', the student movement in Táchira started to protest. Ramírez was the president of the student federation of '*Universidad Nacional Experimental del Táchira*' (UNET).[59] The marches organized in San Cristobal and Mérida were the first big student marches in the country—a year before the April 2002 failed coup. They contacted other universities in the country via the '*Federación de Estudiantes Universitarios de Venezuela*', hoping to construct a national student apparatus. This initiative failed because some university student federation leaders supported the government. 'We tried to form a national union of students with the key university in the capital (*Universidad Central de Venezuela* [UCV]) and all the universities in the country'. Ramírez visited 'most of the experimental universities in the country addressing the need to form a national union of students in each university. Unfortunately, there wasn't enough interest to make it happen'.[60] In other words, there wasn't enough 'grip' for the construction of a national student equivalential chain in Venezuela. Logics of difference subverted this attempt to construct an organized national student movement.

On April 12, 2002, in a televised statement, the Governor of Táchira said: 'what happened in Caracas was coup d'état and incited the "people" to confront him at the Governor's official residence if they wanted him to leave his post'. As a result, many civilians formed an impressive gathering outside the governor's residence. Ramírez, President of the student federation, joined with 2,000 to 3,000 students. The governor left and anti-Chavista demonstrators took the residence. When Chávez reassumed power, 12 individuals were prosecuted by violently organizing an invasion of the residence.[61] Ramírez points out that 'a week before the closure of RCTV on May 28, 2007, students in San Cristobal were the first ones to protest nationwide. Many students were injured. In Táchira, students come from all class sectors; however, the government claims that students are nothing else but rich kids from the capital'.[62] The latter resonates with Casanova's claims.

The above anecdotes give us a glimpse of the lack of communication and internal mechanisms among opposition students in different regions of the country. The way students organized and contested the expansion of the Bolivarian hegemony in Táchira played no role whatsoever in the student movement in Caracas. The appearance of a new opposition force (well broadcasted by the media) in Caracas, contesting the government's decision not to renew RCTV's broadcasting license at the end of May 2007, combined with national media coverage of students speaking in the parliament on June 7 of the same year and of other events, provided a perfect publicity stage for the student leaders representing the *Generación 2007*. With its discourse of reconciliation, humanism, and human rights principles (e.g. freedom of speech, nonviolent action, etc.) articulated in its '*Manos Blancas*' symbol, the student movement became a leading opposition force in 2007. Nonetheless, apart from its fresh, non-partisan, agonistic, and reconciliatory proposal, the movement had no political substance to challenge and successfully displace the popular 'grip' the Bolivarian project enjoyed.

The government's first electoral defeat in the December 2007 referendum (by a margin of less than 2 percent) was partly due to the participation of the *Generación 2007*, which contested the constitutional changes (e.g. indefinite re-election) Chávez intended to implement. However, after its splash of success from the end of May until December 2007, this movement failed to crystallize. Its popularity and success was centered upon student leaders that attracted a lot of media attention after the closure of RCTV at the end of May 2007. This was a serious weakness for the expansion of the student movement. It appears that with no key 2007 student leaders, there were no possibilities to shift the movement beyond the phase of the constitutional referendum and its rejection of the RCTV closure.

Professor Agustin Blanco Muñoz (UCV) states that on May 27, 2008 (a year after the closure of RCTV), 'students gathered to organize the "revival of the student movement", "the *Manos Blancas* movement" or "*Generación 2007*". Student coordinators were new faces to news anchors. The 2007 celebrity student leaders joined political parties. It was obvious that the media were there to see what new student-leader material was available to promote and sell to the highest bidder (political parties)'.[63]

It seems that there was a problematic lack of discourse to sustain the meaning of the student movement after its success in 2007. Blanco Muñoz

132 *Populism in Venezuela*

claims that they were desperately trying to revive the mechanisms that helped students challenge the government a year earlier. It is evident that once key student leaders left, there was no platform to replace them and shift their anti-Bolivarian discourse. In my view, if a well-articulated national student union existed, the movement would have progressed and avoided its dependence on the media publicizing students from Caracas only. Political parties were the ones that benefitted from this flaw. In December 2008, it was announced that Yon Goicoechea joined *Primero Justicia* (centre-right party). Also, in November 2008, Stalin Gonzalez became the candidate of ' *Un Nuevo Tiempo*' (centre-left party), campaigning to be the mayor in the Libertador municipality of Caracas.

I argue that without the closure of RCTV in May 2007, there would have never been a student movement like the one addressed in this chapter. The lack of opposition forces challenging the Bolivarian project gave students the opportunity to fill that void. There was a short-lived 'direction' and 'energy' to challenge the next phase of the populist project. Their discourse had the 'grip' to get the support required in 2007. After 2007, circumstances were different. The students had to find another reason to challenge the government. They found nothing. Conventional opposition party-politics (in spite of its directionless position) quickly recovered its position (overtaken by the young uncontaminated student movement) as the alternative to the Bolivarian project, and subtracted valuable human resources from the already worn-out student project.

The new generation of students is primarily articulating its protest methods by organizing 'hunger strikes' (nonviolent resistance) outside the 'American Organization States' office in Caracas. They seek maximum publicity exposure to inform all presidents in the American continent of the human rights violations (unlawfully jailing students and other individuals) this 'totalitarian government' practices.[64] Cilia Flores (an influential Chavista politician) claims that 'the students are opportunists; with the media and opposition parties they are making a "publicity show". Students are manipulated and exploited by opposition parties who are in search for future political candidates'.[65] Ramírez (a student leader in Táchira) notes that 'if *Manos Blancas* was well articulated, it could have been a symbol of renovation, a Venezuela with new political leadership constructing new political practices and a new framework for the society. It could have been a new political project; however, the presence of circumstantial student groups delimited any incentives to transform this movement into a new political party'.[66]

The student movement failed to expand and crystallize as a new opposition force because the *Generación 2007* movement did not represent the national student population. Even during the process of selecting *Generación 2007* committee members (attended by representatives from universities in Caracas) in May–June 2007, we see how interests/differences among student representatives created internal friction and hence a lack of clear

The Anti-Bolivarian Student Movement 133

common objectives. In retrospect, this movement was not formed to expand beyond its strategy to challenge the government on the basis of its decision not to renew RCTV's broadcasting license. The discourse of 'Manos Blancas', 'humanism', 'reconciliation', 'nonviolent action', and so on didn't have enough significance to the people for it to transcend its initial student setting to include other frontiers and involve other social and political sectors. This student project failed to transcend its initial phase because there was no incentive to surpass opposition political parties and construct an equivalential chain where different anti-Bolivarian demands could be partially subverted by constructing a common radical demand to end this 'socialist' (or any other gripping common signifier [I refer to Laclau's empty signifier]) regime as a symbolic signifier.

If *Generación 2007* had been a national student force (not limited to Caracas university circles) and student leaders that graduated had collectively invested in the construction of a new political party (rather than joining opposition parties), representing the party at different regions of the country, this student movement would have signified something different to other social and political sectors that oppose the crystallization of the Bolivarian project. This shift in student politics would have taken the movement to different dimensions, opening a socio-political platform that could have persuaded Bolivarian supporters to change sides. Outdated and discredited opposition political parties that were failing to get the adequate support from the population, selected *Generación 2007* graduate students as a way to rejuvenate their own campaigning stance, and, for their own political survival, impede the emergence of a new and united anti-Chavista political project—founded by students from different sectors of the country.

CONCLUSION

The *Generación 2007* student movement had a 'splash' of success by challenging Chávez's decision not to renew RCTV's broadcasting license at the end of May 2007, and contributing to the government's first electoral defeat in a constitutional referendum in December 2007. Media coverage was a crucial factor in its short-lived success. Media attention gave the student movement the platform to boost their nonviolent *Manos Blancas* discourse. It also gave student leaders from universities in Caracas the stage to challenge the Bolivarian project as well as promote potential political leaders. By conducting fieldwork research, I learned that the movement seen and heard in the media was not a national student organization but a group of students from Caracas that organized and managed this anti-Bolivarian project. Fieldwork helped me get a fuller picture of this movement and therefore to unpack the flaws in the three diverging interpretations discussed in the previous section. Throughout this chapter, I employed Glynos and Howarth's critical explanation methodology to furnish an analytical

134　*Populism in Venezuela*

approach, along with Laclau's theoretical populist schema of logics of difference and equivalence. These methodological and theoretical approaches helped me flesh out a different outlook on the student movement and decode the narratives addressed in this chapter.

The emergence of a student opposition force, much publicized by constant media coverage, which challenged the government on the streets of Caracas at the end of May 2007 and in the parliament days later, took everyone in this deeply divided society by surprise. The success of this movement was based on the media widely reporting on student leaders and their use of discourses such as reconciliation, human rights, and nonviolent action in their *Manos Blancas* symbol. This movement had ample opportunity to expand and consolidate and to challenge the Bolivarian project under a whole set of different circumstances.

However, the downfall of this *Generación 2007* student movement was its dependence on a handful of student leaders that left the movement when they graduated in 2008 and joined opposition political parties. Also, this movement was not a national representation of students from other states. Its success, thanks to 'media coverage' in 2007, only consisted of selective students based in Caracas. If this movement had tried to evolve by expanding and incorporating other regional student leaders and movements, with the aim of constructing a new political project (detached from conventional opposition political parties), students would have been able to construct and crystallize a viable anti-Bolivarian project and possibly play a key role in displacing Chávez's populist regime. This chapter summarizes the development of the student movement, how the *Generación 2007* succeeded, and its failure to evolve, reproduce itself, and thus challenge the Bolivarian project after 2007.

6 Indefinite Re-election, Gerrymandering, Chávez's Cancer, Grand Missions, and a United Opposition Force

The second chapter of this investigation described the historical context in Venezuela, thus unfolding the socio-political terrain where this populist project was constructed. An alliance of several political parties and social organization named *Polo Patriótico* gave Chávez the platform to persuade Venezuela's discontented electorate to support the institutional change his Bolivarian project advocated in the December 1998 presidential election. The third chapter outlines the processes that de-instituted the *Punto Fijo*/bipartite institutional system, attempts of anti-Bolivarian sectors to reinstitute their 'hegemonic position'. It also narrates the second phase of institutional radicalism, which was the 'mission' social programs created in 2003. These programs aimed to improve the lives of Venezuela's excluded sectors. This chapter concludes by analyzing the emergence and impact of new opposition forces and Chávez's first electoral defeat in a constitutional referendum in December 2007. Chapter 4 is an in-depth analysis of the *Barrio Adentro* mission healthcare program. This fieldwork investigation casts light on its practices, strengths, and inability to provide a 'free' healthcare program in Venezuela. The previous chapter expands on one of the new opposition forces (the student movement) discussed in Chapter 3.

This final chapter addresses key events that occurred in Venezuela after December 2007. The first section assesses the referendum that took place on February 15, 2009. This referendum successfully bypassed the results of the constitutional reform referendum in December 2007, giving Chávez the green light to run for elections indefinitely. The second section analyzes the parliamentary election that took place on September 26, 2010. I describe how the government employed practices of electoral 'gerrymandering' in order to maintain a majority in the parliament. The third section analyses the impact of Chávez's health conditions and popularity after being diagnosed with cancer, the formation of four more 'mission' social programs, and the type of discourse used to affiliate his political project with Simon Bolívar, Venezuela's liberator from Spanish rule. I employ Claude Lefort's theoretical analysis of democracy as an 'empty place' to furnish an appropriate context for the issues raised above.

136 *Populism in Venezuela*

The concluding section of this chapter examines the stance of the opposition political leader Leopoldo López. An analysis of López in this investigation is considered important for the following reasons. First, López can genuinely bill himself as the true resurrection of Simon Bolívar because of his blood ties with Bolívar. Second, López's political encounters with the Bolivarian project and its attempts to decimate López's ambition to run for a political office reveal key aspects of the practices the government employs. And finally, it analyzes the new unified opposition force, the five candidates running for the opposition presidential primary election held on February 12, 2012, and the discursive meaning of sections of the speech given by the opposition's elected presidential candidate, after being announced winner with almost two-thirds of the votes.

6.1   INDEFINITE RE-ELECTION

In Chapter 3, I examined key events from Chávez's inauguration as president in February 1999 until the first Bolivarian defeat during the December 2, 2007 referendum. Chávez's response to this unexpected defeat is addressed in the last section of that chapter (see pages 84–87). He announced that a new offensive was coming: 'a new reform or a rephrased one'. A second referendum that, to some extent, made reference to the constitutional changes rejected in the December 2007 referendum was possible because the parliament was still fully controlled by the government. The changes in the December 2007 referendum used the 'constitutional reform' mechanism for a constitutional review; however the second referendum on February 15, 2009 was framed with another mechanism, which was a 'constitutional amendment'.[1]

In this context, on January 15, 2009, the parliament granted Chávez the authority to modify the constitution and the possibility for the indefinite and continuous re-election of the president, which was later extended to all elected public offices. Chávez argued that wining the referendum was 'vital for the Revolution'.[2] The second referendum went ahead with the claim that it was a different question vis-à-vis the first one. It was indeed different in the context of 'indefinite re-election' because 'all' high-ranking politicians were included, not just the president. The referendum took place on February 15, 2009. The government won with 54.85 percent of the votes (45.14 percent rejected it).[3]

That element of re-election for 'all' politicians in the Chavista camp guaranteed Chávez the full mobilization of his party machinery across the nation. Chávez lost the December 2007 referendum because nearly three million Chavista supporters abstained from voting (see Chávez's speech, page 84 in Chapter 3). A series of events can explain this high level of abstention. The government's decision not to renew the broadcasting license of the private TV channel *Radio Caracas Televisión* (RCTV) on May 28,

2007 had an impact on Chávez's popularity. The anti-Bolivarian student movement emerged, the party *Podemos* deserted the Bolivarian equivalential camp, and Baduel, Chávez's close friend, openly challenged the constitutional reform Chávez proposed in the December 2007 referendum.

The second referendum also helped the Bolivarian project evaluate the electoral terrain throughout the country. For the advancement of the revolutionary process, it was vital to maintain a majority in the coming parliamentary election in September 2010. Eugenio G. Martínez, an election specialist in Venezuela, claims that the results collected in the February 2009 referendum provided the incumbent two outcomes in the parliament (in the context of Distrito Federal, Amazonas, Barinas, Carabobo, Lara, Miranda, Táchira, and Zulia as federal entities) if those votes were used in the September 2010 parliamentary election. First, without district adjustments, the Bolivarian project would have gathered 38 seats and the opposition 34. If district adjustments were put in place, the outcome would have been quite different: 45 seats for the government and 27 for the opposition.[4] These kinds of electoral adjustments are known as 'gerrymandering'.[5] Before elaborating on the impact of these electoral modifications in the parliamentary election in September 2010, I'll describe the origin of gerrymandering and what it entails.

6.2 GERRYMANDERING

The concept of gerrymandering has a cunning history in the U.S. In 1812, Elbridge Gerry was governor of Massachusetts. His party controlled the state legislature. In redrawing senatorial district boundaries after the census of 1810, Gerry's party (Democratic-Republicans) hoped to win more seats by packing opposition voters (Federalists) into a few strongholds while carving out a long, thin Republican district along the northern, western, and southwestern edges of Essex County. When a reporter mapped the new districts in the county, the shape resembled a lizard; his editor exclaimed, 'Salamander! Call it a Gerrymander!'.[6] Gerry, the governor's surname, was blended with Salamander. According to Philip Musgrove, the concept of gerrymandering applies to two distinct forms of electoral representation. 'One is that a gerrymander is any set of districts which gives some advantage to the party which draws the electoral map'.[7] The other one 'is any set of districts which results from a deliberate effort by the districting party to give itself an advantage in future elections'. The first is a matter of *results*; the second is a matter of *intent*.[8] The notion that logically separates these two forms of gerrymandering 'is the notion of what it is possible for a party intent on gerrymandering actually to succeed in doing to benefit itself '.[9]

Manuel Rachadell notes that Venezuela's electoral system works for the interests of the Bolivarian Government.[10] The electoral adjustments known as the *Ley Organica de Procesos Electorales* (LOPE), approved in the

138 *Populism in Venezuela*

parliament in July 2009, were happily received by the *Consejo Nacional Electoral* (CNE) and put into effect for the parliamentarian elections on September 26, 2010. Rachadell describes an interesting case of district gerrymandering adjustment in Caracas. Previously, districts of 'La Vega' and 'Paraiso' in Caracas (i.e. Distrito Federal) were sector 3 in the electoral order. One parliamentarian was elected in this sector. As the voters in these two districts are mainly opposition supporters, the government decided to integrate 'La Vega' and 'Paraiso' (with its parliamentary seat) with three die-hard Chavista (*Chavismo duro*) districts: 'Caricuao', 'Macarao', and 'Antinamo' in sector 5. This adjustment not only crippled the opposition; it also opened possibilities for the government to grab another parliamentary seat.[11] Indeed, two *Partido Socialista Unido de Venezuela* (PSUV) candidates won these seats with 51.83% and 51.79% of the votes in sector 5.[12]

These kinds of adjustments were also implemented in the states of Miranda, Zulia, Carabobo, Barinas, Lara, and Táchira.[13] As Musgrove puts it, this is gerrymandering of *intent*. The government's objective was to keep, against all odds, a majority in the parliamentary election on September 26, 2010. The Chavista platform needed two-thirds majority (110) of the 165 seats. In spite of time and resources aplenty dedicated to the campaign, the incumbent only secured 98 seats with 5,399,574 votes. The opposition's *Mesa de la Unidad Democrática* (MUD)[14] got 65 seats with 5,312,293 votes, and the *Patria Para Todos* (PPT)[15] got 2 seats with 330,260 votes.[16] If we add the MUD and PPT (a party that rejected full acceptance of Chávez's tutelage) votes together, we get 242,979 more vis-à-vis the government.

The Economist notes that 'only blatant gerrymandering of constituencies and an electoral reform that abolished proportional representation allowed Mr Chávez to keep control of the legislature. Even so, he failed to retain the two-thirds majority he had said was vital for his regime's future'.[17] This is a good benchmark of Chávez's popularity. These results give us a prelude to the October 2012 presidential election. The support represented by the 7.3 million votes (62.84 percent) Chávez received for his re-election in December 2006 seems to be fading away. The populist discourse this revolutionary project advocates seems to be losing its 'grip' with Venezuela's popular masses. There are obvious signs of political fragmentation in Chávez's equivalential chain. PPT's desertion of the Bolivarian project reveals that the extent of internal differences is so critical that the 'nodal point' constructed to challenge and displace the *Punto Fijo* establishment in 1998 no longer holds (see pages 56–58 in Chapter 2). The decision of the party *Podemos*, later followed by the PPT, to abandon the Bolivarian project, shows that Chávez and his party in power are failing to adapt and politically galvanize what this revolution aims to achieve. Electoral results are also indicators of people's satisfaction/dissatisfaction with a political project that has governed Venezuela for more than a decade. The next section analyzes Chávez's discourse and strategy after being diagnosed with cancer. It assesses to what extent this has had an impact on his popularity

Indefinite Re-election 139

and analyzes his attempts to discursively reconstruct the Bolivarian Revolution, as he is seeking to improve his popularity and be re-elected in the coming October 2012 presidential election.

6.3 CHÁVEZ'S CANCER, 'GRAND MISSIONS', AND RE-ELECTION

The theme of Chávez's health became a pressing matter for Venezuelans in the second half of 2011. Rumors coupled with genuine concerns about the president's well-being made Chávez's health a hot topic. Lack of official information about Chávez's health condition and why he had stayed in Cuba for so long left many unanswered questions. On June 30, 2011, things became clearer when, from Havana, Chávez informed the nation during a televised speech of the reason for his long absence and health problems. He looked pallid and seemed to have lost weight. Chávez also read the speech, which is unusual, and spoke slowly instead of in his normally energetic and self-assured manner. Nonetheless, it is worth analyzing parts of Chávez 15-minute speech, as it introduces a set of new elements into Chávez's populist discourse:

> [t]oday I read this communiqué to the Venezuelan nation and the international public opinion, for they are waiting to learn about my health . . . I must admit that as for my health, I just planned to do a check up of my left knee. . . . Notwithstanding, in Havana, on Wednesday evening, June 8, here we were again with Fidel the Greatest (*Gigante*) . . . it was not difficult for Fidel to note some discomfort, in addition to my left knee. . . . He queried me almost like a doctor; I made my confession almost like a patient. On that same night, the whole medical breakthrough . . . was made available to us. . . . Hence, a foreign mass in the pelvic area was found, leading to an emergency surgery in the face of the impeding risk of widespread infection. . . . Another set of special . . . studies were conducted and confirmed the existence of an abscessed tumor with cancerous cells. A second surgery removed the tumor . . . I have continued evolving satisfactorily. . . . In the meantime, I have kept and keep informed and in command of the actions of the Bolivarian Government . . . I am immensely grateful for the numerous and enthusiastic expressions of solidarity received from the Venezuelan people and other fellow peoples . . . convinced that all that love, all that solidarity, are the most lofty energy which drive and will drive my willingness to vanquish in this battle that life has put in front of me. I am especially grateful to the Cuban people, Fidel, Raúl, all the medical legion . . . I have been keenly aware of some degree of anguish and uncertainty that has been overwhelming throughout these days . . . in the soul and body of the Venezuelan nation . . . beyond the manipulating attempts of some well-known sectors. . . .

140 *Populism in Venezuela*

From the bottom of my soul and conscience, the human reason, the loving reason, to be precise . . . I feel obliged now to speak to you from deep inside myself . . . I can remember February 4, 1992. That day, I had no choice but to address myself to Venezuela . . . from a road that I felt like leading me to a bottomless *abyss*. From a sort of a dark cavern of my soul, the *"For now"* emerged; afterwards, I plunged. Those ill-fated hours of April 11, 2002 also come to my memory. . . . It was like a painful chant from the bottom of another *abyss*. . . . Again, at this new time of troubles and above all, since the very Fidel Castro the Greatest came to give me the tough news of the cancerous finding, I started begging my Lord Jesus . . . to give me the possibility of speaking to you, not from an *abyss* . . . I think we have achieved it, thank God. . . . And finally, my beloved fellow countrymen and countrywomen; my beloved daughters and sons; my dear comrades; young people, boys and girls of my people; my loyal soldiers . . . my people, all and only one in my heart, I tell you that wanting to speak to you today as I prepare once again to return has nothing to do with myself but with you . . . patriotic people, good people . . . I urge you to continue together climbing up new summits . . . with our Father Bolívar, in the vanguard, to continue climbing up to the summit. . . . Thank God, thank you people . . . Havana, June 30, 2011 . . . From my heart, from my soul, from my supreme hope which is the hope of the people: For Now and Forever we will Live and Win . . .[18]

The underlined portions of Chávez's speech reveal important aspects of his relation with the Cuban regime, how he communicates with '*el pueblo*' of Venezuela, and how he is using this unexpected health problem as an opportunity to reproduce his political discourse:

- Firstly, his act of naming Fidel the Greatest (*Gigante*) gives us an insight into the comradeship these two leaders enjoy. For Chávez, calling Fidel *El Comandante* is no longer appropriate because he is a commander himself (see pages 50–51 in Chapter 2); something higher is required to describe Fidel's authority and achievements. Also, the doctor-patient discussion gives us a glimpse of the mentor-student bond Fidel Castro and Hugo Chávez have developed throughout the years. It seems that Chávez feels admiration for Fidel because he has succeeded in keeping the Cuban Revolution alive since 1958 in spite of the attacks from the U.S. (a common enemy) attempting to overthrow his regime. In other words, Fidel is a role model for Chávez. Fidel's astute ability to stay in power for so long is an indicator of masterful leadership for Chávez. This can partly explain why the advice Chávez receives from Castro tends to have a degree of influence in Chávez's decisions (e.g. see page 110 in Chapter 4). This could also explain why Chávez trusts Cuba's medical apparatus (more than he does Venezuela's) for his own medical checkups and complex surgeries such as the removal of cancerous tumors.

- Second, Chávez carefully articulates his speech by acknowledging the concerns his beloved compatriot followers have raised about his health, and his eagerness to explain his health, emotions, and love to those who worry about his well-being. The word 'abyss' is used to infuse his cancer diagnoses with other critical events in Chávez's life (coups in 1992 and 2002). What Chávez is trying to emphasize is his urgent desire to convey to '*el pueblo*' his feelings during these dark moments because his love for and bond with his core-base Venezuelan supporters are priceless. Chávez's 'all and only one in my heart' is the kind of discourse he employs to 'grip' and galvanize his core supporters. Another valuable component is Chávez describing his frame of mind—i.e. 'From a sort of a dark cavern of my soul'—when the '*Por ahora*' empty signifier emerges (see pages 88–89 in Chapter 2). Furthermore, the insertion of Bolívar in the speech is essential as it signifies that vital element of indefinite fulfillment to come his political platform promotes.
- And, Chávez modifies the Cuban Revolution slogan 'Homeland, Socialism or Death, we will Win' (*Patria, Socialismo o Muerte, Veceremos*); he imported (and added) 'Socialism' in December 2006 (see page 80 in Chapter 3). Referring to his health and other circumstances, Chávez modifies the slogan to: 'For now and Forever we will Live and Win' (*Por ahora y para Siempre, Viviremos y Venceremos*). Obviously, as he is trying to survive and live for the people and further sediment the revolution, Chávez has changed 'Death' to 'Live'—as this is more appropriate for his health (in times of uncertainty), and the Bolivarian project that much depends upon his presence and populist discourse. 'Death' is a promise to fight until the end for the socialist revolution Chávez aims to materialize in Venezuela, and defeat any enemy (e.g. oligarchs, bourgeoisie, the American empire, and so on) that aims to displace it. Nonetheless, at this moment, his prime objective is to fight cancer. What is also interesting is the change of the motto from 'Socialism', the ideology Chávez announced as the next phase of the revolution in December 2006, to his well galvanized '*Por ahora*' signifier, attaching that signifier to '*para siempre*' (forever) and thus giving his 'For now' a sense of validity and open-endedness—19 years after its creation—and reproducing the emotional support he received after his brief speech on February 4, 1992.

On July 28, 2011, less than a month after his speech in Havana, from the presidential balcony in Miraflores—now called *el 'balcón' del pueblo* (the balcony of the people), Chávez celebrated his 57th birthday. His daughter, son in law, and three grandchildren were beside him and a wide selection of supporters below. Apart from talking to the people, Chávez danced and

142 *Populism in Venezuela*

sung '*joropo*' (creole music from the *llanos* [plains] of Venezuela). As he sung, Chávez improvised the lyrics—making reference to his health, emotions, and the people: '*viva la vida, viviré y venceremos* (live life, I'll live, and we'll win) . . . *yo le canto a la vida aquí con ustedes, entendiéndome en un momento tan querido* (I sing to life here with all of you who understand me in a precious moment like this one) . . . *aquí les canto de mi alma con todos ustedes, viva la vida!* (here I sign from my soul with all of you, live life!)'. The people respond when he stops signing: '*pa'lante, pa'lante el Comandante* (Commander, go forward, go forward)'.[19]

Apart from celebrating his birthday weeks after announcing his health condition, this was a valuable opportunity to further sediment the political frontier Chávez represents, strengthen his ties and bond with the people, and confront his enemies:

> *Los escualidos* (the opposition) keep claiming that this is a show only, that I'm not ill at all. Now they are going to say that I even danced and sung in the balcony. Even though I have been defeating this illness, which has been very difficult, new doses of chemotherapy will begin soon; I'll lose my hair soon. No cancerous cells have been found in my body. I have a tough body . . . I invite people to celebrate my 77th birthday in 2031. I said that I would leave in 2021, no way 2021, maybe 2031 . . . I [laughing] heard the American Empire is bankrupt; we could offer Barack Obama a loan. [20]

Even though there have been allegations among opposition sectors that Chávez's cancer narrative is fabricated, seeking to create a sense of sympathy and somehow increase his popularity, to some extent, it has now been widely accepted that Chávez has been recovering from cancer. Nevertheless, specific information stating where and what type of cancer he recovered from is a closely guarded state secret. Still, this health problem seems to be of no concern to Chávez as he is happily inviting people to celebrate his 77th birthday at the balcony of the people. Referring to the comment that the American empire is bankrupt, Chávez wants to discursively emphasize that capitalism provides greater wealth for the few and greater poverty for the many. The democratic socialism the Bolivarian Revolution is constructing defends the less privileged population and works for the well-being of the people.

Chávez has recently concentrated his effort (a decision that seems to be mostly a pre-electoral presidential campaign platform) to create more social programs. Since the creation of '*misión*' social programs in 2003 (see Chapter 3), the government has formed 34 missions to help Venezuela's underprivileged population. Approximately U.S. $39 billion of oil revenues has been allocated to these social programs since 2003. Apparently, these new missions are only attempts to repackage/reproduce other missions, with different names and popular marketing objectives.[21] Part of mission re-branding is the inclusion of the word '*Gran*', thus modifying these new social programs as '*Gran Misiones*' (Grand Missions). If these 'grand missions' materialize and improve the lives of Venezuela's underprivileged population before the presidential election in October 2012, Chávez is likely to get re-elected because these types of missions can generate a sense of gratitude. Let me elaborate on why four of these missions can secure the popular electoral support Chávez needs.

1. *Gran Misión en Amor Mayor* (Grand Mission Love for the Elders): to be eligible for the state pension this mission offers, women have to be above 55 years old and men above 60. The applicant must be part of a nuclear family with an income below the current Bs. 1,548.22 monthly minimum.[22] No previous contributions to build up entitlement are required. If we observe the protests that took place in France when the government decided to overhaul pensions and raise the retirement age from 60 to 62,[23] Chávez's pension program seems to be very generous. This also applies to the austerity measures the British government announced in October 2010, to increase the state retirement age from the current 60 for women and 65 for men to 66 (for both women and men) by 2020.[24]

2. *Gran Misión Vivienda* (Grand Mission Housing): according to Chávez, 'this mission aims to give people their full potential in life. . . . Capitalism has condemned poor people to misery, to live in a miserable '*rancho*' (slum), as if they were already dead. Every day, the Revolution will give more and more of the Venezuelan people a life worth living for; a decent house to live in'. During 2011, three rounds were organized throughout the states of Venezuela for people to register with their identification card.[25] The demand for housing has been so high that in the first and second round, more than 2.3 million families registered for a free property.[26] Chávez has set a target to build more than 153,000 houses in 2011.[27] Nonetheless, government figures stating that this target has been achieved are not available. The 2012 target is to complete 200,000 houses by September 2012 (i.e. before the presidential election on October 7, 2012).[28]

3. *Gran Misión Saber y Trabajo* (Grand Mission Knowledge and Work): the main objective is to reduce employment and underemployment—with particular emphasis on young people and women. This mission seeks to help citizens who are affected by long-term and absolute unemployment. Those who are willing to participate in formation programs and be part of development projects in housing, agriculture, transport, popular tourism, medical assistance, and strategic plans in the Orinoco Belt (heavy crude oil sands) can benefit from this government training/employment scheme. The registration process has been organized in four rounds. The Bolivarian project aims to generate more than 2.8 million new jobs between 2012 and 2019.[29]

144 *Populism in Venezuela*

4. *Gran Misión Hijos de Venezuela* (Grand Mission Sons of Venezuela): this program aims to provide resources to homes that cannot fulfill their basic needs. It is a short-term economic plan helping people overcome conditions of extreme poverty. This mission focuses on four groups of the population: poor pregnant teenagers, pregnant women who live in conditions of poverty, children under age 17 living in poverty, and disabled people of all ages. Critical or extreme poverty is classified as homes in which both parents are unemployed, or in which, if the parents are employed, they receive a salary below the monthly minimum wage. Nuclear families that meet these criteria are eligible to receive BsF 430 per month for each child under 17, up to three children per household. Also, mothers and family members taking care of a disabled family member of any age are entitled to BsF 600 per month.[30]

Chávez inaugurated *Gran Misión Hijos de Venezuela* on December 12, 2011, at the *Anexo Negra Matea de Maternidad de Concepción Palacios* in Caracas. The opening of this mission was televised on all channels of Venezuela. As I was in Caracas during that period, I thought it was a good opportunity to watch and analyze the kind of discourse Chávez and pregnant teenagers articulate. In a green open area inside the maternity hospital, a group of approximately 20 pregnant teenagers and women were seated—listening and speaking to Chávez, who was standing. When Chávez arrived, everybody clapped and cheered. Happy, behind a tree, Chávez said: 'ooh, are you all pregnant? . . . I see'. He asked a teenager, 'when will you give birth?' She said: 'in January'. He replied, 'you'll be one of the first ones on the list! Are you all from Caracas?' They said: 'yes'. As the event progressed, a mixture of teenagers and women expressed their gratitude to the support Chávez has given them. One said: 'I'm with you taking the Revolution forward!'. Chávez gave them opportunities to talk and describe their problems at home, and to make requests for housing, medical assistance, care for elder family members, and financial help. Chávez interacted with them and ordered his team to take notes and deal with their requests. There are interesting points in Chávez's speech and conduct worth pointing out here:

> [t]oday I'm going to sign a law that we'll protect all of you . . . the opposition (*los escualidos*) are saying that I am an irresponsible person giving money away (*regalando plata*) to pregnant women, looking for votes, that he is mad, etc. . . . They are the ones who are mad really. . . . God bless them, I don't want anything bad to happen to anyone. . . . Yesterday, one of them said that this mission encourages pregnancy because if you are pregnant Chávez splashes cash; you know . . . madness . . . they are like that, like mad people . . . they are mad because they are desperate . . .'

Chávez wants to emphasize that in this deeply dichotomized society, he represents and protects the underdog, previously excluded, unskilled, jobless, poor, weak, and so on—in Venezuela. This kind of populist discourse reinforces that vital 'us-them' axis, which seeks to remind the popular mass that the opposition is the enemy. This underpins the importance of the Bolivarian 'equivalential chain' (i.e. the revolution) to *el pueblo*. During the *Gran Misión Hijos de Venezuela* inauguration event, Chávez also reveals interesting aspects of his character, referring to his recent health problem, and how he likes to come close to ordinary people and show a sense of love and care for their well-being:

> Venezuela has experienced 200 years of neglect; we inherited from capitalism atrocious levels of poverty and misery. It is impossible for us to fix it in a decade. I have been here for thirteen years . . . for the last thirteen years we have fought hard without a break. God, please give all us life and health to fight tirelessly for thirteen more years and another thirteen after that . . . I am one of you, I give my life to you: the poor. Medics tell me to slow down, Chávez you work too much. The cancer I got is because stress . . . thank God the tumor has been removed. . . . During the last months, with the pain and thinking that this might be the end, I have been reflecting, this is my weakness. But now, I'm here standing and talking to you! . . . my horse is still, my jumping around has stopped. . . . How old are you, right at the back? 'Fifteen', a teenager says. All my love to you, are you pregnant? She says: 'yes, it is a girl'. Congratulations . . . I'm her symbolic grandfather . . . 'thank you', she said. Come here, come here, she looks like a baby girl, I want to give her a kiss . . . in my eyes she is my daughter . . . look how beautiful she is [Chávez kisses and hugs her]. . . . Are you studying? 'No', she says. Please go back to school, study English, mathematics and teach your daughter . . . God bless you.

Chávez blames capitalism and those who benefitted from this form of political system in the last 200 years, and claims that they are responsible for the poverty and misery many Venezuelans are facing today. These are populist reminders that work by demonizing the 'other' camp, and claiming that the new radical project they are trying to crystallize will bring fulfillment to come to Venezuela's previously excluded sectors. Missions are programs that aim to tangibly materialize, in one form or another to the people, the improvement and empowerment Chávez has promised since 1992. Referring to his health, Chavez compares his years of struggle protecting his beloved *pueblo* with the cancer diagnosed in June 2011. As Chávez notes, 'I am one of you, I give my life to you: the poor'. This intimate relation Chávez has with his core popular-base is vital for his political existence. Chávez shows this love and affection from 'the bottom of my soul and conscience', as he stated in his speech from Havana on June 30, 2011, as well as in his

146　*Populism in Venezuela*

interaction with the pregnant 15-year-old girl and the language he uses in that interaction. This is nothing new in Chávez's discursive practices; both subjects, Chávez and *el pueblo*, feed each other from this close relation. Chávez needs to reproduce this affection not only for political (electoral) reasons, but also for his own cult of personality, and reassure himself that after 13 years in power he can still mobilize the masses.

In a totally different context, we also see an affective logic similar to the brief interaction Chávez had with the pregnant 15-year-old. On December 17, 2011, Chávez visited the '*Panteón Nacional*' (see page 63 in Chapter 3) to commemorate the 181-year anniversary of Simon Bolívar's death. Chávez manifested again his determination to uncover the truth about Bolívar's death because he believes Bolívar was murdered.[31] Chávez stated that 'it is very difficult that Bolívar died of tuberculosis; this is a disease that slowly kills you'. Nostalgically, Chávez also stated that:

> When I saw the bones and skeleton of Bolívar, it looked like a child and I felt like holding it. This skeleton is of a our Liberator because the leg bones I saw are of someone who travelled on horseback many long journeys. . . . Bolívar's time is now because our Liberator didn't belong to the century when he lived. Now is when Bolívar is truly alive. When *el pueblo* wakes up, Bolívar is there with them. . . . Fidel told me: 'Chávez, Bolívar the genius is out of the bottle. There is nothing that can confine him again; the Liberator is commanding all your projects'. . . . Bolívar will be beside me until 2030.[32]

The discursive meaning of Chávez holding and hugging the pregnant 15-year-old and wishing to use the same approach to Bolívar's skeleton because it looks like a child, shows that Chávez sees physical touch as a powerful way to communicate love and transmit, as a central connector, all the different subjects he, as the leader of the Bolivarian project, needs to address. I argue that for Chávez, the presence of Bolívar, as the 'direction' and 'energy'—i.e. 'vector' (see fantasmatic logics—pages 34–36 in Chapter 1)—is vital for the advancement of the revolution. Chávez tries to revitalize the revolution and act as an agent between *el pueblo* and the symbol of nationalist emancipation Bolívar represents.

With the use of a 'horse' as a means of transport in his metaphor (i.e. 13 years fighting without a break for the well-being of the people), and reflecting upon the reason why he has been diagnosed with cancer, Chávez seeks to compare his personal account with that of Bolívar by referring to the leg bones he saw in the sarcophagus. In other words, Chávez believes and tries to reinforce himself (cult of personality) as the 'nodal point' in the equivalential chain where all different sectors (including Bolívar's effort to emancipate *el pueblo* from Spanish rule) are embodied in a totality of different demands (I refer to Laclau's theoretical insights; see pages 17–18 in Chapter 1), which constructed and sustain the hegemonic practices Chávez manages with his populist discourse. Fidel's 'Bolívar the genius is out of the bottle' remark provides Chávez a sense of endorsement from the Greatest (*El Gigante*—as Chávez calls Fidel) of the way Chávez is running the Bolivarian project, and maybe, with Bolívar beside him, of his goal of staying in power until 2030.[33]

After his serious health condition, Chávez has frequently announced his intention to govern Venezuela until 2031.[34] What is fascinating is that after his cancer diagnosis, his popularity has increased. A survey conducted by *Datanálisis*, a Venezuelan polling firm, shows that in October 2011, Chávez's support was 58.9 percent—a 10-point increase—after announcing on June 30 the removal of a tumor. According to Luis Vicente León, president of *Datanálisis,* what the population pays attention to is Chávez's struggle and battle to defeat this illness. People don't seem to notice that Chávez is ill. Electing a sick man to the presidency seems to have no relevance to Venezuela's future.[35]

In other words, Chávez is generally understood by the less privileged population as the underdog symbol of leadership that defends people who have been, in one way or another, antagonized by an external force. *El pueblo* perceives Chávez as 'one of us'. Chávez knows how to challenge and defeat a 'common enemy': the oligarchs, the American empire, bourgeoisies, etc. Emotions of the underdog and the victim suppress emotions of rational electoral decisions. To put it in another way, Chávez is David in the 'David versus Goliath' battle. Chávez's discourse depends greatly on confrontation in order to draw attention to the dichotomic terrain poor Venezuelans have faced for many years. In this context, his populist discourse is articulated, takes shape and makes an impact with his followers and those who oppose him.

When Chávez announced to the people his cancer diagnosis and recovery process, the speech astutely turned it into a populist opportunity. With the word 'abyss' in his speech, he compared this incident with other events of 'abyss': the failed coup on February 1992, a dark moment when his 'For now' appeared, and April 2002, when the enemy temporarily ousted him from the presidency; Chávez manages to shift people's concern, acknowledged in the speech, to sympathy and solidarity. The meaning of the cancer Chávez is recovering from has shifted. This form of resemblance in the context of 'abyss' opens the terrain to suggest indirectly that this is part of an evil plot to overthrow Chávez and dismantle the Bolivarian hegemonic project he leads.[36]

The help people receive before October 7, 2012 from the Grand Missions addressed earlier will be a key factor for Chávez to gather sufficient votes and win the presidency for a third time. If the Chavista apparatus fails to use the time and resources allocated to these 'Grand' programs because of mismanagement and corrupt practices like those discussed at the end of the *Barrio Adentro* analysis (e.g. 20,000 BA workers not being paid), this opportunity to galvanize popular support and thus maintain or increase the 58.9 percent

148   *Populism in Venezuela*

popularity Chávez had in October 2011 could change drastically. Attempts to regain the popularity enjoyed in December 2006 (i.e. 62.84 percent of the vote in the December presidential elections–see page 79 in Chapter 3) by re-branding missions as 'Grand Missions': programs that offer help and assistance, similar with other missions that failed or are no longer active; requires drastic re-thinking and urgent improvement, in order to avoid more disappointment and disillusionment with Venezuela's poor voters.

The parliamentary election on September 26, 2010 was a wake up call and a clear electoral indicator to the Chavista apparatus. Support from the popular base is not infinite. Political sectors need to maintain constant rapport with social sectors in less privileged areas and encourage community participation in the construction, development and management of social programs. Political groups that oppose the regime succeeded in gathering 300,000 more votes than the incumbent. In spite of the gerrymandering tactics the government implemented, the Chavista camp failed to maintain a majority in the parliament. It is possible that the expectations, practices, and illusions (of a better and false imaginary picture of a new world ahead) the Bolivarian project managed to offer to the previously excluded population have lost the 'grip' they once had. It is possible that the transitory fulfillment *misiones* provided to the people from 2003 until December 2006 is to some extent failing to physically and emotionally deliver the help people need to survive and create a fantasy of fulfillment to come with Chávez in power. After years of populist practices as a mode of governance, constant use of the 'us-them' axis demonizing and blaming a 'common enemy' responsible for people's misfortunes might no longer be a convincing form of political discourse to mobilize the masses to the ballot box.

As Miquilena put it, 'Chávez does not understand the difference between an "adversary" and an "enemy"' (see page 68 in Chapter 3). The role of Chávez as a populist leader has been to politically crystallize a variety of different antagonistic emotions as one. If Chávez and his political project stop reminding the people that the 'enemy' is accountable for all evils in Venezuela's society, the Bolivarian project would collapse. Respect for and dialogue with 'adversary' social and political sectors that disagree with governmental and institutional policies could have a detrimental impact on the Bolivarian Revolution. The inclusion of Castro's views and his importance in Chávez's speeches reveal the significance of Castro's advice for Chávez and the mentor-mentee relationship they both enjoy. It is not known to what extent Cuban institutional practices have been incorporated in Venezuela's institutional framework as part of the socialist phase Chávez announced in December 2006. Nonetheless, Chavez's intention to stay in power until 2031 might be a decision that relates with the latter point.

Claude Lefort claims that 'the legitimacy of power is based on the people; but the image of popular sovereignty is linked to the image of an empty place, impossible to occupy, such that those who exercise public authority can never claim to appropriate it'.[37] The results of the constitutional reform referendum in December 2007 rejected Chávez's intention to end presidential term limits,

Indefinite Re-election 149

allowing him to run for re-election indefinitely (see pages 83–87 in Chapter 3). However, in spite of this, Chávez insisted on finding other methods to amend term limits in the constitution and be re-elected indefinitely. As Lefort notes, 'democracy combines these two apparently contradictory principles: on the one hand, power emanates from the people; on the other, it is the power of nobody. And democracy thrives on this contradiction'.[38]

The intention and ability to bypass the December 2007 referendum outcome open a set of questions about the legitimacy of democratic principles practiced in Venezuela today. According to Lefort, 'whenever the latter risks being resolved or already resolved, democracy is either close to destruction or already destroyed'.[39] Chávez's decision to ignore his defeat in December 2007, his use of power to get a favorable outcome in the second referendum on February 15, 2009, and the gerrymandering tactics implemented without any obstruction from a electoral system are clear signs that the Chavista political apparatus uses its power in the name of the 'previously excluded population' to suit its own political agenda.

These kinds of episodes could potential destroy what Venezuelan democracy entails. Problems occur when a political power doesn't respect that 'empty place' in democracy, 'claiming to speak for the people as its unmediated representative . . . it is democracy itself, and not just liberalism, that is being denied. Taken to the extreme populism descends into totalitarianism'.[40] The use of power in public authority to alter rules that were set out to keep democratic principles above individual or political interests opens a terrain where a once thriving democracy becomes a totalitarian state, ruled by a cult leader who enjoys absolute control of an institutional structure that claims to be democratic.

The national significance of Bolívar the Liberator has been used to buff up and give resonance to a political project that calls itself Bolivarian and discursively claims to be the successor of Bolívar's unfinished work. In the next section of this chapter, the symbol of Bolívar will be raised in the context of Leopoldo López: a key opposition political leader who is a blood descendant of Bolívar. To conclude this chapter, I briefly discuss the themes opposition candidates used to campaign for the *Mesa de la Unidad Democrática* (MUD—Coalition for Democratic Unity, earlier discussed) primary election on February 12, 2012, and what type of discourse this internally elected opposition candidate might use to challenge Chávez in the coming October 2012 presidential election.

6.4 THE LEGITIMATE HEIR BY BLOOD TO BOLÍVAR & THE *MESA DE LA UNIDAD DEMOCRÁTICA* CHALLENGES CHÁVEZ'S POPULIST REGIME

Chávez's use of Bolívar for political/nationalistic marketing and continuous campaigning since 1992 is overwhelming. As a discursive tool, attempts to resurrect and benefit from what Bolívar signifies as the focal point of

150   Populism in Venezuela

national identity, and the cultural respect and admiration Bolívar as a national symbol of emancipation epitomizes to the people, are pivotal components in Chávez's populist discourse. Chávez and his political project have branded, constructed, and repeatedly galvanized this 'Bolivarian Revolution' by using Bolívar's footing, as the leader who in the 1820s defeated the Spanish Empire in Venezuela and other Latin American countries, and gave freedom to many people previously exploited by an oppressive ruler.

Nonetheless, this sense of repetitive use of Bolívar, seeking to give a meaning to the cause the Chavista camp advocates, can be counter-productive. A *Barrio Adentro* driver in Táchira, who worked for one year without receiving the promised salary, told me recently, with a lot of resentment, 'I hate Bolívar—he is also Chavista'. It is possible that the constant attempt to politically capitalize on the Bolivarian symbol for the last two decades has contaminated the meaning of Bolívar for people from less privileged sectors in Venezuela. If all these factors were put together, the opposition could potentially argue that Chávez and his regime have abused, distorted, and/or corrupted Bolívar.

If the opposition decides to challenge the Chavistas because they claim to be the true representatives of Venezuela's poor, and therefore feel entitled to use Bolívar and re-interpret the past for their own political objectives, an interesting counter-populist discourse could materialize. Nonetheless, this could also open a new avenue for Chávez to reinforce the underdog/antagonistic discourse that feeds his populist project, thus reminding *el pueblo* of the 'us-them' axis and blame the 'others' responsible for their (us) misfortunes. In my view, the most suitable opposition political leader to articulate the Bolívar theme and challenge Chávez is Leopoldo López: the great, great, great, great, great nephew of Simon Bolívar.[41] During my last visit to Venezuela (December 2011), it was difficult to arrange an interview with López (who was campaigning for the opposition presidential primary election held on February 12, 2012). Luckily, before my departure, I had the opportunity to interview López and ask him, as the legitimate heir by blood of Bolívar, for his view about Chávez's fanatical relation with Bolívar. He stated:

> The use of Bolívar as a focal point for political interests is nothing new in Venezuela's history. After his death in 1830, there have been attempts to use his name. This was intensified in the 1870s when the dictator Guzman Blanco created a currency with the name of Bolívar and tried to transmit his persona based on his relation with Bolívar. In the early twentieth century, another dictator, Juan Vicente Gomez, also branded his project using the name of Bolívar; to such an extent that Gomez's birth and death certificates show the same day and month as Bolívar's. Chávez's government has also made a lot of use of Bolívar. As a nation, we have a strong attachment to our history and collective memory that reminds us of that glorious period of Venezuela's and part of South America's independence. We must feel very proud of our

past. However, I see the use of the past as an excuse for government officials not addressing the future, but wasting time talking about the past. The Venezuela of the twenty-first century must be called to conquer the future; of course, we are connected with our history, but not live the present justifying and reconstructing the past. This is what this government has done: change the narrative of our history . . . yes, I am a descendant of Simon Bolívar, and from my father's side I am related with Cristobal de Mendoza, the first president of Venezuela. I was brought up listening to and always reflecting on the problems of the country: the past, present, and my commitment towards its future. . . . We need a government that genuinely thinks of the present and where Venezuela will be in the future. We are living in conditions of backwardness and stagnation . . . in the last 6–7 years Venezuela has received the highest oil revenue ever; but still, we have to struggle with high levels of inflation, unemployment . . . the biggest problem, which the government puts a blind eye on, is crime. . . . If the government stays in power until 2020, we'll have 500,000 deaths. . . . Returning to your question, I don't have to promote my Bolívar blood. It is a Real Fact. Am I going to use my blood as a political tool? I think we must END that permanent cycle of linking Venezuelan politics, competing on who is more Bolivarian or not, more attached with Bolívar, and so on. Bolívar belongs to ALL VENEZUELANS. What we are trying to do here, I insist on this, it's not who has the most precise interpretation of what happened 100–200 years ago, but who has the right program to deal with the challenges Venezuela will face in the future.[42]

As López pointed out, the use of Bolívar for political and nationalistic interests is not a new phenomenon in Venezuela. Other leaders in Venezuela's history have tried to exploit that eternal pre-eminence the Liberator holds in Venezuela's culture and sense of national identity. Leaders have claimed to have the backing of a fully crystallized and established national signifier. These are attempts to get the backing of the people by challenging a common evil enemy, coupled with a fantasy to get near Bolívar's pedestal. In the context of Chávez, these attempts to resonate with a superior proxy and fulfill what is lacking lend an imaginary sense of grandeur to his populist political project (i.e. the 'vector'—see pages 34–36 in Chapter 1) and seek to promote, in the name of a transcendental nationalistic symbol, a fantasy of fullness/harmony to come to a variety of different unsatisfied and antagonized social sectors in a deeply dichotomized society.

The key purpose of the interview with López was to examine to what extent López would consider using a similar Bolivarian discourse in future elections (thus capitalize on his Bolívar blood as the legitimate heir) to grab the support Chávez has constructed and nurtured over the last 20 years using the name of Bolívar. According to López, political opportunism in the name of Bolívar is an unproductive cycle that needs to end, and Venezuela's

152   *Populism in Venezuela*

nationalistic sentiments should be allowed to evolve independently. Certainly, making reference to the past is an important element of political practice, but narratives of what happened 100–200 years ago should not be used to reinforce focal points in political discourse today. López notes that re-interpreting the past does not alleviate present conditions of backwardness and stagnation in Venezuela and that it will not help the nation react to future challenges. López puts a lot of emphasis on the future of the country. His Bolívar blood appears to play no personal/political role in his ambition to win the presidency. 'Bolívar belongs to ALL VENEZUELANS', López said.

Ways to deal with the high levels of crime and violence that have grown since Chávez took office (more than 19,000 deaths in 2011—the worst ever) has been the main theme in López's primary campaign.[43] However, on January 25, 2012, López announced his decision to drop out of the primary race and endorse Henrique Capriles Randonski. The risk that the government would bar Lopez from office if elected president, because of dubious allegations of corruption that were never tested in court, partly explains why López decided to save his energies and help with his party machinery, assisting a former party colleague who had better chances of winning the primary elections.[44]

The new MUD opposition force, a unifying political project where a wide range of different political parties (three of these political parties were part of the Chavista equivalential chain) and social organizations have managed to construct a viable democratic force by sharing a common objective: to oust Chávez and party officials from power and unite Venezuela. Differences in terms of age and political color seen among the five candidates running in the primary election give us a glimpse of the political diversity seen in the MUD. I start by describing the two main contenders.

The first contender is Henrique Capriles Radonski, a 39-year-old politician, governor of Miranda since 2008, and a key opposition political figure of *Primero Justicia,* a center-right party founded in 1999. During his campaign, Capriles has announced his intention to replace Chávez's socialism with the successful model of the Left applied in Brazil. The second contender is Pablo Pérez, a 42-year-old governor of the oil rich western state of Zulia since 2008 (predecessor of Manuel Rosales—see page 79 in Chapter 3), and an instrumental leader of *Un Nuevo Tiempo,* a center-left party founded in Zulia in 1999. The third candidate in the opposition primary race is Maria Corina Machado, a 44-year-old parliamentarian, co-founder and former president of the civil organization *Súmate* founded in 2002 (see pages 78–79 in Chapter 3), and the first woman in Venezuela to campaign for the presidency; she is an independent right-wing candidate campaigning with a model called 'popular capitalism'. This model proposes to end class contradiction, democratize capital, and hence adjust people's incomes.

The fourth candidate campaigning in the opposition presidential primary is Diego Arria, an experienced 73-year-old diplomat and politician, appointed in the 1970s as the governor of Caracas and government minister. In the early 1990s, Arria was the permanent representative of Venezuela in the United Nations (UN), and held several positions within the UN. On November 21, 2011, Arria filed a complaint before the International Criminal Court (ICC) at The Hague, Netherlands, against Chávez and some of his top aides for crimes against humanity. As an independent, Arria calls for a constituent assembly and amending changes to the constitution adopted in 1999. And finally, there is Pablo Medina, a 65-year-old political veteran who fought in Venezuela's left-wing guerrilla movement, an influential trade union leader, and a co-founder of the left-wing Marxist party *Causa R* in the 1970s and the PPT (a party founded in September 1997). The PPT played an important role in the construction of the antagonistic *Polo Patriótico* camp: the political machinery that helped Chávez get the votes to win the December 1998 presidential election (see pages 78 and 99–105 in Chapter 2). Medina, the candidate of *Movimiento Laboralista* (trade union party), claims that crime is rampant in Venezuela, and that 'the majority of the armed forces are not with Chávez. Those who support Chávez are corrupt and involved in drug trafficking'.[45]

Chávez names the candidates campaigning in the opposition primary election (including the process of different opposition groups in organizing, debating, and uniting as one force) as the '*Majunche*' (inferior, mediocre).[46] This is a new word in Chávez's populist discourse. On January 8, 2012, in his '*N. 376 Aló Presidente*', based on his sources, Chávez stated that 'less than one million of voters will participate in the February 2012 opposition primary election. Who wins the election will be decided abroad'. Chávez also said: 'I doubt the election will take place anyway'.[47] Days before election day, Teresa Albanes, president of MUD's committee, told the press that people working in the public sector were told: 'if you vote, you'll be fired'. Albanes gave no details of the senders or recipients of the messages, for their personal security.[48] [49]

On February 12, 2012, the first opposition primary election went ahead smoothly—with a turnout higher than expected. More than three million voters (3,049,449) participated in choosing their opposition presidential candidate. Henrique Capriles Radonski won with 62.1 percent (1,900,528) of the votes. Pablo Peres came in second with 30.3 percent, followed by Maria Corina Machado with 3.7 percent, Diego Arria with 1.3 percent, and, in fifth place, Pablo Medina with 0.5 percent.[50] The predictions Chávez announced on January 8, 2012 were proved wrong. Capriles had the political support of two former Chavista parties, *Podemos* and the PPT, as well as the *Causa R* and Leopoldo López's *Voluntad Popular*. When Capriles was announced winner of the primary election, from a stage Capriles said:

> [I] want to thank god, our people, all of those that made the effort to vote today . . . we didn't expect such a phenomenal turnout. In spite all the obstacles, threats, more than 3 million people voted. . . . When the people want change, hope defeats fear, because 'good' always defeats

'evil' . . . I hope to be the president of the yellows, the whites, the greens, the blues, the oranges, the reds. I hope to be president of those without color. That's our dream, to govern for everyone . . . campaigning throughout the country, people look at me in my eyes and said: 'Capriles, don't let us down'. I responded: 'failure is prohibited'. We want to construct a different future for everyone, no orders from the Left or the Right. . . . My dream is to unite Venezuela, we are here to unite our people! . . . There is no room for discrimination or hatred in this project . . . the government classifies Venezuelans based on their political color; our experience tells us that we can govern for everyone. I'll work with all my energy to get the trust of all Venezuelans! We want inclusion without exclusion. . . . Venezuelans are tired of confrontation, division; we have seen how someone is excluded by saying what he/she thinks. . . . We have to be united, not only those that disagree with the government, but all of those who want a prosperous Venezuela where everyone is equal! . . . I'll go to all the *Barrios*, villages of the country to see the faces of all Venezuelans . . .[51]

First, Capriles showed his gratitude to the people that went ahead and ignored the threat state employees received of being fired. The discursive meaning of Capriles's use of colors—the yellows (*Primero Justicia*), white (AD), the greens (COPEI), the blues (PPT), the oranges (MAS), the reds (PSUV, PCV, etc.)—unfolds his intention to have a dialogue with any Venezuelan, regardless of his/her political affiliation. The main objective here is to initiate some form of an open dialogue, reconciliation, and accord with the reds, which are the extreme-left parties, organizations, and subjects that exercise the hegemony the Chavista camp has galvanized in recent years. If the 'reds' were to accept Capriles's invitation, 'logics of difference' would gradually erode the dichotomic frontier Chávez's project maintains and reproduces with his populist discourse; and the Chavista 'logics of equivalence' would also lose the much-needed electoral support from Venezuela's less privileged population.

Capriles puts a lot of emphasis in his speech on the meaning of '*todos*' (everyone/all) in his account of the country, as he seeks to represent every Venezuelan regardless of his/her political color. The other word that is also vital in Capriles's speech is '*unir/unidad*' (unite). The significance and motives Capriles aims to address in his discourse are clearly fleshed out as he makes statements such as: 'we want inclusion without exclusion . . . someone is excluded by saying what he/she thinks. . . . Venezuelans are tired of confrontation, division . . . everyone is equal'. Capriles's discourse of unification, inclusion, and equality aims to challenge and gradually displace the populist dichotomic framework Chávez uses in his discourse.

It is difficult to know if Capriles can make an impact with a decisive opposition discourse prior to the presidential election in October 2012, and electorally convince popular sectors that Chávez's populist 'us-them'

Indefinite Re-election   155

axis and demonizing the 'other' discourses are political tactics that no lon-ger 'grip' and mobilize the masses. As Lefort points out, democracy is an empty place that is impossible to occupy. Those who claim to appropri-ate it, insisting that they are the true representatives of the people, can potential destroy the principles of democracy. The future of democracy in Venezuela is grim if Chávez intends to stay in power until 2031—using the type of discourse that further dichotomizes this society and stirs up hatred by demonizing those who disagree with and oppose his regime.

A day after Capriles's victory, he stressed that Chávez's government is stuck in the past, whereas his vision is to create a better future for every-one. He also stated that he was elected to solve problems, not fight with someone, and that he will not stop the social assistance people are cur-rently receiving.[52] This could give us a glimpse of the type of discourse the opposition will be using to get the support of those dissatisfied Chávez supporters who feel excluded once again. Before concluding this final chap-ter, a key question worth mentioning involves to what extent unity among opposition parties within this MUD political alliance can effectively (i.e. by subverting their differences) consolidate a clear objective, which is to over-throw a 'common adversary': Hugo Chavez (not 'enemy'—as this would contradict the pluralistic agonism the opposition advocates). Repressing their own political ambitions and accepting that 'partial totality' (using Laclau's theoretical category—see pages 33–34 in Chapter 1) are necessary to end, via electoral means, the Bolivarian hegemonic project. This won't be an easy task.

For example, Pablo Pérez had the political support of the two *Punto Fijo/* bipartite political parties: AD and COPEI (see page 45 in Chapter 2). Pérez also received the support of MAS: another important party in Venezuela's political affairs in recent decades (see pages 57–59 in Chapter 2). As Pérez lost the primary election, these three parties might get less internal lever-age than others, and therefore fail to exert political power and influence in strategic campaigning decisions, if the opposition wins in October 2012. In my view, there are possibilities that internal friction among opposition par-ties can be as difficult to resolve as the populist attacks the government will throw at Capriles himself, as he wants to maintain a non-confrontational, agonistic campaign. However, in spite of all the internal and external obsta-cles Capriles will have to deal with, his chances of defeating Chávez are a lot higher now—compared with the conditions his predecessor Manuel Rosales confronted back in the December 2006 presidential election.

CONCLUSION

This chapter draws on a set of key political events that occurred in Ven-ezuela after the government's first electoral defeat in December 2007. The first section described the decisions Chávez's government took to further

156   *Populism in Venezuela*

sediment its control of Venezuela's institutional structure. I explained why the district adjustments the government implemented in July 2009 are categorized as gerrymandering, and how this benefitted the government in the September 2010 parliamentarian election. The second section of this chapter discursively analyses the cancer diagnosis Chávez announced to Venezuelans from Havana on June 30, 2011, its political impact, and the type of discourse Chávez used on July 28, 2011—celebrating his birthday from the *balcon del pueblo*.

Another analysis in this chapter is the formation of a new phase of missions called '*Gran Misiones*'. Four of these 'grand' missions are described, with particular emphasis on the *Gran Misión Hijos de Venezuela* (Grand Mission Sons of Venezuela). This analysis gives us a discursive outlook on Chávez's ability to bond with the people and how he naturally manages to sediment his own cult of personality. I also analyzed the theme of Chávez as a populist leader but in another context, which is his affective relationship with Bolívar. The fantasy that Chávez has articulated in his populist discourse lies very much on the new interpretations of the past he constructs, and his role as the leader of the previously excluded population to follow the principles of emancipation Bolívar represents.

Chávez's intention to stay in power until 2030–31 is raised in this chapter, as is his apparent popularity increase after being diagnosed with cancer. If Chávez is not absent from the public eye and appears to be active and recovering, his health condition will be a supplementary topic. Chávez will be making full use of his nationwide mandatory broadcast on all free-to-air TV and radio stations to publicize the success of the 'Grand Missions' programs across the country before October 2012 (with a 45 percent increase in the annual national budget for 2012),[53] present his Sunday '*Aló Presidente*' programs, publicize the struggles and achievements of the Bolivarian Revolution since 1998 as his presidential campaign strategy, and demonize the *majunche* opposition as servants of the American empire, oligarchs, and so on.

The final section of this chapter sought to analyze, in context, how the opposition can make a better use of the Bolivarian symbol, which is pivotal in Chávez's populist discourse. An interview with Leopoldo López, a key opposition political leader in the MUD alliance who happens to be a blood descendant of Bolívar, reveals interesting views about the selfish use of Bolívar's name since his death in 1830. López stresses that Chávez's effort to re-interpret Venezuela's history and make it resonate with the name of Bolívar is counter-productive. Even though López could potentially capitalize upon his Bolívar blood, he believes that this permanent cycle of using the name of Bolívar must end.

This concluding chapter addressed the emergence of a unified opposition force. The 16.53 percent voter turnout (3,049,449 of 18,338,913) in the opposition primary election for a presidential candidate on February 12, 2012 was higher than expected by organizers and government officials.

Henrique Capriles Randonski won with almost two-thirds of the votes. An analysis of the discourse Capriles chose to celebrate his victory gives us a flavor of the political approach and themes (e.g. pluralism, unity, inclusion) Capriles will use for his presidential campaign. It is predictable that Chávez will form a clear populist strategy to attack and discredit Capriles and his opposition project with words and catch-phrases like 'candidate of the American empire', 'the oligarchs', 'the bourgeoisies', 'the anti-homelands', '*majunches*', and so on. However, I stress that Capriles, as a newly elected opposition leader, will have to campaign hard to convince people from popular sectors who still feel excluded (or excluded once again) to trust his call for reconciliation and unification, but also keep that consensus of unity amongst all the opposition political parties that have formed and recently constructed the MUD opposition alliance.

Conclusion

This investigation has undertaken an overall analysis of populism from a wide selection of angles: theoretical approaches, a methodological schema, and a thorough empirical analysis of a case study to determine, to what extent if any, populism is practiced, as well as its emergence, socio-political construction, crystallization, and democratic success. This in-depth analysis of Venezuela's contemporary political crisis uses the genealogical background to contextualize and thus comprehend the nature, practice, and significance of populist discourse and strategies in this deeply dichotomized society.

The application of Laclau's theory of populism with a wide selection of empirical data (see pages 27–31 in Chapter 1) unfolds a new perspective for the analysis and understanding of populist practices. Glynos and Howarth's 'logics approach' galvanizes the theoretical categories Laclau formulates by outlining categories that help us to classify events of unrest and the impact of social and political practices, as well as to identify the meanings of key words, symbols, anecdotes, and so on. The latter casts light on those emotionally driven elements in populist discourse, providing a category for understanding the force and the grip behind these operations.

Laclau's theoretical framework elucidates the process of analyzing and carefully decrypting a country or region where populist practices are claimed to be responsible for the construction of dichotomy and antagonism in a society, and it offers a thorough and well-substantiated approach to understanding the basis of populism and how popular will (i.e. the *popular subject*) manages to challenge and displace a discredited hegemonic project. Revisiting first the research questions of this investigation set out in the introduction, and then the motives and objectives of these research questions as presented in the 'Research strategy' section of Chapter 1, will help us recapture and summarize this study of populist practices in Venezuela.

The first research question sets out to employ Laclau's theoretical approach to populism and determine to what degree the case of Venezuela represents instances of populist politics. This in-depth case study aimed to provide a fuller and more general understanding of the phenomenon of populism. This consisted of exploring the key factors that account for the emergence and reproduction of populism, and to differentiate between populism as a mode of opposition and populism as a mode of governance. As mentioned earlier, Laclau proposes a balanced theoretical contribution to the understanding of populist politics. In Chapter 2, the construction of the Bolivarian 'equivalential chain', and how it democratically succeeded in initiating the displacement of the *Punto Fijo* institutional structure, is empirically reflected. How populism as a mode of governance is articulated, that is, how populist discourse is reproduced and how further radical changes were implemented throughout different phases of a populist project in power, are contextualized in Chapter 3. These facets are highlighted later.

Regarding the second research question of this investigation, I proposed to explore whether a more general account of populism can be applied to this case and used to evaluate existing theories of populism, e.g. those proposed by Canovan or Taggart. The first chapter of this book examines other existing theories of populism and differentiates these outlooks, seeking to unravel the nature of populist practices and elucidate their comprehension vis-à-vis Laclau's approach. I clearly point out why Laclau's theoretical version seems to be better positioned to examine if, and in what context (with the categorical tools he provides), populism is practiced in Venezuela. Apart from analyzing the ins and outs of Venezuelan politics in the last 20 years, this investigation also opens a new window depicting how to employ and analyze empirical data with a populist theoretical approach coupled with the logics methodological schema Glynos and Howarth provide. The value of this research goes beyond analyzing populism in the Venezuelan context. This theoretical and methodological schema can easily be applied to other case studies that seem to constitute instances of populist politics.

Glynos and Howarth's social, political, and fantasmatic 'logics approach' offers new ways and categories to classify narratives and data (e.g. events, practices, symbols, and so on), and to discursively interpret the empirical material selected. For example, it opens a new way to make sense of the significance and impact of a variety of social, political, and emotional factors— previously regarded as irrelevant, or simply not seen before. For instance, the category of social logics gave this investigation a useful approach to the analysis and understanding of the significance of popular mass protests outside the Presidential Palace on April 13, 2002—demanding the return of Chávez to the presidency (after a coup d'état two days earlier). This event was very important because people from the slums spontaneously went down the hills, which in effect was pivotal for the return of Chávez, but also reminded the Bolivarian Government of its promise to construct something honorable for people living in the slums (e.g. social programs like *Barrio Adentro*) and improve the lives of poor Venezuelans. Both social and political logics help us address all these intricate events and present an explanatory perspective on all these social and political events in a fragmented society.

160   Populism in Venezuela

The category of political logics helped this investigation contextualize elements such as the de-institution of the *Punto Fijo* hegemonic order, the construction of the Bolivarian institutional framework and hegemony, and the various attempts these displaced political sectors organized with the intention to challenge and re-establish the institutional power they democratically lost. Political logics in populist practices are constructed on the dimension of equivalence by making reference to an 'us-them' axis. This new political dimension represents the previously excluded people. Its objective is to sediment an institutional structure that helps the poor by radically transforming the way social practices function. These are conceptual devices that help us explain the dynamics of populist discourse. The third category, fantasmatic logics, also provided this case study with a conceptual grammar to investigate the configuration and the forces behind these operations.

A key element of the category of fantasmatic logics, much used throughout this in-depth analysis, is the notion of 'grip'. This element puts into context how specific practices or political projects grip subjects. Grip can be applied to subjects from both camps. That is to say, it can be applied to those who resist the changes a populist project wants to implement, but also encapsulates the 'direction' and 'energy' (i.e. Bolívar as the 'vector') of the radical changes populist politics aim to crystallize for the well-being of underclass subjects. This relation between subjects and populist politics lies in a narrative that deems the enemy (the oligarchs, the corrupt *Punto Fijo* system, *majunches*, etc.) responsible for people's misfortunes, while promising a fullness or harmony to come with this new revolutionary hegemonic order.

Other than its post-structuralist discourse analysis contribution, this investigation also advances our understanding of populism in Venezuela. A wide selection of primary and secondary data was used to conduct this in-depth investigation. Interviews with Luis Miquilena—Chávez's mentor, and key political strategist and broker of the *'Polo Patriótico'* platform, which helped Chávez get elected president in December 1998, and consolidated people's support through referendums for a new constitution in 1999 and 2000—reveals critical aspects of this populist project. It also sheds light on how this new hegemonic project managed to survive after the opposition organized various attempts to dismantle it—events that benefitted the populist government and further fragmented the opposition camp (e.g. the Bolivarian project took complete institutional control of the oil industry in 2003)—and thereby contributes to the literature of populism in Venezuela. The analysis presented in Chapter 3 gives us a way of understanding how dichotomized Venezuela's society is and its impact on political practices.

The next phase of the Bolivarian project, which started in 2003, was a radical plan. Its objective was to construct social programs called 'missions' in poor and marginalized areas to help the previously excluded, encouraging people's direct participation and involvement in these programs. These programs, helping the previously excluded, proved to be a success. A key element contextualized in Chapter 3 is how Chávez articulates a discourse of anti-American hegemony by associating those that oppose his Bolivarian hegemonic project (the elite, oligarchs, neoliberals, etc.) with the minority of the population controlled by the American Empire (e.g. the pawns—'*los peones*'—referring to the role of a pawn in the game of chess; see pages 79 and 84–85 in Chapter 3). As a mode of governance, this is how populist discourse is articulated, maintaining and hardening the dichotomic frontier constructed when the Bolivarian project was in opposition. In December 2006, Chávez was re-elected with more than 60 percent of the votes—announcing 'socialism of the twenty-first century' as the discourse for the next phase of the Bolivarian project. Using his popularity, Chávez organized a referendum in December 2007 to introduce constitutional amendments that would allow him to be re-elected indefinitely. However, in spite of time and resources aplenty, Chávez lost. New opposition forces stopped him.

This is a brief summary of the chronological chain of events discussed and analyzed in Chapters 2 and 3. Laclau's theory of populism coupled with Glynos and Howarth's 'logics approach' provided the theoretical and methodological methods for presenting a descriptive interpretation of populism, by discursively unfolding the nature and impact of populist practices in Venezuela. In Chapter 3, the socio-political significance of the themes analyzed in Chapters 4 and 5 was briefly contextualized, and a rationale was presented for their selection for further analysis.

The in-depth analysis of a healthcare program called Mission '*Barrio Adentro*' (BA) in Chapter 4 contextualized the discursive articulation that formed a new phase of the Bolivarian hegemonic project with direct grassroots popular participation. These are government strategies to materialize in a true sense the institutional radical change promised to their electoral popular-base. My objective was to descriptively address and contextualize elements of the formation and reproduction of Bolivarian populist practices by evaluating how a popular healthcare program for the excluded emerged, the political contestation it created, and how it has managed to advance. Furthermore, my objective was to evaluate the resistance from Venezuela's Medical Federation—aligned with anti-Bolivarian forces. My claim is that this popular program has radically transformed healthcare in Venezuela. However, the future of BA looks uncertain.

Nonetheless, on February 16, 2012 (in spite of its lower-than-expected number of graduates and timeframe), the graduation of 8,150 Venezuelan medics, which is the first promotion of the 'Integrated General Medicine' program chaired by Chávez and accompanied by the Hollywood actor Sean Penn, represented, to some extent, a sign of progress for BA.[1] Yet, the escalation of protests by BA workers demanding clear employment agreements with the government and that salaries be paid may seriously jeopardize improvements achieved in other sectors of this healthcare program (see pages 109–12 in Chapter 4). Failure to solve these problems could seriously affect Chávez's popularity in the 2012 presidential election.

162 *Populism in Venezuela*

Furthermore, on April 2, 2012, a newspaper report stressed that the construction of 1,235 BA II buildings has ceased because of a lack of funds and because building contractors (48 of 54 construction contracts are on hold) have failed to complete the project on time.[2] On the one hand, there is progress, but on the other, internal problems obstruct the development of BA.

Chapter 5 analyzed how an anti-Bolivarian movement known as '*Generación 2007*' was formed, its demands, its methods of challenging the expansion of government control, and why this student movement failed to transform itself as a long-term opposition force. This analysis reveals what the opposition political machinery lacked, and how this new social sector added new discursive elements to the opposition camp in order to challenge the expansion and sedimentation of the Bolivarian hegemonic project. Nonetheless, while it started off with a lot of possibilities and optimism, and seemed to constitute a challenge to the new hegemonic project, it ultimately failed and was absorbed into other opposition political parties.

The students' '*Manos Blancas*' discourse did manage to temporarily challenge the government and symbolized hope for all of those who opposed the Bolivarian project. However, its success was short lived because the movement depended greatly on those student leaders from universities in Caracas who benefitted from the constant media attention in 2007 at the demonstration events in Caracas. The media created an atmosphere in which these leaders nationally represented all students who opposed the Bolivarian project. However, in reality, this was not the case. When these students graduated in 2008, and were thus unable to represent the student movement, there were no substitutes available to fill those key student leadership positions. Unfortunately, these former student leaders joined opposition political parties. In my view, if they collectively tried to construct a new opposition political frontier, capitalizing on their success in challenging the government in 2007, it is possible that this new force could have had the right conditions to contest and ultimately displace the Bolivarian hegemony.

Chapter 6 addressed the referendum that took place on February 15, 2009, giving Chávez the green light to run for the presidency indefinitely. It also addressed the electoral district gerrymandering reforms the government employed to keep control (two-thirds majority) of the parliament in the September 2010 parliamentarian election, which the incumbent didn't get. Furthermore, I analyzed Chávez's discourse from Havana on June 30, 2011, informing Venezuelans of his cancer diagnoses and recovery, the increase of his popularity after announcing his health condition, the formation of four more 'Grand Missions' a year before the October 2012 presidential election, and the type of discourse Chávez uses to connect his political project with Bolívar's struggle for nationalist emancipation from Spanish rule. Moreover, an interview with Leopoldo López, Bolívar's descendant and a key opposition political leader, highlights interesting views about the use of Bolívar for political purposes in Venezuela, and López's perspective on Chávez's regime. This chapter concludes by analyzing the emergence of

Conclusion 163

the *Mesa de la Unidad Democrática* (MUD) opposition force, the candidates in the primary presidential election held on February 12, 2012, and Henrique Capriles Randonski's speech after being declared the winner with 62.1 percent of the votes.

In my view, without populist discourse, there is no Bolivarian hegemony. Populist practices stand on the dichotomic platform constructed when this political project emerged in the late 1990s. Discursively, reproducing the underdog sentiment reconstitutes the significance of the Bolivarian hegemonic project to the previously excluded. The notion of blaming people's misfortunes on the previous regime, the American hegemony, oligarchs, *majunches*, bourgeoisies living in the east of Caracas, and so on aims to discursively re-articulate the 'us-them' frontier. This is the mechanism used to reproduce the nodal point of the Bolivarian hegemonic project in order to maintain the national popular vote, particularly during moments of crisis.

However, because Chávez has been in power since 1999, people's tolerance and their perception that there will be fulfillment to come under Chávez are wearing thin. During my fieldwork visit in September 2010, people from many 'social sectors'[3] complained about poverty, crime, unemployment, inflation, food shortages, the poor supply of water and electricity, lack of infrastructure maintenance and improvement, institutional abuse, and rampant corruption at all levels of government. It appears that there are fewer conditions available for the Bolivarian project to reproduce the populist discourse and thus further sediment its frontier, blaming the oligarchs, the American empire, and so on for people's lack and misfortunes (i.e. the previously excluded). It is difficult to predict how Chávez and his political machinery will act in view of the emergence of an organized opposition force campaigning for a young 40-year-old presidential candidate detached from the ills of pre-1999 governments, and in view of Chávez's fight with cancer, as a new malignant tumor was found in February 2012—in the same place where a cancerous tumor was removed in June 2011. In spite of the incumbent's surplus of financial and logistical resources, a re-election campaign shortly after the removal of another cancerous tumor won't be easy for Chávez and his political machinery throughout the country.

Furthermore, the role of Chávez as a symbolic figure who incorporates and names together all the needs, wants, and problems of the 'people' could be losing its grip after being in power for more than a decade. His populist rhetoric, in which he claims to be a defender working for the well-being of the previously excluded (like himself) against a common enemy, cannot have the same effect because after 14 years in power, problems of poverty have not been solved and a sense of improvement has not yet materialized. How long will it take to complete the Bolivarian hegemonic project? How can we objectively identify what is a fulfilled or hollow promise? The discursive role of leadership in this context opens the terrain for more analysis. To what extent can Chávez expect *'el pueblo'* to support his own sense of enjoyment in the presidency, when his claim that circumstances have not

164   *Populism in Venezuela*

improved as promised because external forces are constantly attempting to displace the revolution seems to be less convincing every day.

Panizza states that 'populism has traditionally been regarded as a threat to democracy'.[4] There is indeed a threat to democracy when a populist does not recognize that 'democracy power is an "empty place" that can only be provisionally occupied'.[5] Lefort's explanation of 'empty place' in his theoretical understanding of democracy' that is, the relation among terms such as 'popular sovereignty', 'the power of nobody', and 'exercise public authority can never claim to occupy it'; helps us deduce the Chavista project from another perspective (see pages 148–49 in Chapter 6).

Chávez's insistence on staying in the presidency when his administration ends in 2012 could have serious implications for Venezuela's democratic system. Of course, it is the people who will decide in the October 2012 presidential election. Nonetheless, Venezuela's 'socialism of the twenty-first century' agenda seems to be decided in a chauvinistic fashion by Chávez only. Chávez hopes to be in power until 2031. If cancer doesn't end his presidency, Chávez might be able to fulfill his ambition. He has already managed to get round his plan to run for re-election indefinitely after his first electoral defeat in the December 2007 constitutional reform referendum. Chávez might have something up his sleeve if further re-adjustments are needed to keep his presidency. This would raise serious questions about the legitimacy of democratic practices in Venezuela.

Notes

NOTES TO THE INTRODUCTION

1. Levine, D. 'The Transition to Democracy: Are There Lessons from Venezuela?', *Bulletin of Latin American Research*, Vol. 4, No. 2 (1985): 58.
2. Gott, R. *Hugo Chávez and the Bolivarian Revolution* (London: Verso, 2005), 13.
3. Ali, T. *Pirates of the Caribbean—Axis of Hope* (London: Verso, 2006), 15.
4. Ali, *Pirates of the Caribbean—Axis of Hope,* 26.
5. Fernandes, S. *Who Can Stop the Drums?—Urban Social Movements in Chávez's Venezuela* (Duke University Press, 2010), 84.
6. Marcano, C., and Barrera Tyszka, A. *Hugo Chávez* (New York: Random House, 2007), 140.
7. Marcano and Barrera Tyszka, *Hugo Chávez,* 141.
8. Hawkins, K. *Venezuela's Chavismo and Populism in Comparative Perspective* (New York: Cambridge University Press, 2010), 6.
9. Hawkins, *Venezuela's Chavismo and Populism in Comparative Perspective,* 5.
10. Stoker's descriptive elements are based on Harnecker's interpretation. Harnecker, M. *Understanding the Venezuelan Revolution—Hugo Chávez Talks to Marta Harnecker* (New York: Monthly Review Press, 2005). Stoker, G. *Why Politics Matters—Making Democracy Work* (London: Palgrave, 2006), 135–36.
11. Stoker, *Why Politics Matters—Making Democracy Work,* 139.
12. Mires, F. *Al Borde del Abismo—El Chavismo y la Contrarrevolución Antidemocrática de Nuestro Tiempo* (Caracas: Debate, 2007), 44–45.

NOTES TO CHAPTER 1

1. Ionescu, G., and Gellner, E. *Populism—Its Meanings and National Characteristics* (London: Weidenfield Goldbacks, 1970), 1–2; Laclau, E. *Politics and Ideology in Marxist Theory: Capialism—Fascism—Populism* (London: Verso, 1977), 145; Canovan, M. *Populism* (London: Junction Books, 1981), 3–4; Westlind, D. *The Politics of Popular Identity: Understanding Recent Populist Movements in Sweden and the United States* (Lund: Lund University Press, 1996), 133; Taggart, P. *Populism* (Buckingham: Open University Press, 2000), 2–3.
2. Canovan, M. *The People* (Cambridge: Polity Press, 2005), 78.
3. Canovan, M. *Populism* (London: Junction Books, 1981), 13.

166 *Notes*

4. Canovan, *Populism*, 13.
5. Canovan, M. *Populism* (London: Junction Books 1981); Canovan, M. 'Two Strategies for the Study of Populism', *Political Studies*, Vol. 30 (1982): 544–52; Canovan, M. '"People", Politicians and Populism', *Government and Opposition*, Vol. 19 (1984): 312–27; cited by Canovan, *The People,* 79.
6. Kazin, M. *The Populist Persuasion: An American History* (New York: Basic Books 1995); Westlind, D. *The Politics of Popular Identity: Understanding Recent Populist Movements in Sweden and the United States* (Lund: Lund University Press, 1996); Laclau, E. 'Populism: What's in a Name?', in Panizza, F. (ed.), *Populism and the Mirror of Democracy* (London: Verso, 2005); cited by Canovan, *The People,* 79.
7. Canovan, *The People,* 79.
8. Canovan, M. 'Populism for Political Theorists?', *Journal of Political Ideologies*, Vol. 9, No. 3 (2004): 242.
9. Canovan, M. 'Taking Politics to the People: Populism as the Ideology of Democracy', in Mény, Y., and Surel, Y. (eds.), *Democracies and the Populist Challenge* (New York: Palgrave Macmillan, 2002), 25.
10. Canovan, 'Taking Politics to the People: Populism as the Ideology of Democracy', 26.
11. Di Tella, Torcuato S. 'Populism into the Twenty-First Century', *Government and Opposition*, Vol. 32, No. 2 (April 1997):188.
12. Di Tella, 'Populism into the Twenty-First Century', 188–90.
13. Kazin, M. *The Populist Persuasion: An American History* (New York: Basic Books, 1995), 2.
14. Kazin, *The Populist Persuasion: An American History,* 3.
15. Canovan,'Populism for Political Theorists?', 244.
16. Taggart, *Populism*, 1.
17. Taggart, *Populism*, 2.
18. Taggart, *Populism*, 2–3.
19. Taggart, *Populism*, 3.
20. Taggart, *Populism*, 3.
21. Taggart, *Populism*, 4.
22. Taggart, *Populism*, 4.
23. Taggart, *Populism*, 5.
24. Taggart, *Populism*, 10.
25. Taggart, *Populism*, 10.
26. Taggart, *Populism*, 95.
27. Taggart, *Populism*, 95.
28. Taggart, *Populism*, 95–96.
29. Taggart, *Populism*, 96–97.
30. Taggart, *Populism*, 97.
31. Panizza, F. 'Introduction: Populism and the Mirror of Democracy', in Panizza, F. (ed.), *Populism and the Mirror of Democracy* (London: Verso, 2005), 3.
32. Panizza, 'Introduction: Populism and the Mirror of Democracy', 3–4.
33. Panizza, 'Introduction: Populism and the Mirror of Democracy', 4.
34. Panizza, 'Introduction: Populism and the Mirror of Democracy', 5–6.
35. Panizza, 'Introduction: Populism and the Mirror of Democracy', 9.
36. Panizza, 'Introduction: Populism and the Mirror of Democracy', 10.
37. Panizza, 'Introduction: Populism and the Mirror of Democracy', 10–11.
38. Panizza, 'Introduction: Populism and the Mirror of Democracy', 11.
39. Panizza, 'Introduction: Populism and the Mirror of Democracy', 11–12.
40. Panizza, 'Introduction: Populism and the Mirror of Democracy', 14.
41. Panizza, 'Introduction: Populism and the Mirror of Democracy', 16–17.

Notes 167

42. Glynos, J. 'Sexual Identity, Identification and Differences', *Philosophy and Social Criticism*, Vol. 26, No. 6 (2000): 85–108; cited by Panizza, 'Introduction: Populism and the Mirror of Democracy', 19.
43. Panizza, 'Introduction: Populism and the Mirror of Democracy', 19.
44. Panizza, 'Introduction: Populism and the Mirror of Democracy', 20.
45. Žižek, S. *The Sublime Object of Ideology* (London: Verso, 1989), 105–6; cited by Panizza, 'Introduction: Populism and the Mirror of Democracy', 26.
46. Panizza, 'Introduction: Populism and the Mirror of Democracy', 26.
47. Panizza, 'Introduction: Populism and the Mirror of Democracy', 29.
48. Canovan, *Populism,* 9; cited by Panizza, 'Introduction: Populism and the Mirror of Democracy', 29.
49. Panizza, 'Introduction: Populism and the Mirror of Democracy', 29.
50. Lefort, C. *The Political Forms of Modern Society: Bureaucracy, Democracy, Totalitarianism* (Cambridge, MA: MIT Press, 1986), 279; cited by Panizza, 'Introduction: Populism and the Mirror of Democracy', 29.
51. Panizza, 'Introduction: Populism and the Mirror of Democracy', 29.
52. Laclau, E., and Mouffe, C. *Hegemony and Socialist Strategy—Towards a Radical Democratic Politics* (London: Verso, 1985); Laclau, E. *New Reflection on the Revolution of Our Time* (London: Verso, 1990); Laclau, E. *Emancipation* (London: Verso, 1996).
53. Laclau, E. *On Populist Reason* (London: Verso, 2005), 67.
54. Laclau, *On Populist Reason*, 68–69.
55. Laclau and Mouffe, *Hegemony and Socialist Strategy—Towards a Radical Democratic Politics*, 105.
56. Laclau, *Emancipation*, 36–46; cited by Laclau, *On Populist Reason*, 69.
57. Laclau, *On Populist Reason*, 69.
58. Laclau, *On Populist Reason*, 69.
59. Laclau, *On Populist Reason*, 69.
60. Laclau, *On Populist Reason*, 70.
61. Laclau, *On Populist Reason*, 70.
62. Laclau, *On Populist Reason*, 70.
63. Laclau, *On Populist Reason*, 70.
64. Laclau, *On Populist Reason*, 70.
65. Laclau, *On Populist Reason*, 70.
66. Laclau, *On Populist Reason*, 70.
67. Laclau, *On Populist Reason*, 71.
68. Laclau, *On Populist Reason*, 71.
69. See: Parker, P. 'Metaphor and Catachresis', in Bender, J., and Wellbery, D. (eds.), *The End(s) of Rhetoric* (Stanford, CA: Stanford UP, 1990), 60–73; cited by Laclau, *On Populist Reason*, 71.
70. Laclau, *On Populist Reason*, 71.
71. Laclau, *On Populist Reason*, 71.
72. Laclau, *On Populist Reason*, 72.
73. Laclau, *On Populist Reason*, 71.
74. Laclau, *On Populist Reason*, 72.
75. Laclau, *On Populist Reason*, 73.
76. Laclau, *On Populist Reason*, 73.
77. Laclau, *On Populist Reason*, 78.
78. Laclau, *On Populist Reason*, 81.
79. Laclau, *On Populist Reason*, 81.
80. Laclau, *On Populist Reason*, 86.
81. Laclau, *On Populist Reason*, 87.

168   *Notes*

82. Laclau, *On Populist Reason*, 88.
83. Laclau, *On Populist Reason*, 89.
84. Laclau, *On Populist Reason*, 95–96.
85. Laclau, *On Populist Reason*, 99.
86. Laclau, *On Populist Reason*, 100.
87. Laclau, *On Populist Reason*, 109.
88. Laclau, *On Populist Reason*, 110.
89. Laclau, *On Populist Reason*, 110.
90. Laclau, *On Populist Reason*, 110.
91. Laclau, *On Populist Reason*, 110.
92. Laclau, *On Populist Reason*, 110.
93. Laclau, *On Populist Reason*, 116–17.
94. In general, this approach can be defined as follows: 'Discourse Theory investigates the way in which social practices articulate and contest the discourses that constitute social reality. These practices are possible because systems of meaning are contingent and can never completely exhaust a field of meaning. In order to unpack and elaborate upon this complex set of statements, we need working definitions of the categories of discursivity, discourse, and discourse analysis'. Howarth, D., and Stavrakakis, Y. 'Introducing Discourse Theory and Political Analysis', in Howarth, D., Norval, A., and Stavrakakis, A. (eds.), *Discourse Theory and Political Analysis* (Manchester: Manchester University Press, 2000), 3. More to the point, Howarth emphasizes in another article a picture of populist discourse. He states that a 'picture' of populism is 'a loose set of features that permits a range of "family resemblance" phenomena to be connected or derived—which might be said to underpin, but in no way determine or exhaust the populist experience. Its function is primarily heuristic rather than strictly explanatory, in that it facilitates the categorization and description of phenomena brought within its orbit'. Howarth, D. 'Populism or Popular Democracy? The UDF, Workerism and the Struggle for Radical Democracy in South Africa', in Panizza, F. (ed.), *Populism and the Mirror of Democracy* (London: Verso, 2005), 203–4. These features are presented in this sub-section—quoting from other papers.
95. Howarth, D. 'Applying Discourse Theory: The Method of Articulation', in Howarth, D., and Torfing, J. (eds.), *Discourse Theory in European Politics: Identity, Policy and Governance* (Basingstoke: Palgrave Macmillan, 2005), 317–49.
96. Laclau, E. 'Constructing Universality', in Butler, J., et al. (eds.), *Contingency, Hegemony, Universality* (London: Verso, 2000), 282–83; cited by Howarth, 'Applying Discourse Theory: The Method of Articulation', 323.
97. Howarth, 'Applying Discourse Theory: The Method of Articulation', 323.
98. Howarth, 'Applying Discourse Theory: The Method of Articulation', 323.
99. Howarth, 'Applying Discourse Theory: The Method of Articulation', 323.
100. Howarth, 'Applying Discourse Theory: The Method of Articulation', 323.
101. Howarth, 'Applying Discourse Theory: The Method of Articulation', 323.
102. Howarth, 'Applying Discourse Theory: The Method of Articulation', 323.
103. Howarth, 'Applying Discourse Theory: The Method of Articulation', 323.
104. Howarth, 'Applying Discourse Theory: The Method of Articulation', 323.
105. Glynos, J., and Howarth, D. *Logics of Critical Explanation in Social and Political Theory* (London: Routledge, 2007), 139.
106. Glynos and Howarth, *Logics of . . . Social and Political Theory*, 139.
107. Glynos and Howarth, *Logics of . . . Social and Political Theory*, 140.
108. Glynos and Howarth, *Logics of . . . Social and Political Theory*, 140.
109. Laclau, E. 'Populism: What's in a Name?', in Panizza, F. (ed.), *Populism and the Mirror of Democracy* (London: Verso, 2005), 34.

110. Laclau, 'Populism: What's in a Name?', 34.
111. Laclau, 'Populism: What's in a Name?', 34.
112. Laclau, 'Populism: What's in a Name?', 34.
113. Laclau, 'Populism: What's in a Name?', 34.
114. Laclau, 'Populism: What's in a Name?', 34.
115. Laclau, 'Populism: What's in a Name?', 35.
116. Laclau, 'Populism: What's in a Name?', 35.
117. Laclau, 'Populism: What's in a Name?', 35.
118. Laclau, 'Populism: What's in a Name?', 36.
119. Laclau, 'Populism: What's in a Name?', 36.
120. Laclau, 'Populism: What's in a Name?', 36.
121. Laclau, 'Populism: What's in a Name?', 36–37.
122. Laclau, 'Populism: What's in a Name?', 37.
123. Laclau, *On Populist Reason* (London: Verso, 2005), 130–31.
124. Laclau, *On Populist Reason*, 131.
125. Laclau, E., and Mouffe, C. *Hegemony and Socialist Strategy* (London: Verso, 1985), 112.
126. Laclau, 'Populism: What's in a Name?', 37.
127. Laclau, 'Populism: What's in a Name?', 38.
128. Laclau, 'Populism: What's in a Name?', 38.
129. Laclau, 'Populism: What's in a Name?', 38.
130. Laclau, 'Populism: What's in a Name?', 38–39.
131. Laclau, 'Populism: What's in a Name?', 39.
132. Laclau, 'Populism: What's in a Name?', 39.
133. Laclau, 'Populism: What's in a Name?', 39.
134. Laclau, 'Populism: What's in a Name?', 39–40.
135. The term 'empty signifier' was earlier discussed in Laclau's framework in Chapter 1, see pages 16–18. Laclau, 'Populism: What's in a Name?', 40.
136. Laclau, 'Populism: What's in a Name?', 40.
137. Laclau, 'Populism: What's in a Name?', 40.
138. Glynos and Howarth, *Logics of . . . Social and Political Theory*, 141.
139. Glynos and Howarth, *Logics of . . . Social and Political Theory*, 141.
140. Glynos and Howarth, *Logics of . . . Social and Political Theory*, 142.
141. Laclau, *On Populist Reason*, 117; cited Glynos and Howarth, *Logics of . . . Social and Political Theory*, 142.
142. Glynos and Howarth, *Logics of . . . Social and Political Theory*, 142.
143. Glynos and Howarth, *Logics of . . . Social and Political Theory*, 142.
144. Glynos and Howarth, *Logics of . . . Social and Political Theory*, 143.
145. Glynos and Howarth, *Logics of . . . Social and Political Theory*, 143.
146. Glynos and Howarth, *Logics of . . . Social and Political Theory*, 143.
147. Laclau and Mouffe, *Hegemony and Socialist Strategy*, 130; cited by Glynos and Howarth, *Logics of . . . Social and Political Theory*, 144.
148. Glynos and Howarth, *Logics of . . . Social and Political Theory*, 144.
149. Glynos and Howarth, *Logics of . . . Social and Political Theory*, 144.
150. Glynos and Howarth, *Logics of . . . Social and Political Theory*, 145.
151. Glynos and Howarth, *Logics of . . . Social and Political Theory*, 145.
152. Glynos and Howarth, *Logics of . . . Social and Political Theory*, 145.
153. Glynos and Howarth, *Logics of . . . Social and Political Theory*, 145.
154. Glynos and Howarth, *Logics of . . . Social and Political Theory*, 145.
155. Glynos and Howarth, *Logics of . . . Social and Political Theory*, 145.
156. Laclau, *On Populist Reason*, 101; cited by Glynos and Howarth, *Logics of . . . Social and Political Theory*, 145.
157. Glynos and Howarth, *Logics of . . . Social and Political Theory*, 145.
158. Glynos and Howarth, *Logics of . . . Social and Political Theory*, 145.

170 *Notes*

159. Glynos and Howarth, *Logics of . . . Social and Political Theory*, 146.
160. Glynos and Howarth, *Logics of . . . Social and Political Theory*, 147.
161. Glynos and Howarth, *Logics of . . . Social and Political Theory*, 147.
162. Glynos and Howarth, *Logics of . . . Social and Political Theory*, 147.
163. Glynos and Howarth, *Logics of . . . Social and Political Theory*, 147.
164. Glynos and Howarth, *Logics of . . . Social and Political Theory*, 150.
165. Glynos and Howarth, *Logics of . . . Social and Political Theory*, 150.
166. Glynos and Howarth, *Logics of . . . Social and Political Theory*, 151.
167. Glynos and Howarth, *Logics of . . . Social and Political Theory*, 151.
168. Glynos and Howarth, *Logics of . . . Social and Political Theory*, 151.
169. Glynos and Howarth, *Logics of . . . Social and Political Theory*, 151–52.
170. Glynos and Howarth, *Logics of . . . Social and Political Theory*, 152.
171. Glynos and Howarth, *Logics of . . . Social and Political Theory*, 119.
172. Glynos and Howarth, *Logics of . . . Social and Political Theory*, 119.
173. Althusser, L. *Lenin and Philosophy, and Other Essays* (New York: Monthly Review Press, 1971), 176; cited by Glynos and Howarth, *Logics of . . . Social and Political Theory*, 119.
174. Zizek, S. *The Sublime Object of Ideology* (London: Verso, 1989); cited by Glynos and Howarth, *Logics of . . . Social and Political Theory*, 119.
175. Glynos and Howarth, *Logics of . . . Social and Political Theory*, 119.
176. Glynos and Howarth, *Logics of . . . Social and Political Theory*, 119.
177. Glynos and Howarth, *Logics of . . . Social and Political Theory*, 119–20.
178. Glynos and Howarth, *Logics of . . . Social and Political Theory*, 120.
179. Glynos and Howarth, *Logics of . . . Social and Political Theory*, 120.
180. The literature of Howarth ('Applying Discourse Theory: The Method of Articulation' [2005]) and Glynos and Howarth (*Logics of Critical Explanation in Social and Political Theory* [2007]) outlines a methodological schema that provides the necessary tools for this research. Theoretically, Laclau (*On Populist Reason* [2005] and 'Populism: What's in a Name?' [2005]) and Laclau and Mouffe (*Hegemony and Socialist Strategy* [1985]) offer a discursive structure to classify and comprehend how social and political mechanisms operate (defend/demand) when a populist phenomenon is mobilised.
181. Glynos and Howarth, *Logics of . . . Social and Political Theory*, 153.
182. Glynos and Howarth, *Logics of . . . Social and Political Theory*, 153.
183. Glynos and Howarth, *Logics of . . . Social and Political Theory*, 152.
184. Stavrakakis, Y. *Lacan and the Political* (London: Routledge 1999), 81; cited by Glynos and Howarth, *Logics of . . . Social and Political Theory*, 145.
185. Howarth, 'Applying Discourse Theory: The Method of Articulation', 329.
186. Howarth, 'Applying Discourse Theory: The Method of Articulation', 329.
187. Months after Chávez's first electoral defeat in December 2007, Baduel was arrested on grounds of corruption. He was detained for only two days. However, the second arrest in April 2009 coincides with Baduel's decision to challenge Chávez in public once again. Baduel was sentenced for seven years and eleven months in prison on corruption charges. Baduel claims that he was convicted on baseless allegations without any evidence or an impartial trail.

NOTES TO CHAPTER 2

1. '*Generación 28*' was the first significant public protest against Gomez. When Gomez died in 1935, key student founders formed major political parties and were the leading figures in national politics until the 1970s. Between 1928 and 1935 they constructed a new socio-political discourse in Venezuela.

Notes 171

2. Coronil, F. *The Magical State: Nature, Money, and Modernity in Venezuela* (Chicago: University of Chicago Press, 1997), 91–94.
3. Coronil, *The Magical State: Nature, Money, and Modernity in Venezuela*, 94.
4. The three political parties were: AD, COPEI (Political Electoral Independent Organization Committee—this Christian democratic party was founded in January 1946 by Rafael Caldera), and Democratic Republic Union (URD). The only party that decided not to participate in this process was the Communist Party (PCV). Thereon, the PCV got involved in the guerrilla movement.
5. *Partido Comunista de Venezuela* (PCV) re-entered the electoral system. However, the majority of PCV members left the party and formed two new parties: *Movimiento al Socialismo* (MAS) and *La Causa Radical* (LCR). I'll elaborate on these parties later.
6. In 1972 the price of crude oil was about U.S. $3.00 per barrel. By the end of 1974 the price quadrupled to over $12.00. From 1974 to 1978 oil prices were relatively flat: $12.21 to $13.55 per barrel.
7. Buxton, J. 'Economic Policy and the Rise of Hugo Chávez', in Ellner, S., and Hellinger, D. (eds.), *Venezuelan Politics in the Chávez Era: Class, Polarization, and Conflict* (Boulder, CO: Lynne Rienner Publishers, 2003), 115.
8. Buxton, J. 'Economic Policy and the Rise of Hugo Chávez', 115.
9. The combination of the Iranian Revolution and the Iraq-Iran War triggered an increase in crude oil prices—from U.S. $14 in 1978 to $35 per barrel in 1981.
10. From 1983 until 1988, 973 protests (665 conventional, 214 confrontational, and 94 violent) demanded the authorities to react to their needs. See Lopez Maya, M. 'Venezuela after the Caracazo: Forms of Protest in a Deinstitutionalised Context', *Bulletin of Latin American Research,* Vol. 21, No. 2 (2002): 203.
11. Naím, M. 'The Launching of Radical Policy Changes, 1989–1991', in Tulchin, J. S., and Bland, G. (eds.), *Venezuela in the Wake of Radical Reform* (Boulder, CO: Lynne Rienner Publishers, 1993), 68.
12. McCoy, J. L. 'Venezuela: Labor and the State in a Party-Mediated Democracy: Institutional Change in Venezuela', *Latin American Research Review,* Vol. 24, No. 2 (1989): 35–68; cited by Coronil, *The Magical State: Nature, Money, and Modernity in Venezuela,* 371.
13. Karl, T. L. 'The Venezuelan Petro-State and the Crisis of "Its" Democracy', in McCoy, J., Serbin, A., Smith, W. C, and Stambouli, A. (eds.), *Venezuelan Democracy under Stress* (Coral Gables, FL: North-South Center at the University of Miami, 1995); cited by Coronil, *The Magical State: Nature, Money, and Modernity in Venezuela,* 371.
14. Naim, M. 'The Political Management of Radical Economic Change: Lessons from the Venezuelan Experience', in Tulchin, J. S., and Bland, G. (eds.), *Venezuela in the Wake of Radical Reform* (Boulder, CO: Lynne Rienner Publishers, 1993), 157.
15. Their founders wanted to make their movement resonate with Bolívar's values of emancipation and equality. In 1983 was the 200th anniversary of Bolívar's birth.
16. The government ordered independent bus drivers to increase the fares by 30 percent. Unfortunately, several ignored this regulation and went ahead with a 100 percent increase. These drastic changes developed into a protest that soon became a national emergency.
17. 'Between 300 to 3,000 dead according to different sources'. 'Former Venezuelan Defense Chief may face charges for 1989 "Caracazo"', *VHeadline—News & Views about Venezuela,* July 31, 2010, http://www.vheadline.com/readnews.asp?id=95056 [accessed November 2010].

172   Notes

18. Coronil, F., and Skurski, J. 'Dismembering and Remembering the Nation: The Semantics of Political Violence in Venezuela', *Comparative Studies in Society and History*, Vol. 33, No. 2 (1991): 327.
19. Kelly, J., and Palma, P. 'The Syndrome of Economic Decline and the Quest for Change', in McCoy, J., and Myers, D. (eds.), *The Unravelling of Representative Democracy in Venezuela* (Baltimore: Johns Hopkins University Press, 2004), 213.
20. The racial element fleshes out vital points of 'power' control. The 'poor/popular' that barely had a Caucasian connection played no role in managing the country. Their labor responsibilities were mostly unskilled, whereas the 'educated' shared a degree (some more than others) of Caucasian blood and maintained professional, managerial, and political positions.
21. *El Nacional.* February 5, 1992. Microfilm archives. Biblioteca Nacional, Caracas, Venezuela.
22. *El Nacional.* February 8, 1992. Microfilm archives. Biblioteca Nacional, Caracas, Venezuela.
23. 'Palabras del teniente-coronel Hugo Chávez 4 el de Febrero de 1992 por la televisión'. *analitica.com* Venezuela. http://www.analitica.com/bitblioteca/hchavez/4f.asp [accessed October 2008].
24. See the term 'empty signifier' in pages 16–18 in Chapter 1. For further reference regarding the use of the category 'empty signifier', see Steven Griggs and David Howarth's article, where they describe how signifiers such as 'freedom to fly', 'sustainable aviation', and 'demand management' are classified as empty signifiers in the context of 'Stop Stanstead Airport Expansion' analysis. Griggs, S, and Howarth, D. 'Populism, Localism and Environmental Politics: The Logic and Rhetoric of the Stop Stanstead Expansion Campaign', *Planning Theory,* Vol. 7, No. 2 (2008): 123–144. Another helpful application of this category is available in Howarth's article, where he analyzes the 'limits of "blackness" as an empty signifier' during the apartheid regime in South Africa. Howarth, D. 'The Difficult Emergence of a Democratic Imaginary: Black Consciousness and Non-Racial Democracy in South Africa', in Howarh, D., Norval, A., and Stavrakakis, A. (eds.), *Discourse Theory and Political Analysis* (Manchester: Manchester University Press, 2000), 168–92.
25. Panizza, F. 'Introduction: Populism and the Mirror of Democracy', in Panizza, F. (ed.), *Populism and the Mirror of Democracy* (London: Verso, 2005), 10.
26. *El Nacional.* February 5, 1992. Microfilm archives. Biblioteca Nacional, Caracas, Venezuela.
27. *El Chiripero* (the cockroaches) was a political alliance of Caldera's political faction from COPEI that formed 'Convergencia' together with a coalition of several medium/small leftist parties and 12 political groups.
28. *El Chiripero* won with a total of 1,710,722 votes (30.46 percent). Caldera's party (Convergencia) only received 956,529 votes (17.03 percent). However, MAS added a crucial 595,042 votes (10.59 percent), to win the election.
29. *'Convergencia'*—campaign ad, 1993.
30. During the first six months of Caldera's administration, the currency collapsed, there was alarming inflation and a major banking crisis, and capital continued to leave the country. Caldera had to bail out the banks. These events added more strain on the poor.
31. Marcano, C., and Barrera Tyzka, A. *Hugo Chávez sin Uniforme: Una Historia Personal* (Barcelona: Debate, 2006), 153–54.
32. Zago, A. *La Rebelión de los Ángeles.* (Caracas: Fuentes Editores, 1992); Cited by Lopez Maya, M. *Del Viernes Negro al Referendo Revocatorio* (Caracas: Alfadil Ediciones, 2005), 167.

Notes 173

33. Lopez Maya, *Del Viernes Negro al Referendo Revocatorio*, 170.
34. Harnecker, M. *Understanding the Venezuelan Revolution—Hugo Chávez Talks to Marta Harnecker* (New York: Monthly Review Press, 2005), 42.
35. Lopez Maya, *Del Viernes Negro al Referendo Revocatorio*, 168.
36. Lopez Maya, *Del Viernes Negro al Referendo Revocatorio*, 167.
37. Chávez in Zago, *La Rebelión de los Ángeles*; cited by Lopez Maya, *Del Viernes Negro al Referendo Revocatorio*, 167.
38. Lopez Maya, *Del Viernes Negro al Referendo Revocatorio*, 167–68.
39. Lopez Maya, *Del Viernes Negro al Referendo Revocatorio*, 169.
40. Lopez Maya, *Del Viernes Negro al Referendo Revocatorio*, 170.
41. Lopez Maya, *Del Viernes Negro al Referendo Revocatorio*, 170.
42. Harnecker, *Understanding the Venezuelan Revolution—Hugo Chávez Talks to Marta Harnecker*, 43.
43. Laclau and Mouffe, *Hegemony and Socialist Strategy*, 112.
44. Harnecker, *Understanding the Venezuelan Revolution—Hugo Chávez Talks to Marta Harnecker*, 43.
45. From 1811 until 1821, when Spanish control ended, the third Republic was established (Venezuela became a province of the Great Colombia). However, in 1830 J. A. Páez—a key independence leader—disagreed with the notion of Venezuela as a province and thus founded the fourth Republic. Chávez represented the fifth Republic.
46. Blanco Muñoz, A. *Venezuela del 04F-92 al 06D-98: Habla el Comandante Hugo Chávez Testimonios Violentos* (Caracas: Cátedra Pío Tamayo, CEHA/IIES/FACES/UCV, 1998), 512–13; cited by Marcano and Barrera, *Hugo Chávez sin Uniforme: Una Historia Personal*, 164–65.
47. Roberts. K. 'Social Polarization and the Populist Resurgence in Venezuela', in Ellner, S., and Hellinger, D (eds.), *Venezuelan Politics in the Chávez Era: Class, Polarization, and Conflict* (Boulder, CO: Lynne Rienner Publishers, 2003), 66.
48. Enrique Salas Romer was an independent congressman from 1983 until 1989. In 1989 with a COPEI party-base, he was elected governor of the industrious state of Carabobo. In 1998, Salas Romer founded the party '*Proyecto Venezuela*' to run for the presidential election in December 1998.
49. 'Estudio de temas municipales'. *Consultores 21*, Caracas, February, 1997; cited by Roberts, 'Social Polarization and the Populist Resurgence in Venezuela', 66.
50. 'La Mayoría de PPT esta con mi candidatura'. *El Universal*, October 16, 1997, http://www.eluniversal.com/1997/10/16/pol_art_16121CC.shtml [accessed February 2008].
51. Harnecker, *Understanding the Venezuelan Revolution—Hugo Chávez Talks to Marta Harnecker*, 62.
52. Further elements of the 'logic of Chavismo' shall be discussed in Chapter 3—based on interviews with Luis Miquilena in December 2007 and March 2008.
53. Harnecker, *Understanding the Venezuelan Revolution—Hugo Chávez Talks to Marta Harnecker*, 62.
54. Harnecker, *Understanding the Venezuelan Revolution—Hugo Chávez Talks to Marta Harnecker*, 62.
55. Medina, M. *El Elegido Presidente Chávez—Un Nuevo Sistema Político* (Bogota, D.C.: Ediciones Aurora 2001), 110.
56. Medina, P. *Rebeliones: Una Larga Conversación con Maria Cristina Iglesias y Farruco Sesto* (Caracas: Edicion del Autor, 1999), 76; cited by Medina, *El Elegido Presidente Chávez—Un Nuevo Sistema Político*, 110.
57. 'PPT Respalda a Hugo Chávez y Constituyente'. *El Universal*, March 8, 1998, http://www.eluniversal.com/1998/03/08/pol_art_08120AA.shtml [accessed February 2008].

174 *Notes*

58. In a survey that included 38 key communities nationwide with a sample of 1,000 cases Chávez started to be the favorable presidential candidate. 'Chávez aventaja en 5 puntos a Sáez'. *El Universal*, April 4, 1998, http://www.eluniversal.com/1998/04/30/pol_art_30116GG.shtml [accessed February 2008].
59. Uzcategui, L. J. *Chávez Mago de las Emociones—Análisis Psicosocial de un Fenómeno Político* (Caracas: Lithopolar Graficas, 1999), 117.
60. 'MAS y Caldera juntos hasta el final'. *El Universal*, January 20, 1998, http://www.eluniversal.com/1998/01/20/pol_art_20102AA.shtml [accessed February 2008].
61. 'Hablaran con los cuatro candidatos independientes—MAS incluyo a Chávez entre sus opciones'. *El Universal*, April 4, 1998, http://www.eluniversal.com/1998/04/20/pol_art_20112C.shtml [accessed February 2008].
62. 'Chávez llamo a la unidad del MAS'. *El Universal*, June 13, 1998, http://www.eluniversal.com/1998/06/13/pol_art_13102AA.shtml [accessed February 2008].
63. Felipe Mújica (president of MAS)—interview by author, Caracas, January 7, 2008.
64. Felipe Mújica, interview by author, Caracas, January 7, 2008.
65. '*Polo Patriotico*': 56.20 percent (MVR: 40.17 percent; MAS: 9.00 percent; PPT: 2.19 percent; PCV: 1.29 percent). *Consejo Nacional Electoral*, December 6, 1998, http://www.cne.gov.ve/estadisticas/e98_01.pdf [accessed October 2008].
66. Ángel Bermúdez, 'Hugo Chávez Frias fue proclamado ayer como presidente electo de la Republica—Insto al Congreso a llamar a referéndo'. *El Universal*, December 12, 1998, http://www.eluniversal.com/1998/12/12/pol_art_12112AA.shtml [accessed February 2008].
67. Salas Römer's coalition: 39.97 percent (Proyecto Venezuela: 28.75 percent; AD: 9.05 percent; COPEI: 2.15 percent). *Consejo Nacional Electoral*, December 6, 1998, http://www.cne.gov.ve/estadisticas/e98_01.pdf [accessed October 2008].
68. Felipe Mújica, interview by author, Caracas, March 16, 2009.
69. 'Discurso de Toma de Posesión'. *Biblioteca Electronica*, Caracas, February 2, 1999, http://www.analitica.com/bitblioteca/hchavez/toma.asp in Spanish. [accessed February 2008].
70. Laclau, E. 'Populism: What's in a Name?', in Panizza, F., *Populism and the Mirror of Democracy*, (London: Verso, 2005), 39.

NOTES TO CHAPTER 3

1. 'Elites Políticas acuden al miedo'. *El Universal*, Caracas, April 23, 1999, http://www.eluniversal.com/1999/04/23/pol_art_23108FF.shtml [accessed August 2009].
2. Rodolfo Cardona. 'Chávez Llamo a Votar la Población'. *El Universal*, Caracas, April 25, 1999, http://www.eluniversal.com/1999/04/25/pol_art_25102BB.shtml [accessed June 2008].
3. Simón Bolívar was born on July 24, 1783 in Caracas, Venezuela. This date is a national bank holiday in honor of the Liberator's struggle for independence/emancipation from Spanish rule.
4. Rodolfo Cardona. 'Simón Bolívar Despertó de Nuevo'. *El Universal*, July 25, 1999, http://www.eluniversal.com/1999/07/25/pol_art_25114AA.shtml [accessed July 2008].

Notes 175

5. Glynos, J., and Howarth, D. *Logics of Critical Explanation in Social and Political Theory* (London: Routledge, 2007), 145.
6. Laclau, *On Populist Reason*, 101; cited by Glynos and Howarth, *Logics of ... Social and Political Theory*, 145.
7. It is important to point out that 53.77 percent (5,907,426) of the electorate abstained. *Consejo Nacional Electoral*, http://www.cne.gov.ve/estadisticas/e001.pdf [accessed July 2008].
8. Marisol Decardi R. 'Debate Constituyente voces del poder "Prometo no defraudar el pueblo"'. *El Universal*, July 26, 1999, http://www.eluniversal.com/1999/07/26/pol_art_26106A2.shtml [accessed July 2008].
9. Harnecker, M. *Understanding the Venezuelan Revolution—Hugo Chávez Talks to Marta Harnecker* (New York: Monthly Review Press, 2005), 49.
10. Harnecker, *Understanding the Venezuelan Revolution—Hugo Chávez Talks to Marta Harnecker*, 49.
11. The abstention was 55.63 percent. 'Resultados Electorales Referendo 15/12/1999'. *Consejo Nacional Electoral*, December 15, 1999, http://www.cne.gov.ve/estadisticas/e012.pdf [accessed August 2009].
12. An experienced politician born in 1919, Coro, Venezuela. His political career was primarily important for his position as the secretary general of a union representing bus drivers in the 1940s. He was involved with various political stages of political struggle in Venezuela and imprisoned during the periods of dictatorial rule. Also, he was the right hand man of the founder (Jovito Villalba) of URD (one of the three political movements in the 'Punto Fijo Pact' in 1961—later excluded by AD and COPEI; see pages 44–45 in Chapter 2). Politically, Miquilena re-appeared when the discourse of Chavismo gained prominent attention in Venezuela. Miquilena was Chávez's ideological mentor and political broker. He was the key strategist and political negotiator of the '*Polo Patriótico*' political platform. During the first years of the Chávez regime, Miquilena held important government posts: president of the Constituent Assembly, president of the National Legislative Commission, senator (his term began in 1999), and minister of Justice and the Interior. By January 2002 the close friendship between Chávez and Miquilena ended due to critical internal disagreements in government, and thus Miquilena decided to resign and join the opposition.
13. Luis Miquilena, interview by author, Caracas, December 19, 2007.
14. Luis Miquilena, interview by author, Caracas, December 19, 2007.
15. Abstention was 5,120,464 (43.69 percent). 'Elecciones 30 de Julio 2000—Presidente de la Republica'. *Consejo Nacional Electoral*, July 30, 2000, http://www.cne.gov.ve/estadisticas/e015.pdf [accessed July 2008].
16. 'Gobernadores Electos'. *Consejo Electoral Nacional*, July 30, 2000, http://www.cne.gov.ve/estadisticas/e021.pdf [accessed July 2008].
17. 'Elecciones 30 de Julio de 2000. Total de Representantes por agrupación política y por entidad'. *Consejo Electoral Nacional*, July 30, 2000, http://www.cne.gov.ve/estadisticas/e041.pdf [accessed July 2008].
18. Apart from 99 PP members in the parliament, indigenous representatives endorsed the decree proposal.
19. 'Tendrá un año para emitir decretos en seis áreas: 38 leyes en total—Asamblea Aprobó la Ley Habilitante'. *El Universal*, November 8, 2000, http://www.eluniversal.com/2000/11/08/pol_art_08111AA.shtml [accessed July 2008].
20. Buxton, J. 'Economic Policy and the Rise of Hugo Chávez', in Ellner, S., and Hellinger, D. (eds.), *Venezuelan Politics in the* Chávez *Era: Class, Polarization, and the Conflict* (Boulder, CO: Lynne Rienner Publishers, 2003), 129.

176 *Notes*

21. Felipe Mújica (President of MAS), interview by author, Caracas, March 16, 2009.
22. 'Hugo Chávez Anuncio Segunda Ley Habilitante'. *El Universal*, November 14, 2001, http://www.eluniversal.com/2001/11/14/pol_art_14102F2.shtml [accessed August 2008].
23. Luis Miquilena, interview by author, Caracas, March 14, 2009.
24. Fedecámaras is composed of chambers of commerce in 12 key trade sectors. During the first administration of the 'center-right' President R. Caldera (1969–74), this federation of commerce established a vital degree of importance in the political system.
25. Luis Miquilena, interview by author, Caracas, March 14, 2009.
26. Luis Miquilena, interview by author, Caracas, March 14, 2009.
27. 'Ortega: Esta latente una huelga general indefinida'. *El Universal*, December 12, 2001, http://www.eluniversal.com/2001/12/12/pol_art_12102CC.shtml [accessed August 2008].
28. 'Gobernabilidad///Debate de alcance nacional—Se multiplica llamado a rectificar'. *El Universal*, November 9, 2001, http://www.eluniversal.com/2001/11/09/pol_art_09102AA.shtml [accessed August 2008].
29. 'Gobernabilidad///La venganza de Ceresole—Chávez en la encrucijada'. *El Universal*, November 12, 2001, http://www.eluniversal.com/2001/11/12/pol_art_12176AA.shtml [accessed August 2008].
30. 'Chávez advierte a la oligarquia: "No se Equivoquen"'. *El Universal*, December 10, 2001, http://www.eluniversal.com/2001/12/10/pol_art_10112HH.shtml [accessed August 2008].
31. 'Gobernabilidad///Comenzaron las mesas de concertación en el parlamento—Dialogo sin entendimiento'. *El Universal*, December 15, 2001, http://www.eluniversal.com/2001/12/15/pol_art_15102AA.shtml [accessed August 2008].
32. Laclau, 'Populism: What's in a Name?, 39. See also Glynos and Howarth's definition of the 'us-them' axis following the 'dimension of equivalence' in the sub-section 'Political Logics'—pages 31–33 in Chapter 1.
33. Luis Miquilena, interview by author, Caracas, December 19, 2007.
34. Carmona Estanga was selected by the Council of Venezuelan-U.S. Businessmen for an upcoming visit to Washington. He was 'labelled as "a highly regarded and influential business leader who has consistently played a critical role in advancing U.S. commercial interests in Venezuela"'. Golinger, E. *The Chávez Decode: Cracking U.S. Interventionism in Venezuela* (Northampton, MA: Olive Branch Press, 2006), 47.
35. Golinger, *The Chávez Decode: Cracking U.S. Interventionism in Venezuela*, 47–48.
36. Golinger highlights that the 'NED had pumped up its spending in Venezuela to a whopping $877,435'. Golinger. *The Chávez Decode: Cracking U.S. Interventionism in Venezuela*, 49.
37. On February 13, 2002, Carlos Ortega met with Otto Reich (Assistant Secretary of State for Western Hemisphere Affairs. From 1986 to 1989 Reich served as U.S. Ambassador to Venezuela) in Washington, D.C. See: www.state.gov/r/pa/prs/dpb/2002/8034.htm. Golinger. *The Chávez Decode: Cracking U.S. Interventionism in Venezuela*, 49.
38. For instance: the National Democratic Institute (NDI) section of the Democratic Party within NDE, the International Republican Institute (IRI) section of the Republic Party within NDE, and the U.S. Agency for International Development (USAID) by using a private company called Development Alternatives, Inc. (DAI).
39. Golinger states: from 2000 to 2006 $34,175,505 of U.S. public funds was used for 'Promoting Democracy in Venezuela'. *The Chávez Decode: Cracking*

U.S. Interventionism in Venezuela, 56. Furthermore, Wilpert claims that 'for 2003 funds reached an all time high of $10 million. Altogether, from 2002 to 2005 the U.S. government provided over $26 million to Venezuelan NGOs ("U.S. Aid Stirs Venezuela's Suspicion," Associated Press, Aug. 27, 2006), with at least $9 million in the pipeline for 2006'. Wilpert, G. *Changing Venezuela by Taking Power—The History and Policies of the Chávez Government* (Verso: London 2007), 170.

40. Sara Carolina Díaz. 'Crisis Naranja /// Tribunal disciplinario estudia sancionar a Didalco Bolívar—MAS Expulsa a siete Diputados'. *El Universal*, January 8, 2002, http://www.eluniversal.com/2002/01/08/pol_art_08104AA. shtml [accessed August 2008].

41. 'Luis Miquilena exigirá rectificación al Presidente'. *El Universal*, January 8, 2002, http://www.eluniversal.com/2002/01/08/pol_art_08104FF.shtml [accessed August 2008].

42. Taymen Hernandez. 'Miguel pusos a su cargo a la orden—Rodríguez Chacin sustituye a Miquilena'. *El Universal*, January 25, 2002, http://www.eluniversal.com/2002/01/25/pol_art_25106DDD.shtml [accessed August 2008].

43. Milagros Socorro. 'De Enero a Enero /// La sociedad civil tomo las calles—¿Escualidos? ¡Ya no Mas!'. *El Universal*, January 24, 2002, http://www.eluniversal.com/2002/01/24/pol_art_24102AA.shtml [accessed August 2008].

44. Coronil, F., and Skurski, J. 'Dismembering and Remembering the Nation: The Semantics of Political Violence in Venezuela'. *Comparative Studies in Society and History*, Vol. 33, No. 2 (1991): 328.

45. Gustavo Mendez. 'Guerra de desgaste/Se asegura prestación de servicios básicos CTV acude a la huelga indefinida'. *El Universal*, April 11, 2002, http://www.eluniversal.com/2002/04/11/pol_art_11110AA.shtml [accessed August 2008].

46. Nelida Fernández Alanzó. 'Guerra de Desgaste/Entre desacatos y manifestaciones—El Este le da carta de despido a Chávez'. *El Universal*, April 11, 2002, http://www.eluniversal.com/2002/04/11/pol_art_11102AA.shtml [accessed August 2008].

47. Freddy Bernal (a Chavista mayor of Caracas) called Ortega (president of CTV) irresponsible using the national TV station, by leading that march to stage a confrontation with Chávez's supporters outside Miraflores. Source: Bartley, K., and O'Briain, D. *The Revolution Will Not be Televised* (DVD—Power Pictures, 2003).

48. Kelly, J. 'Origines y consecuencias de la Constitución Bolivariana', in Francés, A. and Machado Allison, C. (eds.), *Venezuela: la crisis de abril* (Caracas: Ediciones IESA, 2002), 44. These observations resonate with Fedecámaras's unsuccessful attempt to make a pact in the National Assembly and invalidate Chávez's 49 Decree Laws (see pages 66–68) and the abdication of moderate Chavistas (Miquilena and MAS—see page 69–70 in this chapter).

49. Kelly, 'Origines y Consecuencias de la Constitución Bolivariana', 45.

50. Cannon, B. 2004. 'Venezuela, April 2002: Coup or Popular Rebellion? The Myth of a United Venezuela', *Bulletin of Latin America Research*, Vol. 23, No. 3 (2004): 295–96.

51. Márquez, P. 'Diario de una Oligarca Escualida: Reaccion de la Clase Media', in Francés, A., and Machado Allison, C (eds.), *Venezuela: La Crisis de Abril* (Caracas: Ediciones IESA, 2002), 117.

52. Roberto Giusti. 'Jornada Decisiva/Helicópteros sobrevolaron Miraflores—Carmona presidiría Junta de Gobierno'. *El Universal*, April 12, 2002, http://www.eluniversal.com/2002/04/12/pol_art_12190AA.shtml [accessed August 2008].

178   *Notes*

53. Carmona Estanga, P. 'Decreto del Gobierno Provisional de Pedro Carmona Estanga'. In *Observatorio Social de América Latina* (2002) Year III, 7: 27–8; cited by Cannon, 'Venezuela, April 2002: Coup or Popular Rebellion? The Myth of a United Venezuela', 296.
54. Bartley and O'Briain, *The Revolution Will Not be Televised* (DVD—Power Pictures, 2003).
55. 'Simpatizantes de Hugo Chávez manifestaron en Fuerte Tiuna'. *El Universal*, April 13, 2002, http://www.eluniversal.com/2002/04/13/pol_art_13105CC. shtml [accessed August 2008].
56. The media blamed the Chavistas (Bolivarian Circle) shooting protestors from the Puente (bridge) Llaguno. This was continuously shown on private TV channels. However, from another angle, it is obvious that there is no march on the street below the bridge; it appears that the shooters are defending the Chavista march—stopped on each side of the bridge (minutes: 24:00). The opposition march might have looked for cover below the bridge. Another vital piece of evidence in John Pilger's documentary is that the CNN correspondent Otto Neustald in Caracas mentions that on April 10, he was called and informed that 'on April 11, the march will go to Miraflores. The message was that there will be deaths and a—recorded footage—of twenty high ranking officials will appear speaking against the Chávez government demanding the resignation . . . it was all planned' (minutes: 25:45). Pilger, J. *The War on Democracy by John Pilger* (Youngheart Entertainment Granada Productions, October 2007): (duration: 1:33.36). http://www.venezuelanalysis.com/video/2705 [accessed August 2008].
57. Bartley and O'Briain, *The Revolution Will Not be Televised* (DVD—Power Pictures, 2003).
58. 'Reconstrucción/Casa Blanca evita hablar de golpe de Estado—Washington elogia a militares'. *El Universal*, April 13, 2002, http://www.eluniversal. com/2002/04/13/pol_art_13111AA.shtml [accessed August 2008].
59. Bartley and O'Briain, *The Revolution Will Not Be Televised* (DVD—Power Pictures, 2003).
60. Marcano, C., and Barrera Tyzka, A. *Hugo Chávez* (New York: Random House, 2007), 180.
61. 'Con infiltrados lograron el rescate'. *El Universal*, April 15, 2002, http:// www.eluniversal.com/2002/04/15/pol_art_15114CC.shtml [accessed August 2008].
62. Bartley and O'Briain, *The Revolution Will Not be Televised* (DVD—Power Pictures, 2003).
63. Lopez Maya, M. *Del Viernes Negro al Referendo Revocatorio* (Caracas: Alfadil Ediciones, 2005), 270.
64. 'Carmona exige investigación profunda de los hechos del 11A'. *El Universal*, May 11, 2002, http://www.eluniversal.com/2002/05/11/pol_art_11108CC. shtml [accessed August 2008].
65. 'Defensa de Ramírez Pérez afirma que el Presidente si Renuncio'. *El Universal*, May 14, 2002, http://www.eluniversal.com/2002/05/14/pol_art_14109BB. shtml [accessed August 2008].
66. Founded in 2002, '*Coordinadora Democrática*' was an alliance of different political ideologies, civil society groups, and Venezuelan non-governmental organizations.
67. 'Oposición/Discurso de Rosendo activo coalición—Oposición se cohesiona para enfrentar a Chávez's'. *El Universal*, May 13, 2002, http://www.eluniversal.com/2002/05/13/pol_art_13104AA.shtml [accessed August 2008].
68. Lopez Maya, *Del Viernes Negro al Referendo Revocatorio*, 270.
69. Lopez Maya, *Del Viernes Negro al Referendo Revocatorio*, 272–73.

Notes 179

70. 'La Renuncia negociada es la salida'. *El Universal*, December 10, 2002, http://www.eluniversal.com/2002/12/10/pol_art_10104BB.shtml [accessed August 2008].
71. Lopez Maya, *Del Viernes Negro al Referendo Revocatorio*, 273.
72. 'Conflictividad/Presidente de la CTV invita a declararse en "desobediencia"—"El Único golpista convicto y confeso es usted señor Chávez"'. *El Universal*, December 28, 2002, http://www.eluniversal.com/2002/12/28/pol_art_28104AA.shtml [accessed August 2008].
73. 'La gente piensa, la gente actúa—"Ese Pueblo que te puso allí, ahora no te quiere"'. *El Universal*, December 6, 2002, http://www.eluniversal.com/2002/12/06/pol_art_061102SS.shtml [accessed August 2008].
74. Taymen Hernandez. 'Conflictibilidad/De como los oficialistas administran la política de repliegue—Base Chapista mantiene la linea'. *El Universal*, December 22, 2002, http://www.eluniversal.com/2002/12/22/pol_art_22107AA.shtml [accessed August 2008].
75. Lopez Maya, *Del Viernes Negro al Referendo Revocatorio*, 274.
76. Lopez Maya, *Del Viernes Negro al Referendo Revocatorio*, 274.
77. Panizza, F. 'Introduction: Populism and the Mirror of Democracy', in Panizza, F. (ed.), *Populism and the Mirror of Democracy* (London: Verso, 2005), 20
78. Gott, R. *Hugo Chávez and the Bolivarian Revolution* (London: Verso, 2005), 238–39.
79. Wilpert, G. *Changing Venezuela by Taking Power—The History and Policies of the Chávez Government* (London: Verso, 2007), 25.
80. Wilpert, *Changing Venezuela—The History and Policies of the Chávez Government*, 25.
81. Some of the missions are as follows: '*Misión Habitat*' (to solve family and communal problems related with construction and urban issues—and a communal panel to evaluate land aspects for the improvement of neighborhoods); '*Misión Identidad*' (a direct branch with the identity institution to help with issues such as identity cards); '*Misión Madres de Barrio*' (to help housewives in need and find ways to improve their conditions of extreme poverty through communal and social programs); '*Misión Milagro*' (eye treatment with Cuba-Venezuela cooperation for those with no economic means); '*Misión Miranda*' (a military program to develop and train a reserve branch of the Forces); '*Misión Negra Hipolita*' (a program to help homeless people with an emphasis on children in the streets); '*Misión Piar*' (to help workers in the mining industry and environmental concerns); '*Misión Villanueva*' (to equally redistribute the space throughout the country, inspect the current development of new infrastructural programs, and help those that live in inhuman conditions at *barrios*). *Gobierno Bolivariano de Venezuela—Misiones*. http://www.gobiernoenlinea.ve/miscelaneas/misiones.html#robinson [accessed August 2008].
82. '*Súmate* is a civil organisation founded in 2002 that promotes the free exercise of citizen's political rights, and the discussion of matters of public interest. It aims to defend, facilitate, and back the political rights accorded to citizens by the constitution. Impartial and independent citizen participation in democratic processes is a vital element of this organisation. It has no links with political movements.' *Súmate—Construimos Democracia*. http://www.sumate.org/nosotros.html [accessed August 2008].
83. Eugenio Martinez. 'Revocatorio para el 29 de Febrero'. *El Universal*, September 26, 2003, http://www.eluniversal.com/2003/09/26/pol_art_26102X.shtml [accessed August 2008].
84. 'Diputado compara a la ONG con la maquinaria Adela—Ismael Garcia critica a Sumate y la entrega de formas al CNE'. *El Universal*, August 22, 2003,

180 *Notes*

http://www.eluniversal.com/2003/08/22/pol_art_22104EE.shtml [accessed Aug. 2008].

85. Alfredo Rojas. 'Presidente señala que oposición no mueve al pueblo'. *El Universal*, August 22, 2003, http://www.eluniversal.com/2003/08/22/pol_art_22104AA.shtml [accessed August 2008].
86. Golinger, *The Chávez Decode: Cracking U.S. Interventionism in Venezuela*, 109–10.
87. Golinger, *The Chávez Decode: Cracking U.S. Interventionism in Venezuela*, 113.
88. Lopez Maya, *Del Viernes Negro al Referendo Revocatorio*, 279.
89. I met people that signed in November–December 2003 and were shocked that their signature was in the 'repair' list. Also, a 'list' of those who signed in the recall referendum named '*Tascón* List' was used to identify who was against the Bolivarian project. This list was commonly used in governmental offices to determine various forms of citizens' eligibility: passports, grants, jobs in the public service, etc.
90. *Consejo Nacional Electoral—Referéndum Presidencial 2004*, http://www.cne.gov.ve/referendum_presidencial2004/ [accessed August 2008].
91. 'Venecuba' means Venezuela's Cubanisation—importing Cuban ideology and projects such as *Misión Barrio Adentro* consisting of Cuban doctors working in *barriadas*. Agustin Blanco Muñoz. 'Súmate: ¡No votaras!'. *El Universal*, November 28, 2005, http://www.eluniversal.com/2005/11/28/pol_art_28102D.shtml [accessed August 2008].
92. Maria Lilibeth Da Corte. 'Parlamentarias/Rangel denuncio que opositores "susuran" a la FAN—Chávez alerta sobre Golpe Electoral'. *El Universal*, December 2, 2005, http://www.eluniversal.com/2005/12/02/pol_art_02106A.shtml [accessed August 2008].
93. Manuel Rosales had been governor of the state of Zulia since 2000. Prior to his electoral success in Zulia he founded a political party called '*Un Nuevo Tiempo*'. He was a parliamentarian AD politician from 1983 until 1994.
94. Eugenio Martinez. 'Campaña 2006// Entrevista Vicente Díaz, rector del Consejo Nacional Electoral "Es imposible que exista un fraude"—Díaz garantiza que el secreto del voto esta resguardado'. *El Universal*, December 2, 2006, http://www.eluniversal.com/2006/12/02/elecc_art_97051.shtml [accessed September 2008].
95. 'Eleccion presidencial 3 de dicimbre de 2006'. *Consejo Nacional Electoral*, December 3, 2006, http://www.cne.gov.ve/divulgacionPresidencial/resultado_nacional.php?color=2&e=06 [accessed August 2008].
96. Elvia Gomez. 'Presidencial 2006—"Reconocemos que hoy nos vencieron" Manuel Rosales se comprometió a continuar recorriendo el país'. *El Universal*, December 4, 2006, http://www.eluniversal.com/2006/12/04/elecc_art_98447.shtml [accessed September 2008].
97. 'Chávez asume por tercera vez la presidencia constitucional de Venezuela—10.01.2007. Presidential Inauguration 2007'. State TV channel: *Venezolana de Televisión*, January 10, 2007, http://www.youtube.com/watch?v=wqBHPMDJe0Y [accessed September 2008].
98. 'Insulza y la Iglesia otra vez en la mira del Mandatario'. *El Universal*, January 11, 2007, http://www.eluniversal.com/2007/01/11/pol_art_138158.shtml [accessed September 2008].
99. Tovar Arroyo, G. *Estudiantes por la Libertad—Pensamiento y Documentos de la Generación 2007* (Caracas: Los Libros de El Nacional, 2007), 122.
100. 'Estudiantes de la UCAB y la USB protestan en apoyo a RCTV'. *El Universal*, May 25, 2007, http://politica.eluniversal.com/2007/05/25/rctv_ava_estudiantes-de-la-uc_25A874209.shtml [accessed September 2008].

Notes 181

101. '17 heridos dejan refriega en Chacao este Lunes'. *El Universal*, May 29, 2007, http://www.eluniversal.com/2007/05/29/pol_art_17-heridos—dejan-re_ 303151.shtml [accessed September 2008].

102. Sara Carolina Díaz. 'Podemos aboga por dialogo pero la Asamblea llama a la calle. "Ya esta bueno de confrontaciones", indico el diputado Ismael García'. *El Universal*, May 30, 2007, http://www.eluniversal.com/2007/05/30/pol_ art_podemos-aboga-por-di_303813.shtml [accessed September 2008].

103. General Raul Baduel was one of the four founders (including Chávez) of the '*Movimiento Bolivariano Revolucionario*' (see pages 46–47 in Chapter 2) in 1982. Baduel also ordered the return of Chávez to the Presidential Palace in April 2002 (see page 72 in this chapter). And he was minister of defense from June 2006 until July 2007.

104. Maria Daniela Espinoza. 'Baduel llama a votar NO ante la reforma "fraudulenta"—Para ex ministro de Defensa, propuesta lleva al "pueblo como ovejas al matadero"'. *El Universal*, November 6, 2007, http://www. eluniversal.com/2007/11/06/pol_art_baduel-llama-a-votar_580618.shtml [accessed September 2008].

105. 'Para Chávez, era su "hermano de toda la vida"—Salvo al Presidente en Abril 2002, pero no participo en el golpe 4F 1992'. *El Universal*, November 6, 2007, http://www.eluniversal.com/2007/11/06/pol_art_para-chavez,-era-su_580345.shtml [accessed September 2008].

106. 'Podemos se une al Bloque del No'. *El Universal*, November 6, 2007, http:// www.eluniversal.com/2007/11/06/pol_art_podemos-se-une-al-bl_580847. shtml [accessed September 2008].

107. Gustavo Mendez. 'La Violencia sello marcha Estudiantil—La PM y GN disolvieron la concentración con bombas lacrimógenas'. *El Universal*, November 2, 2007, http://www.eluniversal.com/2007/11/02/pol_art_la-violencia-sello-m_574558.shtml [accessed September 2008].

108. The extent of the changes was vast; it is worth pointing out the following: abolish presidential term limits, allowing for indefinite re-election of the president (not allowed for any other political post), increase the presidential term from six to seven years, lower the voting age from 18 to 16, expand social security benefits to workers in the informal economy, and so on.

109. Abstention: 44.11%. 'Referendo de la Reforma Constitucional'. *Consejo Electoral Nacional*, December 2, 2007, http://www.cne.gov.ve/divulgacion_referendo_reforma/index.php?tipo_consulta=0&cod_estado=0&cod_ municipio=0&cod_parroquia=0&cod_centro=0&num_mesa=0 [accessed September 2008].

110. 'Primer discurso de Chávez después de su primera derrota 4/5'. *YouTube*, The Presidential Palace, December 3, 2007, http://www.youtube.com/watch ?v=thUyMLA1_90&feature=related [accessed September 2008].

111. 'General Baduel'. *Globovisión—Rueda de Prensa—YouTube*. December 3, 2007, http://www.youtube.com/watch?v=A79UMVbg1AM&feature=relate d [accessed September 2008].

112. Chávez: 'Fue una Victoria de mierda'. *Venezolana de Televisión—YouTube*. December 5, 2007, http://www.youtube.com/watch?v=ed7gB2MmSmM&fe ature=related [accessed September 2008].

113. Panizza, 'Introduction: Populism and the Mirror of Democracy', 29.

NOTES TO CHAPTER 4

1. 'Bipartite' means the party-political accord (between *Acción Democrática* and *Comité de Organización Política Electoral Independiente* [COPEI], the

182   *Notes*

political parties that ruled Venezuela since 1958) that formed a constitutional/institutional framework from 1961 until 1998.

2. Of which three are health related programs: '*Barrio Adentro*' (integrated healthcare), '*Mission Milagros*' (ophthalmological treatment), and '*Mission Sonrisa*' (advanced dental surgery).

3. Magallanes, R. 'La Igualdad en la República Bolivariana de Venezuela (1999–2004)' *Revista Venezolana de Economía y Ciencias Sociales*, Vol. 11 (2005), pp. 71–99; Castellanos, P. L. 'Notas sobre el Estado y la Salud en Venezuela', *Cuadernos de la Sociedad Venezolana de Planificación* (1982), pp. 69–121; Grossi, R. *Acción Sanitaria en Venezuela y Presupuestos 1936–1971*, (Caracas: Ministerio de Salud y Asistencia Social, 1972), 190; cited by Regional Office of the World Health Organization. 'Mission Barrio Adentro: The Right to Health and Social Inclusion in Venezuela', *Pan American Health Organization*, Caracas,Venezuela (July 2006), 5–6.

4. Castellanos, P. L. 'Notas sobre el Estado y la Salud en Venezuela', *Cuadernos de la Sociedad Venezolana de Planificación* (1982); cited by Regional Office of the World Health Organization. 'Mission Barrio Adentro: The Right to Health and social Inclusion in Venezuela', 6.

5. Naím, M. *Paper Tigers & Minotaurs: The Politics of Venezuela's Economic Reforms* (Washington, D.C.: Carnegie Endowment for International Peace, 1993); Buxton, J. 'Venezuela', in Buxton, J., and Phillips, N. (eds.), *Case Studies in Latin American Political Economy* (New York: Manchester University Press, 1999),162–84; cited by Muntaner, C., Armada, F., Chung, H., Mata, R., Williams-Brennan, L., and Benach, J. 'Venezuela Health Reforms—Venezuela's Barrio Adentro: Participatory Democracy, South-South Cooperation and Health Care for All', *Social Medicine,* Vol. 3, No. 4 (2008): 234.

6. Muntaner et al., 'Venezuela Health Reforms . . . Health Care for All', 234.

7. Homedes, N., and Ugalde, A. 'Las Reformas de Salud en América Latina: Una Visión Crítica a Través de Dos Estudios de Caso', *Revista Panamericana de Salud Pública*, Vol.17, No. 3 (2005); Terris, M. 'Witnesses to History: The Caracas Explosion and the International Monetary Fund 5–130', *Journal of Public Health Policy*, Vol. 10, No. 1 (1989): 149; De Vos, P., De Ceukelaire, W., and Van der Stuyft, P. 'Colombia and Cuba, Contrasting Models in Latin American's Health Sector Reform', *Tropical Medicine & International Health*, Vol. 11, No. 10 (2006): 1604–12; cited by Alvarado, C. H., Martínez, M. E., Vivas-Martínez, S., Gutiérrez, N. J., and Metzger, W. 'Cambio Social y Política de Salud en Venezuela', *Medicina Social*, Vol. 3, No. 2 (2008): 114.

8. Rincón, M., and Rodríguez, I. 'Consideraciones Generales sobre la Política y Gestión de la Salud en Venezuela (1900–2003)', *FERMENTUM*, Vol. 14, No. 41 (September–October 2004), 503–32; cited by Alvarado et al. 'Cambio Social y Política de Salud en Venezuela', 115–16.

9. Homedes, N., and Ugalde, A. 'Las Reformas de Salud en América Latina: Una Visión Crítica a través de Dos Estudios de Caso', *Revista Panamericana de Salud Pública*, Vol. 17, No. 3 (2005); cited by Alvarado et al., 'Sección Especial: Reformas Progresistas en Salud . . . Cambio Social y Política de Salud en Venezuela', 116.

10. Diaz Polanco, J. 'El Papel del Financiamiento en los Procesos de Reforma del Sector Salud el Caso de Venezuela', in Díaz Polanco, J. (ed.), *La Reforma de Salud en Venezuela: Aspectos Políticos e Institucionales de la Descentralización de la Salud en Venezuela* (Caracas: Fundación Polar, 2001): 124–45;

Notes 183

cited by Muntaner et al., 'Venezuela Health Reforms . . . Health Care for All', 234.

11. Muntaner et al., 'Venezuela Health Reforms . . . Health Care for All', 234–35.
12. *Plan Estratégico Social*. (Caracas: Ministerio de Salud y Desarrollo Social, 2002).
13. Instituto Nacional de Estadística. Summary of Social Indicators 1997–2008 [translation]. Available at http://www.ine.gob.ve [accessed June 9, 2008]; cited by Briggs, C. L., and Mantini-Briggs, C. 'Confronting Health Disparities: Latin American Social Medicine in Venezuela', *American Journal of Public Health*, Vol. 99, No. 3 (2009): 549.
14. Menéndez E. L., and Di Pardo, R. B. *De Algunos Alcoholismos y Algunos Saberes: Atención Primaria y Proceso de Alcoholización*. (Mexico City: CIESAS, 1996); cited by Briggs and Mantini-Briggs, 'Confronting Health Disparities', 549.
15. Yamada, S. 'Latin American Social Medicine and Global Medicine', *American Journal of Public Health*, 93 (2003), 1994–96; cited by Briggs and Mantini-Briggs, 'Confronting Health Disparities', 549.
16. Briggs C. L, and Mantini-Briggs, C. 'Confronting Health Disparities . . . in Venezuela', 550.
17. Alvarado, C. H, Martinez, M. E., Vivas-Martinez, S., Gutiérrez, N.J.,and Metzger, W. 'Cambio Social y Política de Salud en Venezuela', *Medicina Social*, Vol. 3, No. 2 (2008): 113–29; cited by Briggs, C. L., and Mantini-Briggs, C. 'Confronting Health Disparities . . . in Venezuela', 550.
18. Ruben Alayón Monserat, a sociologist at the Universidad Central de Venezuela (UCV), was working for the revolutionary government as the director of socio-economic affairs in the Libertador municipality in Caracas in 2003.
19. Alayón, M. R. 'Barrio Adentro: Combatir la Exclusion Profundizando la Democracia', *Revista Venezolana de Economía y Ciencias Sociales*, Vol. 11 (September–December 2005): 240.
20. Wilpert, G. *Changing Venezuela by Taking Power—The History and Policies of the Chávez Government* (Verso: London 2007), 62–63.
21. Glynos, J., and Howarth, D. *Logics of Critical Explanation in Social and Political Theory* (London: Routledge, 2007), 141.
22. Alayón, 'Barrio Adentro . . . Democracia', 240.
23. Alayón, 'Barrio Adentro . . . Democracia', 222–44.
24. Patruyo, T. 'El Estado Actual de las Misiones Sociales: Balance sobre su Proceso de Implementación e Institucionalización'. *Instituto Latinoamericano de Investigaciones Sociales* (April, 2008), 35.
25. Alayón, 'Barrio Adentro . . . Democracia', 244.
26. 'Misión Médica Cubana Barrio Adentro. Estadísticas Anuales. Unidad Central de Información', *Misión Médica Cubana*, Caracas, Venezuela (2006); cited in 'Mission Barrio Adentro: The Right to Health and Social Inclusion in Venezuela', *Pan American Health Organization*, Caracas, Venezuela (2006), p. 26.
27. Alayón, 'Barrio Adentro . . . Democracia', 219.
28. Alayón, 'Barrio Adentro . . . Democracia', 221.
29. Alayón, 'Barrio Adentro . . . Democracia', 222–25.
30. Alayón, 'Barrio Adentro . . . Democracia', 226–27.
31. *El llanero* means the plainsman. Calabozo is the second biggest city of Guárico (pop. 154,000). It is an agricultural inland town in *Los Llanos* of Venezuela.
32. Luis Lara (president of the communal assembly), interview by author, Carrasquelero–Calabozo, Guárico, March 20, 2009.

184 *Notes*

33. When Luis Lara (the newly elected communal president) was interviewed, the key topic in the communal assembly was how to prosecute the former communal president, who unlawfully used the government's Communal Bank loan funds (Bs 397 million; approx. U.S. $189,000)—given to Carrasquelero for communal projects—for personal expenses. Lara stressed that communal corruption is also practiced in other *barrios* of Calabozo.
34. Luis Lara, interview by author, Carrasquelero—Calabozo, Guárico, March 20, 2009.
35. Luis Lara, interview by author, Carrasquelero—Calabozo, Guárico, March 20, 2009.
36. Doña Nuñez (health committee [*Comité de Salud*] coordinator), interview by author, BA I in Caricuao, Caracas. April 14, 2009.
37. Discursively, *Barrio Adentro* is as follows. An accurate translation of what *Barrio* means varies according to the use of the Spanish language in other regions; in the Venezuelan context: *Barrio*: 'slum/ghetto'—*Adentro*: 'deep'. Thus, **Barrio Adentro** means **Deep in the Slums**.
38. Doña Nuñez, interview by author, BA I in Caricuao, Caracas. April 14, 2009.
39. Regional Office of the World Health Organisation. 'Mission Barrio Adentro: The Right to Health and Social Inclusion in Venezuela'. *Pan American Health Organization*, Caracas, Venezuela (July 2006), 36–37.
40. Laclau, E. *On Populist Reason* (London: Verso, 2005), 117; quoted by Glynos and Howarth, *Logics of Critical Explanation in Social and Political Theory*, 142.
41. Alayón, 'Barrio Adentro . . . Democracia', 221.
42. Glynos and Howarth, *Logics of . . . Social and Political Theory*,104.
43. Glynos and Howarth, *Logics of . . . Social and Political Theory*,104.
44. Hugo Chávez. *Program N. 155—Aló Presidente*. Desde la Capilla de la alcaldía del Municipio Libertador, Caracas. July 6, 2003.
45. D'Elia, Y. 'Las Misiones Sociales en Venezuela: una aproximación a su compresión y análisis', *Instituto Latinoamericano de Investigaciones Sociales* (2006), 29–30
46. Patruyo, 'El Estado Actual de las Misiones', 36.
47. Patruyo, 'El Estado Actual de las Misiones', 38.
48. Patruyo, 'El Estado Actual de las Misiones', 39.
49. Patruyo, 'El Estado actual de las Misiones', 39.
50. 'Presidencia de la Republica'. Decreto N. 2.745—14 de diciembre de 2003. Published at the *Gaceta Oficial de la Republica Bolivariana de Venezuela*. Caracas, lunes de 26 de enero de 2004—Número: 37. 865.
51. Muntaner et al., 'Venezuela Health Reforms . . . Health Care for All', 238–39.
52. Muntaner et al., 'Venezuela Health Reforms . . . Health Care for All', 239.
53. Muntaner et al., 'Venezuela Health Reforms . . . Health Care for All', 239
54. Muntaner et al., 'Venezuela Health Reforms . . . Health Care for All', 239
55. Patruyo, 'El Estado Actual de las Misiones', 49
56. Muntaner et al., 'Venezuela Health Reforms . . . Health Care for All', 240.
57. Muntaner et al., 'Venezuela Health Reforms . . . Health Care for All', 240.
58. Patruyo, 'El Estado Actual de las Misiones', 50.
59. 'Barrio Adentro IV: 16 hospitales se construyen actualmente en el país', *Tribuna Popular,* December 12, 2012, http://www.pcv-venezuela.org/index. php?option=com_content&view=article&id=405:barrio-adentro-iv-16-hospitales-se-construyen-actualmente-en-el-pais&catid=2:nacional&Itemid=3 [accessed April 13, 2012].

Notes 185

60. Muntaner et al., 'Venezuela Health Reforms . . . Health Care for All', 240.
61. Muntaner et al., 'Venezuela Health Reforms . . . Health Care for All', 239.
62. Muntaner et al., 'Venezuela Health Reforms . . . Health Care for All', 240.
63. On June 15, 2005, *Program N. 225—Aló Presidente*, Chávez inaugurated the first 30 CDIs and SRIs. The president announced that 600 CDIs and SRIs, as well as 35 TACs, were going to be operational in 2005. Patruyo, 'El Estado Actual de las Misiones', 39.
64. Patruyo, 'El Etado Actual de las Misiones', 39.
65. D'Elia, 'Las Misiones Sociales en Venezuela . . . Análisis'; cited by Patruyo, 'El Estado Actual de las Misiones', 46–47.
66. Patruyo mentions that on June 2005, the first CDIs and SRIs inaugurated *Barrio Adentro* II. The aim was to build 600 CDIs and SRIs that year; however, only 60 were built. Of the 35 CATs, none were built. Patruyo, 'El Estado Actual de las Misiones', 47.
67. Patruyo, 'El Estado Actual de las Misiones', 49.
68. Gobierno Bolivariano de Venezuela—Ministerio del Poder Popular para la Comunicación e Información. 'Lanzamiento del Sistema Publico Metropolitano de Salud y reinauguración del Bloque C del Hospital General del Este Dr. Domingo Luciani'. *Imprenta Nacional* (February 2006), 15.
69. Patruyo, 'El Estado Actual de las Misiones', 49–50
70. Patruyo, 'El Estado Actual de las Misiones', 50.
71. Briggs C. L., and Mantini-Briggs, C. 'Confronting Health Disparities: Latin American Social Medicine in Venezuela.' *American Journal of Public Health*, Vol. 99, No. 3 (March 2009): 549.
72. Jaen, M. H. *El Sistema de Salud en Venezuela: Desafios* (Caracas: IESA, 2001); Urbaneja, M. L. *Privatizacion en el Sector Salud en Venezuela* (Caracas: CENDES, 1991); cited by Briggs, C. L., and Mantini-Briggs, C. 'Confronting Health Disparities . . . in Venezuela', 550.
73. Briggs C. L, and Mantini-Briggs, C., 'Confronting Health Disparities . . . in Venezuela', 550.
74. Ceaser, M. 'Cuban Doctors Provide Care in Venezuela's Barrios', *The Lancet*, Vol. 363, No. 9424 (2004): 1874–75; cited by Briggs, C. L., and Mantini-Briggs C. 'Confronting Health Disparities . . . in Venezuela', 550.
75. Laclau, *On Populist Reason,* 117; quoted by Glynos and Howarth, *Logics of . . . Social and Political Theory,* 142.
76. Glynos and Howarth, *Logics of . . . Social and Political Theory,* 142.
77. Glynos and Howarth, *Logics of . . . Social and Political Theory,* 142.
78. Vivian Castillo. 'Gremio Medico se declara en conflicto por crisis laboral—FMV analiza acciones para exigir mejoras salariales y condiciones laborales'. *El Universal*, September 13, 2007, http://politica.eluniversal.com/2007/09/13/pol_art_gremio-medico-se-dec_469209.shtml [accessed May 21, 2009].
79. 'Douglas León Natera afirma que déficit de médicos ronda 42%—en poco más de dos años emigraron cerca de 2 mil 400 medicos'. *El Universal*, February 06, 2009, http://www.eluniversal.com/2009/02/06/pol_art_douglas-leon-natera_1257474.shtml [accessed May 23, 2009].
80. Glynos and Howarth, *Logics of . . . Social and Political Theory,* 142–43.
81. D'Elia, Y., and Cabezas, L. F. 'Las Misiones Sociales en Venezuela'. *Instituto Latinoamericano de Investigaciones Sociales* (May 2008), 11.
82. Alvarez, C. 'Venezuela's Oil-Based Economy'. *Council of Foreign Relations,* February 9, 2009, http://www.cfr.org/publication/12089/venezuelas_oilbased_economy.html [accessed July 25, 2009].
83. D'Elia and Cabezas, 'Las Misiones Sociales en Venezuela', 11.

186   *Notes*

84. Patruyo, 'El Estado Actual de las Misiones', 61.
85. Observatorio Comunitario por el Derecho a la Salud. Informe sobre el Derecho a la Salud en Venezuela 2007; cited by D'Elia and Cabezas, 'Las Misiones Sociales en Venezuela', 12.
86. Dr. Elidía Narron, interview by author, Carrasquelero—Calabozo, Guárico, March 19, 2009.
87. Seven students in the module were studying 'Integrated General Medicine' (six years altogether to graduate [three years of General Medicine, the other three in medical specialisation]).
88. Students Delgado, I. and Horopesa, J. and Cuban Medic, interview by author, BA I in Caricuao, Caracas, April 14, 2009.
89. The three regions are (1) State of Táchira, (2) Calabozo, in the State of Guárico, (3) Caricuao in Libertador municipality, Capital District, Caracas.
90. Interview with Cuban Medic, Cordero—San Cristobal, Táchira, March 27, 2009.
91. He was very annoyed when I asked his name: 'you don't need it' he said. Interview with a Cuban Medic, Altos de Gallardin—San Cristobal, Táchira, March 27, 2009.
92. Interview with Cuban medic, BA I bloque 10–11 in Mucuritas, Caricuao, Caracas, April 14, 2009.
93. In all the BA modules/centers I saw pictures of Chávez, Fidel Castro, Che Guevara, Jose Martí (1853–1895; Cuban national hero who fought for Cuban independence against Spain) and Simon Bolívar. All these nationalist leaders are displayed together—resembling a religious altar discourse.
94. CDI 'Dr. Rafael Rangel', Caricuao, Caracas, April 14, 2009.
95. 'Poblacion de Caricuao orgullosa de su CDI "Dr. Rafael Rangel"'. *Venta Bolivariana.org.ve* January 7, 2009, http://www.ventanabolivariana.org.ve/index.php/Poblacion-de-Caricuao-orgullosa-de-su-CDI-Dr.-Rafael-Rangel. html [accessed May 29, 2009].
96. Señora Yolanda, Vicario 1, Calabozo, SRI BA II
97. Señor Chicho, *Barrio* Carrasquelero, Calabozo BA I
98. A patient, Bloque 10–11 Mucuritas, Caricuao, BA I
99. All mission finances are directly administered from the state oil corporation—avoiding ministerial/political obstacles.
100. 'Economia—Resultados primer trimestre 2009: Claves para entender la tormenta'. *análisisvenezuela—Análisis Estratégico para la toma de decisions—Reporte seminal de ODH Grupo Consultor.* 19: Vol 3. 20 al 26 de mayo 2009: 9, http://www.whatsnextvenezuela.com/docs/AnalisisVenezuela_19_090520cc. pdf [accessed June 15, 2010]. Furthermore, a PDVSA Government financial report states that Venezuela's oil industry provided in 2007 U.S. $7.136 billion for social programs (missions). However, this figure declined (from January 1 to September 30, 2008) to U.S. $2.201 billion. *Barrio Adentro I, II,* and *III* received U.S. $114 million during that period. See: 'Informe operacional y financiero—Periodo de nueve (9) meses terminado el 30 de septiembre de 2008—La Nueva PDVSA Con Visión Soberana, Popular y Revolucionaria'. *Petróleos de Venezuela, S.A y sus filiales (PDVSA),* http://www.pdvsa.com/interface.sp/database/fichero/free/4357/429.PDF [accessed August 13, 2010].
101. This is also the case with nurses *'Defensores de Salud'* from various regions of the country protesting in Caracas because the government has not paid their salaries. 'En foto Barrio Adentro no Paga'. *Noticias 24,* April 18, 2008, http://www.noticias24.com/actualidad/noticia/13590/en-fotos-barrio-adentro-no-paga/ [accessed May 30, 2009].
102. The report states that CDIs are not receiving catering expenses, air conditioners are not working, workers are having to buy cleaning products, and

litter is not being collected. The workers consist of stewards, nurses, maids, ambulance drivers, and others.

103. Sara Carolina Díaz. 'Alerta que Barrio Adentro esta en "riesgo letal"—trabajadores de la misión denunciaron ante el parlamento irregularidades'. *El Universal*, July 17, 2009, http://www.eluniversal.com/2009/07/17/pol_art_alertan-que-barrio-a_1476191.shtml [accessed July 25, 2009].

104. Reyes Theis. 'Chávez declaró en emergencia la salud en Venezuela—dos mil módulos de Barrio Adentro no tiene médicos, según el mandatario'. *El Universal*, September 20, 2009, http://www.eluniversal.com/2009/09/20/pol_art_chavez-declaro-en-em_1574464.shtml [accessed September 20, 2009].

105. Even though the target to train and integrate 20,000 Venezuelans into the program by 2010 did not materialize, in November 2011, Claudio Aoun Soulie, the president of Venezuela's National Academy of Medicine, made some interesting remarks about the quality of the integral medical training 8,300 (11,700 less than the 20,000 target) Venezuelan medical students have been receiving. Aoun Soulie stressed that the Academy, the scientific community, and the FMV have expressed on many occasions their concerns about the 'poor' academic, practical, ethical, and technical standards of the training. These students have had no training in key issues like laboratories, tropical medicine, biochemistry, and pharmacology, no experience in morgues or Venezuelan pathology; they are trained via video conferences, not in the emergency operating theatres in the main hospitals of the country. 'Entrevista Claudio Aoun Soulie, Presidente de la Academia Nacional de la Medicina—"8.300 médicos comunitarios jamás han pisado un quirófano"'. *El Universal*, October 30, 2011, http://www.eluniversal.com/nacional-y-politica/111030/8300-medicos-comunitarios-jamas-han-pisado-un-quirofano [October 30, 2011].

106. 'Recursos Sociales bajo control de Chávez se multiplicarán por siete en 2010—La decisión de Chávez de seguir concentrando funciones demuestra la poca confianza que tiene en sus ministros, explicó el analista político José Vicente Carrasquero'. *El Nacional*, November 24, 2009, http://elnacional.com/www/site/p_contenido.php?q=nodo/110071/Nacional/Recursos-sociales-bajo-control-de-Ch%E1vez-se-multiplicar%E1n-por-siete-en-2010 [accessed November 24, 2009].

107. 'Empleados de Barrio Adentro protestan frente al Palacio de Miraflores'. *Noticias24*, November 17, 2010, http://www.noticias24.com/actualidad/noticia/181071/emplados-de-barrio-adentro-protestan-frente-al-palacio-de-miraflores-por-pago-salarial/ [accessed February 11, 2011].

NOTES TO CHAPTER 5

1. Cristina Hossne. 'Estudiantes de la UCAB y la USB protestan en apoyo a RCTV'. *El Universal*, May 25, 2007, http://politica.eluniversal.com/2007/05/25/rctv_ava_estudiantes-de-la-uc_25A874209.shtml [accessed September 2009]. 'UCEVISTAS protestaron en la autopista Francisco Fajardo cierre de RCTV'. *El Universal*, May 25, 2007, http://politica.eluniversal.com/2007/05/25/rctv_ava_ucevistas-protestaro_25A874355.shtml [accessed September 2009].

2. '17 heridos dejan refriega en Chacao este Lunes'. *El Universal*, May 29, 2007, http://www.eluniversal.com/2007/05/29/pol_art_17-heridos—dejan-re_303151.shtml [accessed September 2008].

3. Marianela Rodriguez and Nora Beatriz Sánchez. '14 heridos, uno de gravedad en disturbios en Carabobo y Mérida'. *El Universal*, May 29, 2007, http://

188 Notes

www.eluniversal.com/2007/05/29/pol_art_14-heridos,-uno-de-g_302826. shtml [accessed July 2010].

4. 'Estudiantes exigen derecho de palabra en el Parlamento'. *El Universal*, June 2, 2007, http://www.eluniversal.com/2007/06/02/pol_art_estudiantes-exigen-d_306982.shtml [accessed July 2010].

5. Sara Carolina Díaz. 'Estudiantes tendrán derecho de palabra en el parlamento'. *El Universal*, June 6, 2007, http://www.eluniversal.com/2007/06/06/pol_art_estudiantes-tendran_310723.shtml [accessed July 2010].

6. Iralis Fragiel. 'Chávez dice que estudiantes que protestan son "peones del imperio"'. *El Universal*, June 7, 2007, http://www.eluniversal.com/2007/06/07/pol_ava_chavez-dice-que-estu_07A881457.shtml [accessed, July 2010].

7. 'Douglas Barrios hace su intervención ante la Asamblea Nacional'. *Estudiantes en la AN—YouTube Play*, June 7, 2007, http://www.youtube.com/wat ch?v=3Vt8JPXNIGQ&translated=1 [accessed, July 2010].

8. 'Estaremos dando la cara'. *El Universal*, June 3, 2007, http://www.eluniversal.com/2007/06/03/pol_apo_estaremos-dando-la_306748.shtml [accessed July 2010].

9. Enrique Krauze describes the role of Gustavo Tovar Arroyo as the teacher/mentor of Yon Goicoechea (a key figure in the student movement), as well as 'other student leaders'. Krauze, E. *El Poder y el Delirio* (Barcelona: Tuspuets Editores, S.A. 2008), 140–41.

10. Tovar Arroyo, *Estudiantes por la Libertad . . . de la Generación 2007*, 104–5.

11. Tovar Arroyo, *Estudiantes por la Libertad . . . de la Generación 2007*, 122–23

12. Tovar Arroyo, *Estudiantes por la Libertad . . . de la Generación 2007*, 124

13. Rayma López (student leader of the *Universidad Pedagógica Experimental Libertador*), interview by author, Caracas, March 4, 2009.

14. Rayma López, interview by author, Caracas, March 4, 2009.

15. Tovar Arroyo, *Estudiantes por la Libertad . . . de la Generación 2007*, 126–27.

16. Javier Pereira. 'David Smolansky: La prioridad estudiantil es la resistencia al paquetazo'. *Venezuela Real—Información y Opinión,* September 7, 2008, http://venezuelareal.zoomblog.com/archivo/2008/09/07/david-Smolansky-La-prioridad-estudiant.html [accessed August 2010].

17. Rayma López, interview by author, Caracas, March 4, 2009.

18. Katherina Hruskovec G. 'Manos de Libertad. ¡Basta de ser espectadores! ¡Estamos cansados de la división y la polarización!'. *El Universal*, June 12, 2007, http://www.eluniversal.com/2007/06/12/opi_45885_art_manos—delibertad_310569.shtml [accessed June 2, 2009].

19. Rayma López, interview by author, Caracas, March 04, 2009.

20. Álvarez, A. '¿Venezuela: La Revolución Pierde Su Encanto? Venezuela: Is the Revolution Losing Its Charm?' *Revista de Ciencia Política*, Vol. 28, No. 1 (2008): 405–6.

21. Tovar Arroyo, *Estudiantes por la Libertad . . . de la Generación 2007*, 58–59.

22. Tovar Arroyo, *Estudiantes por la Libertad . . . de la Generación 2007*, 62–4.

23. Tovar Arroyo, *Estudiantes por la Libertad . . . de la Generación 2007*, 109.

24. See Sharp, G. *The Politics of Nonviolent Action*. Gene Sharp with the editorial assistance of Marina Finkelstein. (Boston: Extending Horizons Books; Porter Sargent Publisher, 1973). Tovar Arroyo, *Estudiantes por la Libertad . . . de la Generación 2007*, 80–83.

Notes   189

25. Tovar Arroyo, *Estudiantes por la Libertad . . . de la Generación 2007*, 83–84.
26. Tovar Arroyo, *Estudiantes por la Libertad . . . de la Generación 2007*, 84.
27. Tovar Arroyo, *Estudiantes por la Libertad . . . de la Generación 2007*, 109.
28. Glynos and Howarth, *Logics of Critical Explanation in Social and Political Theory*, 146.
29. Casanova, R. 'La Revuelta de Estudiantes Venezolanos del 2007—El Levantamiento Político de una Nueva Generación'. *Cuadernos del Cendes año 26 n. 70 Tercera Época* (January–April 2009): 100.
30. Casanova, 'La Revuelta de Estudiantes . . . Nueva Generación', 101.
31. Morles, V., Medina Rubio, E., and Alvarez Bedoya, N. *La Educacion Superior en Venezuela*. (Caracas: Lesalc/Unesco, 2003); cited by Casanova, 'La Revuelta de Estudiantes . . . Nueva Generación', 106.
32. Casanova, 'La Revuelta de Estudiantes . . . Nueva Generación', 106.
33. Casanova, 'La Revuelta de Estudiantes . . . Nueva Generación', 103.
34. Casanova, 'La Revuelta de Estudiantes . . . Nueva Generación', 104.
35. Casanova, 'La Revuelta de Estudiantes . . . Nueva Generación', 104–5.
36. Casanova, 'La Revuelta de Estudiantes . . . Nueva Generación', 118.
37. Casanova, 'La Revuelta de Estudiantes . . . Nueva Generación', 99–116.
38. Casanova, 'La Revuelta de Estudiantes . . . Nueva Generación', 105–17.
39. Casanova, 'La Revuelta de Estudiantes . . . Nueva Generación', 107.
40. Casanova, 'La Revuelta de Estudiantes . . . Nueva Generación', 105–16.
41. Unidad de Análisis Estrategico/Univesidad del Pueblo. *El Movimiento de las "Manos Blancas"* (Mérida, Venezuela: UNIVER-SO, 2009), 1–2. http://www.scribd.com/doc/10957786/El-Movimiento-de-Las-Manos-Blancas1 [accessed June 4, 2009].
42. Unidad de Análisis . . . Univesidad del Pueblo . . . *"Manos Blancas"*, 2–3.
43. Unidad de Análisis . . . Univesidad del Pueblo . . . *"Manos Blancas"*, 3.
44. Unidad de Análisis . . . Univesidad del Pueblo . . . *"Manos Blancas"*, 4.
45. This symbol was also used by a movement in Georgia (2003) with the word 'enough' to oust Eduard Shevardnad. There was also a Russian anti-Putin movement using the word 'defense'. Unidad de Análisis . . . Univesidad del Pueblo . . . *"Manos Blancas"*, 4.
46. Unidad de Análisis . . . Univesidad del Pueblo . . . *"Manos Blancas"*, 8–9.
47. Unidad de Análisis . . . Univesidad del Pueblo . . . *"Manos Blancas"*, 5–8.
48. 'Yon Goicoechea, ganador del premio Milton Friedman por la libertad'. *The Milton Friedman Prize for Advancing Liberty*. April 24, 2008, http://www.elcato.org/special/friedman/index.html [accessed June 6, 2009].
49. Rayma López, interview by author, Caracas, March 4, 2009.
50. Prada says: the police shoot from a distance less than four meters, which is totally illegal. Jhonny Prada, interview by author, San Cristobal, Táchira, March 25, 2009.
51. Jhonny Prada (student leader of private universities in Táchira—*Instituto Universitario de la Frontera* [IUFRONT]), interview by author, San Cristobal, Táchira, March 25, 2009.
52. The location and time of this meeting was very secretive right from the start. The student leader who informed me of this event couldn't attend, but contacted me with another student organizing the event. After constant government phone tapping since May 2007, and the interest of foreign journalists who sympathized with the government in interviewing them and attending their internal meetings, a sense of suspicion and distrust regarding non-participants like me was understandable. After the event, Lopez told me that during the meeting, many of them called her asking if I was trustworthy or not. Unfortunately, this documentary was never released. Caracas, January 7, 2008.

190 *Notes*

53. Student leaders like Fabricio Briceño (also from UCV) expressed their experience and opposition to this new phase of the Bolivarian project. Caracas, January 7, 2008.
54. 'Es un proceso de Resistencia al gobierno'. *El Universal*, June 3, 2007, http://www.eluniversal.com/2007/06/03/pol_apo_es-un-proceso-de-re_306746. shtml [accessed August 14, 2010].
55. Tovar Arroyo, *Estudiantes por la Libertad . . . de la Generación 2007*, 110.
56. Laclau, E. 'Populism: What's in a Name?', in Panizza, F. (ed.), *Populism and the Mirror of Democracy* (London: Verso, 2005), 38.
57. Glynos and Howarth, *Logics of Critical Explanation in Social and Political Theory*, 139.
58. Jhonny Prada, interview by author, San Cristobal, Táchira, March 25, 2009.
59. Danny Ramírez, interview by author, San Cristobal, Táchira, March 31, 2009.
60. Danny Ramírez, interview by author, San Cristobal, Táchira, March 31, 2009.
61. Ramírez was sentenced to six years in jail. In December 2007, Chávez decreed an amnesty for political prisoners. He graduated in jail. Danny Ramírez, interview by author, San Cristobal, Táchira, March 31, 2009.
62. Danny Ramírez, interview by author, San Cristobal, Táchira, March 31, 2009.
63. 'Agustin Blanco Muñoz.'¿Cuál movimiento estudiantil?'. *Opinión—El Universal*, May 30, 2008, http://www.eluniversal.com/2008/05/30/opi_1725_art_cual-movimiento-est_30A1623239.shtml
64. 'Estudiante Julio Rivas en libertad se unio a la huelga de hambre en la sede de la OEA'. *El Nacional*, September 29, 2009, http://www.el-nacional. com/www/site/p_contenido.php?q=nodo/101298/Nación/Estudiante-Julio-Rivas-en-libertad-se-unió-a-la-huelga-de-hambre-en-la-sede-de-la-OEA [accessed Sept. 29, 2009].
65. Ocarina Espinoza, 'Presidenta de la AN asegura que oposicion usa a estudiantes para logros politicos'. *El Universal*, October 1, 2009, http://www. eluniversal.com/2009/10/01/pol_ava_presidenta-de-la-an_01A2822253. shtml [accessed October 1, 2009].
66. Danny Ramírez, interview by author, San Cristobal, Táchira, March 31, 2009.

NOTES TO CHAPTER 6

1. Brewer-Carías, A. R. 'Venezuela 2009 Referendum on Continuous Reelection: Constitutional Implications' (Paper for the Panel Discussion on *Venezuela Referendum: Public Opinion, Economic Impact and Constitutional Implications*, Americas Society/Council of the Americas, New York, February 9, 2009), 4. http://ilas.columbia.edu/images/uploads/workingpapers/Allan_Brewer-Carias-_Venezuela_2009_Referendum_on_Continuous_Re-Election,_Constitutional_Implications.pdf [accessed February 1, 2012].
2. *Aló Presidente*, January 11, 2009; cited by Brewer-Carías, 'Venezuela 2009 Referendum on Continuous Reelection: Constitutional Implications', 7.
3. 'ReferendoAprobatorio de la Enmienda Constitucional'. *Consejo Nacional Electoral*, February 15, 2009, http://www.cne.gob.ve/divulgacion_referendo_enmienda_2009/ [accessed November 2010].
4. Martínez, G. E. 'La LOPE y el CNE cambiaron el sistema politico venezolano', in Derecho Electoral en Venezuela—*Centro de Estudios de Politica*

Notes 191

Proyectiva, Segunda Edición Aniversaria (Noviembre–Diciembre 2009); cited by Rachadell, M. 'El Sistema Electoral en la Ley Orgánica de Procesos Electorales', *Provincia*, No. 23 (enero–junio 2010): 152.

5. Rachadell, 'El Sistema Electoral en la Ley Orgánica de Procesos Electorales', 152.
6. See Dean, J. W. 'The Gerrymander', *New England Historical and Genealogical Register*, Vol. 46 (1892): 374–83; cited by Mark Monmonier, *Bushmanders & Bullwinkles* (Chicago and London: The University of Chicago Press, 2001), 1–2.
7. Sickels, R. J. 'Dragons, Bacon Strips and Dumbbells—Who's Afraid of Reapportionment?' *Yale Law Journal*, Vol. 75 (July 1966): 1300–08; cited by Philip Musgrove, *The General Theory of Gerrymandering*, American Politics Series Editor: Randall B. Ripley, Ohio State University Series Number: 04–034 Vol. 3 (Sage Publications/Beverly Hills/ London), 6.
8. O'Rourke, T. P. *Reapportionment: Law, Politics, Computers.* (Washington, D.C.: Amer. Enterprise Inst. Domestic Affairs Study, 1972), 38; cited by Philip Musgrove (1977) *The General Theory of Gerrymandering*, 6.
9. Musgrove, *The General Theory of Gerrymandering*, 6.
10. Rachadell, 'El Sistema Electoral en la Ley Orgánica de Procesos Electorales', 138.
11. Rachadell, 'El Sistema Electoral en la Ley Orgánica de Procesos Electorales', 147.
12. 'Resultados por estado—Nación', *El Nacional*, September 28, 2010, 5.
13. Rachadell, 'El Sistema Electoral en la Ley Orgánica de Procesos Electorales', 147–48
14. The MUD, formed in January 2009, has become an organized and united anti-Bolivarian alliance of political parties. In June 2009, 11 political parties were members of the MUD alliance. By April 2010, the MUD expanded 'to around 50 political parties, of which 16 were national in scope (the rest regional), and had support from some other social organisations and opinion groups'. See: Marquez, H. 'Opposition Plans Return to Opposition Congress'. *IPSNews*, April 27, 2010, http://ipsnews.net/news.asp?idnews=51218 [accessed November 2010].
15. In 2008, Chávez called for all small political parties in the Bolivarian Alliance to become members of his party *Partido Socialista Unido de Venezuela* (PSUV) and comply with party candidate selection procedures. This caused the breakaway of the PPT party from Chávez's equivalential chain. However, the PPT did not join the opposition camp.
16. 'Divulgación Elecciones Parlamentarias', *Consejo Nacional Electoral*, September 26, 2010, http://www.cne.gob.ve/divulgacion_parlamentarias_2010/ [accessed November 2010].
17. 'Venezuela's legislative election—The Revolution checked—The opposition bounces back'. *The Economist*, September 30, 2010, http://www.economist.com/node/17149092?story_id=17149092 [accessed November 2010].
18. 'Hugo Chávez tiene cancer y fue operado en Cuba, Fidel anuncio la noticia'. *Misceláneas De Cuba* on *YouTube*, June 30, 2011, http://www.youtube.com/watch?v=moXw_hiPUHc [accessed January 12, 2012].
19. 'Chávez celebra su cumpleaños desde el balcón del pueblo 57 años'. *Venezolana de Televisión* on *YouTube*, July 26, 2011, http://www.youtube.com/watch?v=oif1a_CfV8c [accessed February 6, 2012].
20. 'Chávez, en su cumpleaños, asegura que no tiene ni una célula cancerígena'. *El Nacional*, July 28, 2011, http://www.el-nacional.com/www/site/p_contenido.php?q=nodo/225070/Nación/Chávez,-en-su-cumpleaños,-asegura-que-no-tiene-ni-una-célula-cancer%C3%ADgena [accessed February 6, 2012].

192 Notes

21. Mayela Armas. 'Presidente Chávez en nueve años ha creado 34 misiones', *El Universal*, December 23, 2011. Page 6.
22. 'Registro Nacional de la Gran Mision en Amor Mayor Venezuela'. *Gobierno Bolivariano de Venezuela*, http://www.conapdis.gob.ve/index.php/registro-nacional-de-la-gran-mision-en-amor-mayo-venezuela [accessed January 28, 2012].
23. 'Pension rallies hit French cities', *BBC*, September 7, 2010, http://www.bbc.co.uk/news/world-europe-11204528 [accessed January 29, 2012].
24. Dan Hyde. 'When Will you Retire?'. *This is Money*, December 1, 2011, http://www.thisismoney.co.uk/money/pensions/article-1679780/New-state-pension-age-retirement-dates-calculator.html [accessed January 29, 2012].
25. 'Gran Misión Vivienda Venezuela'. *Gobierno Bolivariano de Venezuela*, http://www.mcti.gob.ve/Servicios/Registro_Vivienda_Venezuela/ [accessed January 29, 2012].
26. 'Familias inscritas en la Misión Vivienda supera los 2 millones'. *El Universal*, August 9, 2011, http://www.eluniversal.com/2011/08/09/familias-inscritas-en-la-mision-vivienda-supera-los-2-millones.shtml [accessed January 29, 2012].
27. Mayela Armas. 'En un semestre Gobierno prevé terminar 140,000 viviendas'. *El Universal*, July 12, 2011, http://www.eluniversal.com/2011/07/12/en-un-semestre-gobierno-preve-terminar-140000-viviendas.shtml [accessed January 29, 2012].
28. 'Gobierno prevé cumplir meta de viviendas de 2012 para septiembre'. *El Universal*, January 9, 2012, http://www.eluniversal.com/economia/120109/gobierno-preve-cumplir-meta-de-viviendas-de-2012-para-septiembre-imp [accessed January 30, 2012].
29. 'Gran Misión Saber y Trabajo Venezuela'. *Gobierno Bolivariano de Venezuela* http://www.venezueladeverdad.gob.ve/content/gran-misión-saber-y-trabajo-venezuela [accessed January 30, 2012].
30. 'Gran Misión Hijos de Venezuela'. *Gobierno Bolivariano de Venezuela* http://www.minci.gob.ve/infografias/67/210050/gran_mision_hijos.html [accessed January 30, 2012].
31. On July 17, 2010, 'Chávez ordered Bolívar's tomb to be opened because he suspects he was murdered. Most accounts maintain Bolívar died of tuberculosis in Colombia in 1830. More than 50 experts including criminal investigators and forensic pathologists have been examining the remains to see if Bolívar was the victim of a conspiracy rather than a disease'. 'Venezuela's Chávez exhumes hero Simon Bolívar's bones'. *BBC*, July 17, 2010, http://www.bbc.co.uk/news/world-latin-america-10669051 [accessed February 2, 2012].
32. Vásquez, S. A. 'Chávez: El cadaver de Bolívar me pareció el de un niño', *El Nacional*, December 18, 2011. Page 3.
33. The journalist Miguel Pedrero claims that Hugo Chávez and Fidel Castro not only admire each other, help each other, and share similar political views; they also share personal beliefs in African gods and in the power of magic or contact with supernatural entities. 'Las prácticas mágicas de ambos lideres, al descubierto—Hugo Chávez y Fidel Castro, unidos por lo oculto'. *Akasico*, June 1, 2009, http://www.akasico.com/noticia/2043/Conspiraciones/hugo-chavez-fidel-castro-unidos-oculto.html [accessed February 3, 2012]. It is widely speculated in Venezuela, among opposition supporters, that Chávez practices Cuban '*brujeria*' and '*paleria*': Afro-Cuban witchcraft that uses human bones and skulls to call upon the spirits. See: 'Venezuela: los restos de Bolívar estaban "degradados" y requerían exhumación'. *Información y Análisis de América Latina*, July 28, 2010, http://www.infolatam.

com/2010/07/28/venezuela-restos-bolivar-exhumacion-forense/ [accessed February 3, 2012]. A report in the *New York Times* states that 'Political movements drawing strength from the remains of the dead are not new here or elsewhere in Latin America'. According to Lyman Johnson, a historian at the University of North Carolina who specializes in Latin America's body cults, '"Disputes over bodies are disputes over power, power over the past and power in the present. . . . These powerful meanings force new life into long-dead bodies"'. Simon Romero, 'Building a New History by Exhuming Bolívar'. *The New York Times,* August 3, 2010, http://www.nytimes.com/2010/08/04/world/americas/04venez.html [accessed February 3, 2012].

34. Yapp, Robin, 'Hugo Chávez compared to Hitler after vow to rule until 2031'. *The Telegraph,* July 26, 2011, http://www.telegraph.co.uk/news/worldnews/southamerica/venezuela/8663863/Hugo-Chavez-compared-to-Hitler-after-vow-to-rule-until-2031.html ; N. Mastronardi. 'Hugo Chávez: He resuelto gobernar hasta 2031'. *Correo del Orinoco,* December 15, 2011, http://www.correodelorinoco.gob.ve/avances/he-resuelto-gobernar-hasta-2031/[accessed February 3, 2012].

35. 'Datanálisis: popularidad de Chávez aumenta en dos meses tras anunciar su emfemedad'. *Informe21.com,* October 5, 2011, http://informe21.com/hugo-chavez/datanalisis-popularidad-chavez-aumenta-10-puntos-dos-me-ses-anunciar-su-enfermedad [accessed February 3, 2012].

36. This kind of plot discourse was reaffirmed on December 28, 2011, when Chávez, from the Military Academy in Caracas, suggested that the U.S. might be using a secret weapon to give Latin American leaders cancer. The Argentinean President Cristina Fernández de Kirchner, the Brazilian President Dilma Rouseff and her predecessor Lula Da Silva, the Paraguayan President Fernando Lugo, and Chávez, starting an electoral year for the presidency, were diagnosed with cancer. Chávez also stated that 'Fidel always told me, these people have developed technologies, you are too careless, be careful with what you eat, someone could pinch you with a needle'. Furthermore, Chávez claimed that 'the opposition and their American advisers are preparing the ground to claim that the results of the Presidential elections on October 7, 2012 are rigged . . . opposition candidates are campaigning everywhere. It is only now that they pay attention to the *barrios*. They always despised *el pueblo*; but now, they are running around hugging elderly housewives and children'. Maria Lilibeth Da Corte, 'Para Chávez EEUU induce cancer a líderes de la region'. *El Universal,* December 29, 2011, http://www.eluniversal.com/nacional-y-politica/111229/para-chavez-eeuu-induce-can-cer-a-lideres-de-la-region [accessed February 4, 2012]; 'Hugo Chávez: Es muy extraño, cancer en varios presidentes latinoamericanos en muy poco tiempo'. *Venezolana de Televisión* on *YouTube*, December 29, 2011, http://www.youtube.com/watch?v=7CqddV_XKp8 [accessed February 4, 2012].

37. Lefort, C. *The Political Forms of Modern Society: Bureaucracy, Democracy, Totalitarianism* (Cambridge, MA: MIT Press, 1986), 279.

38. Lefort, *The Political Forms . . . Bureaucracy, Democracy, Totalitarianism,* 279.

39. Lefort, *The Political Forms . . . Bureaucracy, Democracy, Totalitarianism,* 279.

40. Panizza, F. 'Introduction: Populism and the Mirror of Democracy', in Panizza, F. (ed.), *Populism and the Mirror of Democracy* (London: Verso, 2005), 29.

41. Leopoldo López was a successful and popular mayor of Caracas's Chacao district from 2000 until 2008. His plan to run for mayor of greater Caracas in the November 2008 local and regional elections was barred from standing

194 *Notes*

on June 23, 2008, on account of unproven corruption allegations that were never tested in court. This ban was due to last until 2014. After investigating López's ban, on September 16, 2011, the Inter-American Court of Human Rights (IACHR) unanimously ruled that López should be allowed to run for office. Chávez's Government condemned IACHR's interference in internal affairs, 'saying the ruling would only be applied if the Supreme Court found it compatible with the Venezuelan constitution. . . . It was therefore not surprising that the court, which has a record of dancing to the government's tune, failed to uphold the ruling'. Nonetheless, López was '"temporarily barred from holding public office". Astutely, the court opted to reassess and issue a ruling on whether López can take office as president if and only if he wins the election'. See: 'Venezuela's presidential campaign—as clear as MUD'. *The Economist,* October 23, 2011, http://www.economist.com/blogs/americasview/2011/10/venezuela's-presidential-campaign [accessed on February 12, 2012].

42. Leopoldo López, interview by author, Chacao—Caracas, December 27, 2011.
43. 'López asegura que a Chávez no le importa el problema de la inseguridad'. *El Universal,* January 12, 2012, http://www.eluniversal.com/nacional-y-politica/primarias-2012/120112/lopez-asegura-que-a-chavez-no-le-importa-el-problema-de-la-inseguridad [accessed February 12, 2012].
44. Elvira Gómez. '"Voten por Capriles que estarán votando por López"—Leopoldo López declinó su aspiración a favor de Henrique Capriles'. *El Universal,* January 25, 2012, http://www.eluniversal.com/nacional-y-politica/120125/voten-por-capriles-que-estaran-votando-por-leopoldo-lopez [accessed February 12, 2012].
45. '"Llegare hasta al final porque soy garantía para derrotar al presidente Chávez"—Pablo Medina: "El dilemma es la bota militar o la Venezuela democrática"'. *Notitarde,* February 4, 2012, http://www.notitarde.com/notitarde/plantillas/notitarde/inota.aspx?idart=1551270&idcat=32681&tipo=2 [accessed February 13, 2012].
46. '¡Lacen su majunche que lo barreremos en las presidenciales de 2012!'. *YouTube,* May 1, 2011, http://www.youtube.com/watch?v=avzK2Vm9h3Q [accessed February 13, 2012].
47. Ender Ramírez Padrino. 'Chávez duda que se realicen primarias opositoras'. *El Nacional,* January 8, 2012, http://www.el-nacional.com/noticia/17028/16/Chavez-duda-que-se-realicen-primarias-opositoras.html [accessed February 13, 2012].
48. These 'you'll be fired' threats were interpreted by state employees and the MUD as an attempt to revise a list similar to the '*Tascón* List' (see page 180n89). The MUD responded, ensuring voters that the secrecy of the vote was secured because voting rolls would be destroyed 48 hours after the opposition primary election. 'MUD denuncia "amenazas" a empleados públicos para que no voten en las primarias', *El Nacional,* February 8, 2012, http://www.el-nacional.com/noticia/21714/64/MUD-denuncia-amenazas-a-empleados-publicos-para-que-no-voten-en-las-Primarias.html [accessed February 13, 2012].
49. According to Ricardo Sanguino, a Chavista parliamentarian, in 2010, there were approximately 2.5 million Venezuelans working in the public sector. Hugo Pietro/Última Noticias, 'La economía según Ricardo Sanguino'. *analitica.com,* June 7, 2010, http://www.analitica.com/va/economia/opinion/8415876.asp [accessed February 13, 2012].
50. 'Primarias 2012—Cifra de votantes de las primarias cierra en 3.040.449'. *El Universal,* February 13, 2012, http://www.eluniversal.com/nacional-y-

politica/primarias-2012/120213/cifra-de-votantes-de-las-primarias-cierra-en-3040449 [accessed February 14, 2012].

51. 'Henrique Capriles Randonski Candidato Definitivo Presidencia de Venezuela 2012/ Video 01'. *Globovisión* on *YouTube*, February 12, 2012, http://www.youtube.com/watch?v=ffVn73dsqsk [accessed February 13, 2012].

52. 'Capriles: este gobierno solo habla del pasado, nosotros del futuro'. *El Universal*, February 13, 2012, http://www.eluniversal.com/nacional-y-politica/primarias-2012/120213/capriles-este-gobierno-solo-habla-del-pasado-nosotros-del-futuro [accessed February 13, 2012].

53. See: 'Crecimiento electoral'. *Tal Cual*, February, 16, 2012, http://www.talcualdigital.com/Nota/visor.aspx?id=66300&tipo=AVA [accessed February 16, 2012].

NOTES TO THE CONCLUSION

1. 'Presidente Chávez encabeza acto de I Promoción de Médicos Integrales'. *El Universal*, February 16, 2012, http://www.eluniversal.com/nacional-y-politica/120216/presidente-chavez-encabeza-acto-de-i-promocion-de-medicos-integrales [accessed February 16, 2012].

2. 'SALUD | Falta de recursos y fallas en control interno golpearon a la misión—1.235 obras de Barrio Adentro II se encuentran paralizadas'. *El Universal*, April 2, 2012, http://www.eluniversal.com/nacional-y-politica/120402/1235-obras-de-barrio-adentro-ii-se-encuentran-paralizadas [accessed April 2, 2012].

3. My observations are based on what I heard from people before and after the parliamentarian election at newsagents, buses, underground (Metro Caracas), etc., and also from reading and listening to news-reports, radio, and television news-updates.

4. Panizza, F. 'Introduction: Populism and the Mirror of Democracy', in Panizza, F. (ed.), *Populism and the Mirror of Democracy* (London: Verso 2005), 29.

5. Lefort, C. *The Political Forms of Modern Society: Bureaucracy, Democracy, Totalitarianism* (Cambridge, MA: MIT Press, 1986), 279; cited by Panizza, 'Introduction: Populism and the Mirror of Democracy', 29.

Bibliography

Alayón, M. R. 'Barrio Adentro: Combatir la Exclusion Profundizando la Democracia', *Revista Venezolana de Economía y Ciencias Sociales*, Vol. 11 (September–December 2005): 219–44.

Ali, T. *Pirates of the Caribbean—Axis of Hope* (London: Verso, 2006).

Althusser, L. *Lenin and Philosophy, and Other Essays* (New York: Monthly Review Press, 1971).

Alvarado, C. H., Martinez, M. E., Vivas-Martinez S., Gutiérrez N. J., and Metzger W. 'Cambio Social y Política de Salud en Venezuela', *Medicina Social*, No. 3 (2008): l13–29.

Álvarez, A. '¿Venezuela: La Revolución Pierde Su Encanto? Venezuela: Is the Revolution Losing Its Charm?', *Revista de Ciencia Política*, Vol. 28, No. 1 (2008): 405–32.

Alvarez, C. 'Venezuela's Oil-Based Economy', *Council of Foreign Relations,* February 9, 2009, http://www.cfr.org/publication/12089/venezuelas_oilbased_economy.html [accessed, July 25, 2009].

Armada, F., Muntaner, C., Chung, H., Williams-Brennan, L., and Benac, J. 'Barrio Adentro and the Reduction of Health Inequalities in Venezuela: An Appraisal of the First Years', *International Journal of Health Services*, Vol. 39, No. 1 (2009): 161–87.

Bartley, K., and O'Briain, D. *The Revolution Will Not Be Televised* (DVD; Power Pictures, 2003).

Blanco Muñoz, A. *Venezuela del 04F-92 al 06D-98: Habla el Comandante Hugo Chávez Testimonios Violentos* (Caracas: Cátedra Pío Tamayo, CEHA / IIES / FACES / UCV, 1998).

Brewer-Carías, A. R. 'Venezuela 2009 Referendum on Continuous Reelection: Constitutional Implications' (Paper for the Panel Discussion on Venezuela Referendum: Public Opinion, Economic Impact and Constitutional Implications, Americas Society/Council of the Americas, New York, February 9, 2009), 1–7. http://ilas.columbia.edu/images/uploads/workingpapers/Allan_Brewer-Carias-Venezuela_2009_Referendum_on_Continuous_Re-Election,_Constitutional_Implications.pdf [accessed February 1, 2011].

Briggs, C. L., and Mantini-Briggs, C. 'Confronting Health Disparities: Latin American Social Medicine in Venezuela', *American Journal of Public Health*, Vol. 99, No. 3 (2009): 549–55.

Buxton, J. 'Venezuela', in Buxton, J., and Phillips, N. (eds.), *Case Studies in Latin American Political Economy* (New York: Manchester University Press, 1999), 162–84.

Buxton, J. 'Economic Policy and the Rise of Hugo Chávez', in Ellner, S., and Hellinger, D. (eds.), *Venezuelan Politics in the Chávez Era: Class, Polarization, and Conflict* (Boulder, CO: Lynne Rienner Publishers, 2003), 113–30.

198 Bibliography

Cannon, B. 'Venezuela, April 2002: Coup or Popular Rebellion? The Myth of a United Venezuela', *Bulletin of Latin America Research*, Vol. 23, No. 3 (2004): 285–302.

Canovan, M. *Populism* (London: Junction Books, 1981).

Canovan, M. 'Two Strategies for the Study of Populism', *Political Studies*, Vol. 30 (1982): 544–52.

Canovan, M. '"People", Politicians and Populism', *Government and Opposition*, Vol. 19 (1984): 312–27.

Canovan, M. 'Taking Politics to the People: Populism as the Ideology of Democracy', in Mény, Y., and Surel, Y. (eds.), *Democracies and the Populist Challenge* (New York: Palgrave Macmillan, 2002), 25–44.

Canovan, M. 'Populism for Political Theorists?', *Journal of Political Ideologies*, Vol. 9, No. 3 (2004): 241–52.

Canovan, M. *The People* (Cambridge: Polity Press, 2005).

Carmona Estanga, P. 'Decreto del Gobierno Provisional de Pedro Carmona Estanga', in *Observatorio Social de América Latina* (2002) Year III, 7: 27–28.

Cartaya,V., Magallanes, R., and Domínguez, C. *Venezuela: Exclusion and Integration: A Synthesis in the Building?* (Ginebra: International Institute for Labor Studies, 1997).

Casanova, R. 'La Revuelta de Estudiantes Venezolanos del 2007—El Levantamiento Político de una Nueva Generación', *Cuadernos del Cendes Año 26 n. 70 Tercera Época* (January–April 2009): 99–123.

Castellanos, P. L. 'Notas sobre el Estado y la Salud en Venezuela', *Cuadernos de la Sociedad Venezolana de Planificación* (1982): 69–121.

Ceaser, M. 'Cuban Doctors Provide Care in Venezuela's Barrios', *Lancet*, Vol. 363, No. 9424 (2004): 874–75.

Coronil, F. *The Magical State: Nature, Money, and Modernity in Venezuela* (Chicago: University of Chicago Press, 1997).

Coronil, F., and Skurski, J. 'Dismembering and Remembering the Nation: The Semantics of Political Violence in Venezuela', *Comparative Studies in Society and History*, Vol. 33, No. 2 (1991): 288–337.

Dean, J. W. 'The Gerrymander', *New England Historical and Genealogical Register*, Vol. 46 (1892): 374–83.

D'Elia, Y. 'Las Misiones Sociales en Venezuela: Una Aproximación a Su Compresión y Análisis', *Instituto Latinoamericano de Investigaciones Sociales* (October 2006), 1–227.

D'Elia, Y., and Cabezas, L. F. 'Las Misiones Sociales en Venezuela', *Instituto Latinoamericano de Investigaciones Sociales* (May 2008),1–17.

De Vos, P., De Ceukelaire, W., and Van der Stuyft, P. 'Colombia and Cuba, Contrasting Models in Latin American's Health Sector Reform', *Tropical Medicine & International Health*, Vol. 11, No. 10 (2006): 1604–12.

Di Tella, T. S. 'Populism into the Twenty-First Century'. *Government and Opposition*, Vol. 32, No. 2 (1997): 187–200.

Diaz Polanco, J. 'El Papel del Financiamiento en los Procesos de Reforma del SectorSalud el Caso de Venezuela', in Díaz Polanco, J. (ed.), *La Reforma de Salud en Venezuela: Aspectos Políticos e Institucionales de la Descentralización de la Salud en Venezuela* (Caracas, Venezuela: Fundación Polar, 2001), 124–45.

Fernandes, S. *Who Can Stop the Drums?—Urban Social Movements in Chávez's Venezuela* (Duke University Press, 2010).

Glynos, J. 'Sexual Identity, Identification and Differences', *Philosophy and Social Criticism*, Vol. 26, No. 6 (2000): 85–108.

Glynos, J., and Howarth, D. *Logics of Critical Explanation in Social and Political Theory* (London: Routledge, 2007).

Bibliography 199

Golinger, E. *The Chávez Decode: Cracking U.S. Interventionism in Venezuela* (Northampton, MA: Olive Branch Press, 2006).

Gott, R. *Hugo Chávez and the Bolivarian Revolution* (London: Verso, 2005).

Griggs, S., and Howarth, D. 'Populism, Localism and Environmental Politics: The Logic and Rhetoric of the Stop Stanstead Expansion Campaign', *Planning Theory*, Vol. 7, No. 2 (2008): 123–44.

Grossi, R. *Acción Sanitaria en Venezuela y Presupuestos, 1936–1971* (Caracas: Ministerio de Salud y Asistencia Social, 1972).

Harnecker, M. *Understanding the Venezuelan Revolution—Hugo Chávez Talks to Marta Harnecker* (New York: Monthly Review Press, 2005).

Hawkins, K. *Venezuela's Chavismo and Populism in Comparative Perspective* (New York: Cambridge University Press, 2010).

Homedes, N., and Ugalde, A. 'Las Reformas de Salud en América Latina: Una Visión Crítica a través de Dos Estudios de Caso', *Revista Panamericana de Salud Pública*, Vol. 17, No. 3 (2005): 83–96.

Howarth, D. *Discourse* (Buckingham: Open University Press, 2000).

Howarth, D., and Stavrakakis, Y. 'Introducing Discourse Theory and Political Analysis', in Howarth, D., Norval, A., and Stavrakakis, A. (eds.), *Discourse Theory and Political Analysis* (Manchester: Manchester University Press, 2000), 1–23.

Howarth, D. 'The Difficult Emergence of a Democratic Imaginary: Black Consciousness and Non-Racial Democracy in South Africa', in Howarth, D., Norval, A., and Stavrakakis, A. (eds.), *Discourse Theory and Political Analysis* (Manchester: Manchester University Press, 2000), 168–92.

Howarth, D. 'Applying Discourse Theory: The Method of Articulation', in Howarth, D., and Torfing, J. (eds.), *Discourse Theory in European Politics: Identity, Policy and Governance* (Basingstoke: Palgrave Macmillan, 2005), 316–49.

Howarth, D. 'Populism or Popular Democracy? The UDF, Workerism and the Struggle for Radical Democracy in South Africa', in Panizza, F. (ed.), *Populism and the Mirror of Democracy* (London: Verso, 2005), 202–23.

Ionescu, G., and Gellner, E. 'Introduction', in Ionescu, G., and Gellner, E. (eds.), *Populism: Its Meanings and National Characteristics* (London: Weidenfeld Goldbacks, 1970), 1–5.

Jaen, M. H. *El Sistema de Salud en Venezuela: Desafíos* (Caracas, Venezuela: IESA, 2001).

Karl, T. L. 'The Venezuelan Petro-State and the Crisis of "Its" Democracy', in McCoy, J., Serbin, A., Smith, W. C, and Stambouli, A. (eds.), *Venezuelan Democracy under Stress* (Coral Gables, FL: North-South Center at the University of Miami, 1995), 33–58.

Kazin, M. *The Populist Persuasion: An American History* (New York: Basic Books, 1995).

Kelly, J. 'Origines y Consecuencias de la Constitución Bolivariana', in Francés, A., and Machado Allison, C. (eds.), *Venezuela: La Crisis de Abril* (Caracas: Ediciones IESA, 2002), 37–45.

Kelly, J., and Palma, P. 'The Syndrome of Economic Decline and the Quest for Change', in McCoy, J., and Myers, D. (eds.), *The Unravelling of Representative Democracy in Venezuela* (Baltimore: Johns Hopkins University Press, 2004), 202–30.

Krauze, E. *El Poder y el Delirio* (Barcelona: Tuspuets Editores, S.A., 2008).

Laclau, E. *Politics and Ideology in Marxist Theory. Capitalism—Fascism—Populism*(London: Verso, 1977).

Laclau, E., and Mouffe, C. *Hegemony and Socialist Strategy—Towards a Radical Democratic Politics* (London: Verso, 1985).

Laclau, E. *New Reflection on the Revolution of Our Time* (London: Verso, 1990).

200 Bibliography

Laclau, E. *Emancipation* (London: Verso, 1996).

Laclau, E. 'Constructing Universality', in Butler, J., Laclau. E., and Žižek, S. (eds.), *Contingency, Hegemony, Universality: Contemporary Dialogues on the Left* (London: Verso, 2000), 281–307.

Laclau, E. *On Populist Reason* (London: Verso, 2005).

Laclau, E. 'Populism: What's in a Name?', in Panizza, F. (ed.), *Populism and the Mirror of Democracy* (London: Verso, 2005), 32–49.

Lefort, C. *The Political Forms of Modern Society: Bureaucracy, Democracy, Totalitarianism* (Cambridge, MA: MIT Press, 1986).

Levine, D. 'The Transition to Democracy: Are There Lessons from Venezuela?', *Bulletin of Latin American Research*, Vol. 4, No. 2 (1985): 47–61.

Lopez Maya, M. 'Venezuela after the Caracazo: Forms of Protest in a Deinstitutionalised Context', *Bulletin of Latin American Research*, Vol. 21, No. 2 (2002): 199–218.

Lopez Maya, M. *Del Viernes Negro al Referendo Revocatorio* (Caracas: Alfadil Ediciones, 2005).

Magallanes, R. 'La Igualdad en la República Bolivariana de Venezuela (1999–2004)', *Revista Venezolana de Economía y Ciencias Sociales*, Vol. 11 (2005):1171–99.

Marcano, C., and Barrera Tyzka, A. *Hugo Chávez sin Uniforme: Una Historia Personal* (Barcelona: Debate, 2006).

Marcano, C., and Barrera Tyzka, A. *Hugo Chávez* (New York: Random House, 2007).

Márquez, P. 'Diario de una Oligarca Escualida: Reaccion de la Clase Media', in Francés, A., and Machado Allison, C. (eds.), *Venezuela: La Crisis de Abril* (Caracas: Ediciones IESA, 2002), 111–19.

Martínez, G. E. 'La LOPE y el CNE cambiaron el sistema politico venezolano', in Derecho Electoral en Venezuela—*Centro de Estudios de Politica Proyectiva*, Segunda Edición Aniversaria (Noviembre–Diciembre 2009): 61–8.

McCoy, J. L. 'Venezuela: Labor and the State in a Party-Mediated Democracy: Institutional Change in Venezuela', *Latin American Research Review*, Vol. 24, No. 2 (1989): 35–68.

Medina, M. *El Elegido Presidente Chávez—Un Nuevo Sistema Político* (Bogota, D.C.: Ediciones Aurora, 2001).

Medina, P. *Rebeliones: Una Larga Conversación con Maria Cristina Iglesias y Farruco Sesto* (Caracas: Edicion del Autor, 1999).

Menéndez, E. L., and Di Pardo, R. B. *De Algunos Alcoholismos y Algunos Saberes: Atención Primaria y Proceso de Alcoholización.* (Mexico City: CIESAS, 1996).

Mires, F. *Al Borde del Abismo—El Chavismo y la Contrarrevolución Antidemocrática de Nuestro Tiempo* (Caracas: Debate 2007).

Monmonier, M. *Bushmanders & Bullwinkles* (Chicago and London: The University of Chicago Press, 2001).

Morles, V., Medina Rubio, E., and Alvarez Bedoya, N. *La Educacion Superior en Venezuela* (Caracas: Lesalc/Unesco, 2003).

Muntaner, C., Armada, F., Chung, H., Mata, R., Williams-Brennan, L., and Benach, J. 'Venezuela Health Reforms—Venezuela's Barrio Adentro: Participatory Democracy, South-South Cooperation and Health Care for All', *Social Medicine,* Vol. 3, No. 4 (2008): 232–46.

Musgrove, P. *The General Theory of Gerrymandering,* American Politics Series, Ripley, R. B. (ed.), Ohio State University Series Number: 04–034 ,Vol. 3 (Beverly Hills and London: Sage Publications, 1977).

Naím, M. *Paper Tigers & Minotaurs: The Politics of Venezuela's Economic Reforms* (Washington, D.C.: Carnegie Endowment for International Peace, 1993).

Bibliography 201

Naím, M. 'The Launching of Radical Policy Changes, 1989–1991', in Tulchin, J. S., and Bland, G. (eds.), *Venezuela in the Wake of Radical Reform* (Boulder, CO: Lynne Rienner Publishers, 1993), 39–94.

Naím, M. 'The Political Management of Radical Economic Change: Lessons from the Venezuelan Experience', in Tulchin, J. S., and Bland, G. (eds.), *Venezuela in the Wake of Radical Reform* (Boulder, CO: Lynne Rienner Publishers, 1993), 147–78.

O'Rourke, T. P. *Reapportionment; Law, Politics, Computers* (Washington, D.C.: Amer. Enterprise Inst. Domestic Affairs Study, 1972).

Pan American Health Organization. 'Mission Barrio Adentro: The Right to Health and Social Inclusion in Venezuela', *Pan American Health Organization*, Caracas, Venezuela (July 2006).

Panizza, F. 'Introduction: Populism and the Mirror of Democracy', in Panizza, F. (ed.), *Populism and the Mirror of Democracy* (London: Verso, 2005), 1–31.

Parker, P. 'Metaphor and Catachresis', in Bender, J., and Wellbery, D. (eds.), *The End(s) of Rhetoric* (Stanford, CA: Stanford UP, 1990), 60–73.

Patruyo, T. 'El Estado Actual de las Misiones Sociales: Balance sobre Su Proceso de Implementación e Institucionalización', *Instituto Latinoamericano de Investigaciones Sociales* (April 2008), 1–89.

Pilger, J. *The War on Democracy by John Pilger* (Youngheart Entertainment Granada Productions, October 2007).

Rachadell, M. 'El Sistema Electoral en la Ley Orgánica de Procesos Electorales', *Provincia*, No. 23 (enero–junio 2010): 127–155.

Regional Office of the World Health Organisation. 'Mission Barrio Adentro: The Right to Health and Social Inclusion in Venezuela', *Pan American Health Organization*, Caracas, Venezuela (July 2006).

Rincón, M., and Rodríguez, I. 'Consideraciones Generales sobre la Política y Gestión de la Salud en Venezuela (1900–2003)', *FERMENTUM*, Vol. 41, No. 14 (September–October, 2004): 503–32.

Roberts. K. 'Social Polarization and the Populist Resurgence in Venezuela', in Ellner, S., and Hellinger, D. (eds.), *Venezuelan Politics in the* Chávez *Era: Class, Polarization, and Conflict* (Boulder, CO: Lynne Rienner Publishers, 2003), 55–72.

Sharp, G. *The Politics of Nonviolent Action*. Gene Sharp with the editorial assistance of Marina Finkelstein (Boston: Extending Horizons Books; Porter Sargent Publisher, 1973).

Sickels, R. J. 'Dragons, Bacon strips and Dumbbells—Who's Afraid of Reapportionment?' *Yale Law Journal*, Vol. 75 (July 1966): 1300–08

Stavrakakis, Y. *Lacan and the Political* (London: Routledge, 1999).

Stoker, G. *Why Politics Matters—Making Democracy Work* (London: Palgrave, 2006).

Taggart, P. *Populism* (Buckingham: Open University Press, 2000).

Terris, M. 'Witnesses to History: The Caracas Explosion and the International Monetary Fund 5–130', *Journal of Public Health Policy*, Vol. 10, No. 1 (1989): 149–52.

Tovar Arroyo, G. *Estudiantes por la Libertad—Pensamiento y Documentos de la Generación 2007* (Caracas: Los Libros de El Nacional, 2007).

Unidad de Análisis Estrategico/Univesidad del Pueblo. *El Movimiento de las "Manos Blancas"* (Mérida, Venezuela: UNIVER-SO, 2009), 1–10. http://www.scribd.com/doc/10957786/El-Movimiento-de-Las-Manos-Blancas1 [accessed June 4, 2009].

Urbaneja, M. L. *Privatizacion en el Sector Salud en Venezuela* (Caracas,: CENDES, 1991).

Uzcategui, L. J. *Chávez Mago de las Emociones—Análisis Psicosocial de un Fenómeno Político* (Caracas: Lithopolar Graficas, 1999).

202 Bibliography

Westlind, D. *The Politics of Popular Identity: Understanding Recent Populist Movements in Sweden and the United States* (Lund: Lund University Press, 1996).

Weyland, K. 'Neopopulism and Neoliberalism in Latin America: Unexpected Affinities', *Studies in Comparative International Development*, Vol. 31, No. 3 (1996): 3–31.

Wilpert, G. *Changing Venezuela by Taking Power—The History and Policies of the Chávez Government* (London: Verso, 2007).

Yamada, S. 'Latin American Social medicine and Global medicine', *American Journal of Public Health*, Vol. 93 (2003): 1994–96.

Zago, A. *La Rebelión de los Ángeles* (Caracas: Fuentes Editores, 1992).

Žižek, S. *The Sublime Object of Ideology* (London: Verso, 1989).

Index

A
abyss 140–1, 147
Acción Democratica (AD) 1, 44–6, 56–7, 67, 154, 171n4, 175n12, 181n1
affect 20–2; affection 18, 81, 107, 145–6; affective 18, 21–2, 35, 38, 49, 51, 146, 156
agonism 45, 68, 155; agonistic 68, 70, 74, 83, 86, 119, 131, 155
Alayón Monserat, R. 92, 94, 104, 183n18
Ali, T. 3
Aló Presidente 97–9, 153, 156, 184n44, 185n63, 190n2
Althusser, L. 36
Álvarez, A. 120
Amazonas 137
America 10, 69, 79; American 10, 57, 79, 84–7, 141, 147, 156–7, 161, 163, 193n36; *see also* United States
American Organization States (AOS) 74, 78, 80, 132
antagonism 13, 34, 47, 49, 51, 59, 61, 109, 129, 158; antagonistic 19–23, 28, 30, 34, 49, 52, 60, 68, 102, 114, 148
apartheid 25, 31, 34, 129, 172n24
Arias Cardenas, F. 65
armed forces 2, 39–40, 46–7, 63, 71, 73, 86, 90, 93, 99, 153
Arria, D. 152–3
Baduel, R. 6, 39–40, 46, 73, 81, 83, 85–8, 137, 170n187, 181n103
barbarism 47; barbaric 70
Barinas 67, 137–8
Barrera Tyzka, A. 3

Barrio Adentro (BA) 77, 89, 92, 95, 97–8, 101, 108–13, 135, 147, 150, 159, 161, 180n91, 184n37, 185n66, 186n100
Barrios, D. 116, 123
Bernal, F. 93, 177n47
Betancourt, R. 44
Blanco Muñoz, A. 131
Bolívar, S. 1–4, 7, 32, 40, 44, 46, 49–50, 53–5, 63–5, 133, 135–6, 140–1, 146–7, 149–52, 156, 160, 162, 171n15, 174n3, 186n93, 192n31

B
Bolivarian Circles (*Circulos Bolivarianos*) 53, 93
Bolivarian Movement (MBR 200) 46, 49–55, 60, 74, 83
Bolivia 63
Briceño, F. 118, 190n53
Briggs, C. L. 91, 102
British 143
Bush, G. 79
Buxton, J. 66

C
Calabozo 94, 106–8, 183n31, 184n33; *see also* Carrasquelero
Caldera, R. 45, 49, 52, 57–8, 127, 171n4, 172n27, 176n24
cancer 7, 39, 135, 138–42, 145–7, 156, 162–4, 193n36; *see also* Chávez, H. and cancer
Cannon, B. 71
Canovan, M. 5, 8–10, 15, 41, 159
Carabobo 137–8, 173n48
Caracazo 2, 47, 49, 51, 60, 65, 70, 90, 92, 96, 171n17

204 *Index*

Caricuao 95, 106–10
Carmona Estanga, P. 69–72, 176n34
Carrasquelero 94, 106–8, 183n31, 184n33; *see also* Calabozo
Carrasquero J.V. 110
Carter Center 74, 78
Casanova, R. 121–7, 131
Castro, F. 3, 51, 80, 93, 110, 140, 186n93, 192n33,
Caudillo 44, 62, 65
Causa R (*La Causa Radical*) 153, 171n5
Chávez, H. 2, 6–7; and *Barrio Adentro* (BA) 77, 89, 92, 97–8, 101, 109, 111, 147, 159; and cancer 7, 39, 135, 138–42, 145–7, 156, 162–4, 193n36; and Castro, Fidel 3, 51, 80, 93, 110, 139–40, 146–7, 186n93, 192n33, 193n36; and the February 1992 coup d'état/coup 2, 6, 43, 48–9, 51–3, 58, 60, 65, 96, 117, 120, 141, 147; and the April 2002 coup d'état /coup 6, 39, 70, 72, 74–6, 81, 85–6, 91–2, 104, 117, 126, 130, 141, 159; and cult of personality/leader 146, 149, 156; and Miquilena 40, 56, 65–6, 68–9, 88, 148, 160, 175n12; and populist 4, 6, 40, 43, 49, 52, 56, 58, 62–4, 68, 70, 80, 82, 86–9, 104, 111–13, 129, 134, 138–9, 141, 145, 147–8, 150–1, 153–7, 159–61, 163–4; and socialism 80, 86–8, 108, 121, 141–2, 152; and totalitarianism 87, 149
Chiripero 52, 58, 172n27
Christ 4, 71, 80, 86; *see also* Jesus
clientelism 1, 45–7, 59
Colombia 63, 173n45, 192n32
Comandante 50–1, 56–7, 59, 140, 142
Comité de Organización Política Electoral Independiente (COPEI) 45, 49, 57, 154–5, 171n4, 172n27, 173n48, 175n12
Comité de Organización Política
Confederación de Trabajadores de Venezuela (CTV) 67–70
Consejo Nacional Electoral (CNE) 78–79, 138
constitution (Bolivarian—1999) 6, 53, 55, 58, 62–5, 68, 70, 73, 77, 80, 83–4, 86–8, 96, 136, 160–1
constitution (*Punto Fijo*—1961) 44, 54–5, 57, 62, 65, 90

Convergencia 52, 172n27
Coordinadora Democratica 74, 178n66
Coronil, F. 44, 46, 70
corruption 1, 45, 48, 51, 54–5, 57–8, 60, 65, 109, 111, 113, 152, 163, 170n187, 184n33, 194n41; corrupt 1, 3, 11, 14, 43, 46, 49, 52, 55, 60, 66, 110, 147, 153, 160; corrupters 65, 68
coup d'état (April 2002) *see* Chávez, H. and the April 2002 coup d'état / coup
coup d'état (February 1992) *see* Chávez, H. and the February 1992 coup d'état/coup
coup d'état 44, 79
crystallization 94, 97, 133, 158
Cuba 80, 100, 102, 105–6, 109–10, 113, 139–40, 179n81; Cuban 3, 6, 40, 72, 80, 87, 89, 93, 95, 97–8, 100–13, 139–41, 148, 186n93, 192n33; *see also* Venecuba

D

D'Elia, Y. 105
deficient being 19, 20, 22, 122, 129
demonize 15, 18, 82, 110, 126, 156; demonization 17
desires 3, 13, 35, 70, 109, 113, 141
Di Tella, Torcuato S. 10
dichotomy 10, 16, 67–8, 86, 158; dichotomic 19–20, 29, 55–6, 60, 97, 129, 147, 154, 161, 163
dictator 44, 122, 124, 126, 150; dictatorial 44, 59, 122, 124, 128, 175n12; dictatorship 73, 124–5
difference 15–18, 25, 29, 31–2, 47–8, 50–1, 54, 57–8, 60, 65, 68–71, 80, 83, 100, 109, 111, 116, 120, 123, 127, 130, 132, 138, 148, 155
discourse 16, 29, 26, 50–1, 59, 104, 111, 148, 168n94; Bolivarian 53, 57, 73, 76, 87; opposition 59, 70, 72, 82, 85, 103, 105, 114, 116, 118–20, 130–1, 133–4, 153–4; populist 9, 59, 62–4, 67–8, 79, 86, 108, 138–40, 144–6, 150, 154
dislocation 14, 32, 36–7, 43, 47, 51, 58, 60, 65, 87, 129; dislocatory event 39, 44, 48, 51, 60; dislocatory moment 36, 60, 96

Index 205

Distrito Federal 137–8

E
Ecuador 63
emancipation 3, 44, 49–50, 55, 63, 68,
  72, 146, 150, 156, 162, 171n15,
  174n3
emotions 21, 26, 49–51, 141, 147–8;
  emotional 9, 36, 43, 59, 109,
  129, 141, 159; emotionally 22,
  26, 48, 148, 158
Empire 79, 84–6, 141–2, 147, 150,
  156–7, 161, 163
empty signifier 15–18, 20–2, 30–1,
  43, 51, 60, 84, 120, 133, 141,
  169n135, 172n24
England 2
enjoyment 35–7, 163
equivalence 15, 17–20, 22, 24–6,
  29–30, 32–3, 35, 38, 41, 50, 52,
  57, 69, 82, 87, 109, 128–9, 134,
  154, 160, 176n32; equivalential
  17–23, 28–32, 35, 41, 48–9, 53,
  55–8, 60, 63, 69, 88, 111–12,
  120, 127, 129–30, 138, 145–6,
  152, 159, 191n15
escualido 142, 144
ethics 36–7, 95, 109
excluded 6, 17–19, 22, 33, 36–7, 43,
  47–51, 53, 56, 58, 60–1, 67–8,
  73, 76–7, 88–94, 96–7, 101–4,
  108–9, 111–13, 118, 126, 129,
  135, 145, 148–9, 154–7, 160–1,
  163

F
fantasmatic logics 5, 24, 33–8, 42–3,
  48, 63, 68, 87, 146, 159–60
fantasy 22, 33–5, 38, 47, 148, 151, 156
Fedecámaras 66–9, 70, 72, 176n24,
  177n48
*Federación de Estudiantes Universi-
  tarios de Venezuela* 130
Federación Medica Venezolana (FMV)
  91, 102–5, 108, 187n105
Fermín, C. 57, 65
Fernandes, S. 3
Flores, C. 132
France 1 43

G
Gallegos, R. 44, 106
Gandhi, M. 121
García, I. 78, 82

Generación 2007 81, 121, 126–7, 129,
  131–4
Generación 28 44, 121, 170n1
Germany 129
Gerry, E. 137
gerrymandering 7, 135, 137–8, 148–9,
  156, 162
Globovisión 79, 117
Glynos, J. 5, 8, 14, 23–7, 31–8, 41–3,
  61, 63, 65, 87, 92, 96, 103,
  112–13, 115, 122, 128, 130,
  133, 158–9, 161
God 59, 64, 72–3, 79–80, 140, 144–5,
  153, 192n33
Goicoechea, Y. 118, 124–5, 130, 132,
  188n9
Golinger, E. 69, 78
Gómez, J.V. 44, 150
Gonzales, S. 118, 124
Gott, R. 3, 76
Gran Misiones 143, 148, 156
Gran Viraje 47
Griggs, S. 172n24
grip 33, 50, 59, 63, 76, 84, 92, 108–9,
  114, 119, 122, 125–6, 129–32,
  138, 141, 148, 155, 158, 160,
  163; gripping 6, 33, 51, 63, 120,
  133; gripped 22, 51, 60, 111, 120
Guárico 94, 183n31
Guevara, E. (*Che*) 108, 186n93
Gutierrez, R. 82, 115
Guzman Blanco, A. 150

H
Harnecker, M. 64, 165n10
Hawkins, K. 4
Health committees (*Comités de Salud*)
  93, 100, 109
hegemonic 18–19, 21–3, 32–3, 52, 65,
  68, 72, 74, 96, 103, 112, 122,
  124; order 5, 12, 55, 61–2, 64,
  67, 72, 96–7, 104, 119–22,
  128, 160; position 32, 61, 65,
  101–5, 109, 135; practices 55,
  67, 70, 116, 123, 146; project
  52, 57, 63, 65, 68, 70, 72, 74,
  77, 79–80, 89, 93, 111, 114–15,
  119, 124, 126, 129, 147, 155,
  158, 160–3
hegemony 13, 15–16, 18, 22–3, 25,
  30–1, 55–6, 67, 69–70, 77, 86,
  92, 104, 116, 129, 131, 154,
  160–3
Herrera Campins, L. 1, 45

206   *Index*

Howarth, D. 5, 8, 23–6, 31–43, 61,
  63, 65, 87, 92, 96, 103, 112–13,
  115, 122, 130, 133, 159, 161,
  168n94, 172n24, 176n32

I
Inter-American Court of Human
  Rights (IACHR) 194n41
International Criminal Court (ICC)
  153
International Monetary Fund (IMF)
  46–7

J
Jesus 140

K
Kazin, M. 10
Kelly, J. 48, 71
Krauze, E. 188n9

L
Laclau, E. 5, 8, 11, 15–33, 39–43, 47,
  53, 60–1, 63, 68, 87, 96, 102–3,
  111, 113, 115, 128–9, 133–4,
  146, 155, 158–9, 161, 176n32
Land Reform 66–8
Lara 137–8
Lara, L. 94–5, 183n32
LASM (Latin American Social Medicine) 91, 104
Lefort, C. 15, 87, 135, 148–9, 155, 164
llanero 94, 183n31
logics; of apartheid 25, 31, 34; of
  difference 19, 20–2, 25–6, 28,
  33, 35, 41, 87, 128–9, 154; of
  equivalence 15, 19, 22, 24–6,
  32–3, 35, 38, 41, 50, 52, 57, 87,
  128, 134, 154; fantasmatic 5,
  24, 33–8, 42–3, 48, 63, 68, 87,
  146, 159–60; of fantasy 34–7,
  122; of Chavismo 60; of the
  market 25–6; political 5, 24–7,
  31–6, 38, 42, 48, 63, 92, 96,
  103, 159–60, 176n32; social
  24–6, 28, 31–3, 37–8, 42, 130,
  159
Lopez Maya, M. 53–4, 75, 171n10
López, L. 7, 40, 136, 149–50, 153,
  156, 162, 193n41
López, R. 117–19, 126, 188n14
love 21, 73, 80, 139, 141, 143, 145–46;
  beloved 83, 140–1, 145
Lusinchi, J. 1, 46

Luther King, M. 121

M
Machado, M.C. 152–3
Majunche 153, 156–7, 160, 163
Manos Blancas 118–22, 124–6, 128,
  131–4, 162
Manos Negras 120, 127
Mantini Briggs, C. 91, 102
Marcano, C. 3
Martí, J. 3, 186n93
Martínez, G.E. 137
Massachusetts 137
Medina, M. 56
Medina, P. 56, 153
Mérida 130
Mesa de la Unidad Democrática
  (MUD) 7, 138, 149, 152–3,
  155–7, 163, 191n14, 194n48
Milagros, Misión 182n2
Milosevic, S. 125
Milton Friedman Prize for Advancing
  Liberty 125
Miquilena, L. 40, 56, 65–6, 68–9, 88,
  148, 160, 175n12
Miraflores 2, 71–3, 86, 111, 141,
  177n47, 178n56
Miranda 137–8, 152, 179
misfortunes 22, 30, 148, 150, 160, 179
Miss Universe 1, 55
missions (*misiones*) 77, 88–9, 94, 143,
  148, 156, 179n81, 186n100
Mouffe, C. 16, 42
Movimiento al Socialismo (MAS) 40,
  47, 52, 56–9, 66, 69, 78, 81–3,
  88, 154–5, 171n5, 172n28,
  174n65 177n48
Movimiento Electoral del Pueblo
  (MEP) 56
Movimiento V Republica (MVR)
  54–7, 59, 69, 82, 174n65
Mújica, F. 40, 58–9, 66
mulato-mestizo 2
Muntaner, C. 99–101
Musgrove, P. 137

N
Naím, M. 46
nationalism 3, 8, 12–13; nationalistic
  13, 149, 151–2
neoliberal 2, 6, 23, 43, 45, 47–9, 51–2,
  59, 67, 70, 72, 74, 79, 90–1,
  102, 116, 121–3, 127, 161; neoliberalism 69

Index 207

Netherlands 153
nodal point 29, 31–2, 51, 54, 57, 89,
     109, 138, 146, 163

O

Obama, B. 142
oligarchs 14, 22, 67, 69–70, 82, 106,
     108, 141, 147, 156–7, 160–1,
     163; oligarchy 3, 13, 20, 30,
     60, 68
Orinoco Belt 143
Ortega, C. 69, 71, 176n37, 177n47

P

Palma, P. 48
Panama 63
Panizza, F. 8, 10, 13–15, 22, 51, 76,
     87, 164
Panteón Nacional 63, 146
Partido Comunista de Venezuela
     (PCV) 56, 82, 171n4, 171n5,
     174n65,
Partido Socialista Unido de Venezuela
     (PSUV) 138, 154, 191n15
Patria o Muerte, Venceremos 80
Patria Para Todos (PPT) 56–7, 138,
     153–4, 174n65, 191n5
*Patria, Socialismo o Muerte, Vecer-
     emos* 80, 141
Patruyo, T. 98–101, 106, 185n66
Pérez, C.A. 1, 45, 46–9, 51, 58, 90
Perú 63
Petkoff, T. 47
Petróleos de Venezuela, S.A. (PDVSA)
     71, 74–5, 79, 109, 186n100,
Pilger, J. 178n56
pluralism 21, 68, 70, 74, 116, 157
political logics 5, 24–7, 31–6, 38, 42,
     48, 63, 92, 96, 103, 159–60,
     176n32; *see also* difference;
     equivalence (equivalential); logics
Polo Patriótico, 56–8, 60–2, 65, 69,
     135, 153, 160, 174–5
Por ahora 43, 50–1, 54, 60, 84, 117,
     120, 141
*Por Ahora y para Siempre, Viviremos y
     Venceremos* 141
Prada, J. 127, 130, 189n50, 189n51
Primero Justicia 132, 152, 154
privatization 47, 90–1, 96, 102, 112
Puchi, L. 58
Punto Fijo 44–6, 52, 54–7, 59–62, 65,
     68, 89, 135, 138, 155, 159–60,
     175n12

R

Rachadell, M. 137–8
racial 76, 172n20; racially 70
Radio Caracas Televisión (RCTV) 79,
     80–3, 114–20, 123, 125, 131–3,
     136
Ramírez, D. 126, 130–2
Randonski Capriles, H. 7, 152, 157,
     163
Reagan, R. 20, 122
recall 75, 77–9, 180n89
reconciliation 116, 119–21, 125–9,
     131, 133–4, 154, 157
*Red Democrática Universitaria Estu-
     diantil* 118, 126
referendum 6–7, 39, 53, 62–5, 68, 72,
     75, 78–9, 83–7, 89, 96, 118,
     120, 131, 133, 135–7, 148–49,
     160–2, 180n89; *see also* recall
Resistencia 118
Roberts. K. 55
Rosales, M. 79, 152–5

S

Sáez, I. 55, 57–60
Salas Römer, E. 55, 57–60
San Cristobal 40, 107, 127, 130–1
Sánchez, R. 118, 124, 127
Serbia 125, 128
Sharp, G. 121–2, 124–5, 127–8
Skurski, J. 70
social logics 24–6, 28, 31–3, 37–8, 42,
     130, 159; *see also* fantasmatic
     logics; political logics
Sonrisa, Misión 97
South Africa 25–6, 34, 129, 172n24
Spain 43, 186n93
Stoker, G. 4, 165n10
Súmate 78–9, 82, 152, 179n82
sword (Bolívar) 63
symbol (symbolic) 14, 21–2, 30, 35,
     38, 48, 56–7, 159; of Bolívar 2,
     7, 32, 44, 49–50, 63, 65, 146,
     149, 150–1, 156; of Chávez
     50–1, 76, 126, 145, 147, 163; of
     Manos Blancas 118–20, 122,
     124, 125, 128, 131–4

T

Tablante, C. 57
Táchira 40, 107, 109, 126–8, 130–2,
     137–8, 150
Taggart, P. 5, 8, 10–13, 22, 37, 41, 159
Tascón List 180n89, 194n48

208   *Index*

Thatcher, M. 10, 122
thick description 93
totalitarian 15, 73, 132; totalitarianism
   87, 149
Tovar Arroyo, G. 117–18, 120–2, 124,
   126–9, 188n9

U
Ugalde, L. 123
underdog 13, 20, 22, 29, 51, 55–6,
   62, 120, 125, 145, 147, 150,
   163
Unión Republicana Democratica
   (URD) 45, 171n4, 175n12
United Kingdom 57; *see also* British;
   England
United Nations (UN) 153
United States 4; *see also* America/
   American
Universidad Católica Andres Bello
   (UCAB) 115, 123–4
Universidad Central de Venezuela
   (UCV) 115, 121, 130, 183n18
Universidad Metropolitana 116

*Universidad Nacional Experimental
   del Táchira* (UNET) 130
Universidad Simon Bolívar (USB) 115
Universidad Socialista del Pueblo 121,
   124
'us-them' axis 16, 30, 32, 43, 55, 58,
   60, 68, 70, 80, 113, 145, 148,
   150, 160, 176n32
Uzcategui, L. 57

V
'vector' 34–6, 50, 53, 55, 63–5, 146,
   151, 160
Venecuba 78, 180n91
Viernes Negro 1, 46
Voluntad Popular 153

W
Washington Consensus 2, 47–8, 52
Wilpert, G. 92, 177n39

Z
Žižek, S. 14
Zulia 137–8, 152, 180n93